British Politics and Society from Walpole to Pitt 1742–1789

Each volume in the 'Problems in Focus' series is designed to make available to students important new work on key historical problems and periods that they encounter in their courses. Each volume is devoted to a central topic or theme, and the most important aspects of this are dealt with by specially commissioned essays from scholars in the relevant field. The editorial Introduction reviews the problem or period as a whole, and each essay provides an assessment of the particular aspect, pointing out the areas of development and controversy, and indicating where conclusions can be drawn or where further work is necessary. An annotated bibliography serves as a guide for further reading.

PROBLEMS IN FOCUS SERIES

British Politics and Society from Walpole to Pitt 1742–1789

EDITED BY

JEREMY BLACK

MACMILLAN

First published 1990

Published by
MACMILLAN EDUCATION LTD
Houndmills, Basingstoke, Hampshire RG21 2XS
and London
Companies and representatives
throughout the world

Printed in Singapore

British Library Cataloguing in Publication Data
British politics and society from Walpole to Pitt, 1742–
1789. — (Problems in focus series).
1. Great Britain, 1727–1820
I. Black, Jeremy   II. Series
941.07′2
ISBN 0–333–45488–X
ISBN 0–333–45489–8 (pbk)

Contents

To
Jeremy and Karl
Good Friends and Fellow Toilers

Preface

It is a great privilege to be asked to edit a second volume in this distinguished series. Rereading the preface of *Britain in the Age of Walpole* (1984), I find that the remarks I made then are equally pertinent for this book. Despite the problems inevitable in collective enterprises, this volume was produced without any disagreement. Differing views are presented, as is only healthy, and the work as a whole testifies not only to the very vigorous nature of current historical scholarship on this period but also to the genuine excitement that currently characterises work and debate on the century. Unfortunately it is a period that receives insufficient attention in schools and many institutions of higher education. This is curious as, despite the supposed greater interest and importance of the neighbouring centuries, the eighteenth is both interesting on its own terms and important in such crucial matters as economic developments, imperial history and Anglo-Scottish relations. Historiographical questions are important but they do not swamp the subject as they appear, for example, to do in the mid-seventeenth century. As students both in schools and in higher education are increasingly encouraged to turn to project work, hopefully more will be guided to the eighteenth century, a period of interest and relatively legible handwriting.

I beg to acknowledge the gracious permission of Her Majesty the Queen to make use of papers in the Royal Archives at Windsor. I would also like to thank the Marquess of Bute and Lady Lucas. Thanks are also due to the British Academy, the Huntington Library, the Staff Travel and Research Fund of Durham University and the Wolfson Foundation. I should like to thank the other contributors for their assistance and Vanessa Graham for her patient help. This book is dedicated to two friends who are also historians of the period. In so doing I am thanking many other historians who have provided valuable encouragement and friendship.

J. M. B.

Introduction

JEREMY BLACK

A CENTRAL theme of the essays in this book is the relationship between change and continuity, and it is a crucial question in work on the second half of the eighteenth century. The popular image of the period is one of both: the economic transformation suggested by the term industrial revolution and the sense of timeless order, confidence and ease created by the stately homes of the age. The question is addressed directly by Roy Porter in a powerful essay that challenges the view of a stable Church–State recently presented by Jonathan Clark. Clark places religion, especially the teachings of the Church of England, at the centre of English society and stresses the ideological and religious underpinning of conservatism and stability more obviously than other scholars, who have also claimed that the period was characterised by social stability. Clark argues that the political opposition to the monarchical, aristocratic, Anglican regime came not so much from political radicals, whom he treats as a small and inconsequential group, but rather from religious radicals.[1] Without fully probing the matter, Clark terms England an *ancien régime* society, thus asserting that the path of her development had not departed from that of the rest of Europe. Unhappy about Clark's typology of social history, Porter argues that it is misleading to see change as a cause or consequence of instability, but that instead it could benefit and be utilised by the existing system. Readers who wish to follow this controversy should also read Clark's *English Society 1688–1832*.

Though Porter personalises the debate, it is fair to state that of late considerable attention has been devoted by a number of scholars towards the strength of religious sentiment, the continued predominance, political, social and ideological, of

1

the aristocracy, and the conservative nature of political and social ideology. This development reflects recent empirical work and a general shift in interest. There has been a widespread shift from interest in dissent, and an interpretation of authority as based on power and operating through coercion, to one that stresses willingness to accept inegalitarian social, political and ideological theories and ways of life. Similarly, a consent model of European society has developed and absolutism has been redefined, as the product of cooperation between central government and social elites, rather than as 'something' that the state 'does' to elites. Britain can be discussed in these terms. By referring, for example, to the relative weakness of the Court, the size of the capital, the role of towns and international trade, it is possible to suggest that in some fashion England was unique and that the term *ancien régime* should not be applied to her. It is certainly possible to demonstrate differences between England and particular European states. Equally it is possible to suggest similarities. England was not alone in having to define relationships with a new dynasty, or with subordinate European territories, or with colonies with a substantial white population. Local government in England was primarily self-government by the social elite and this generated the primary political problem: that of persuading the elite to govern in the interest of the centre. This was a problem that existed whatever the state of high political struggles and it would have been all too familiar to many continental monarchs, well aware of the limitations and compromises of their rule.

If it is argued that there was one model of continental government and society, then it is easy to suggest that England should not be termed an *ancien régime*, as it is simple to demonstrate differences. However, it is more accurate to point to the diversity that characterised continental circumstances and developments. To that extent the term *ancien régime* is misleading if it is taken to denote a uniform situation and consistent change. If, instead, a European pluralism is advanced, then England can be more easily comprehended as a country which, like all others, had both particular and comparable features and developments. The myth of English uniqueness appears even less satisfactory from the perspective of

Ireland and Scotland. The British *ancien régime* was based on the dominance of the British Isles by the English elite, a dominance based on coercion, but increasingly dependent on the willingness of the Irish, Scottish and Welsh elites to accept English political and cultural leadership,[2] a situation that was not without parallels elsewhere in Europe, as for example in the Habsburg hereditary lands. The view of English society advanced by Clark is essentially that of a late-baroque society, characterised by a powerful church, a profound religious faith, patriarchal notions, a monarchy that was strong because it was desired and generally supported, and social dominance by the senior ranks of a comprehensive landed hierarchy. Therefore it is essentially describing a stable conservative society, albeit a society complicated until mid century by the ideological challenge posed by Jacobitism. This analysis offers much of value but its static, structural nature is a weakness, as is the tendency to minimise the role and autonomy of the middling orders and to marginalise government, policy and debate, other than in religious topics. This revisionist interpretation accords with much work on eighteenth-century continental Europe, where notions such as dechristianisation and the rise of bourgeois consciousness are under challenge. However, it is necessary to complement work on clerical ideology and the role of Anglicanism in English culture[3] with studies of the religious beliefs of the bulk of the population, a subject discussed by David Hempton. The extent to which at the parochial level the Church–State enjoyed respect and deference is unclear. It is also by no means clear that the idiom of a Church–State entailed stability and precluded domestic strife. It certainly did not do so in Scotland and Ireland. There the religious establishment, Presbyterian in Scotland and Anglican in Ireland, denied rights and opportunities to much of the population, especially the numerous Episcopalians in Scotland, who until the Revolution Settlement of 1689 had been the established group in Scotland, and the Catholic majority of the Irish population, whose position had deteriorated markedly as a result of the Settlement, which in Ireland, as in Scotland, had to be enforced. Thus, the Revolution Settlement helped to create the basis of instability in Scotland and Ireland. Though, as Bruce Lenman discusses, patronage and the use of local political managers kept both, from the point of view of London, 'quiet' for long periods, their instability posed serious security problems on a number of occasions, most obviously in Scotland in 1715 and 1745 and in Ireland in 1798, while the management of Irish politics became a growing problem from mid century.

There was change in eighteenth-century Britain, and this change cannot be really understood if the notion of an inflexible Church–State, its stability challenged unsuccessfully by Jacobitism and later by Jacobinism, is adopted. Clark's valuable analysis, which captures the flavour of British political culture in the first half of the century, appears increasingly adrift in the second half. Catholic Emancipation, parliamentary reform and the repeal of the Test and Corporation Acts may have been kept at bay, and the extent of economic change in the Industrial Revolution and of urban radicalism in the 1760s and 1790s may have been exaggerated, but it would be wrong to suggest that change was marginal. The consequences of conquering two empires, one in India, the other in North America, and of devising several systems of imperial regulation were of economic and political significance in Britain, and this is discussed by William Hausman and Peter Marshall. Even if the numerical indices of industrialisation were less impressive than used to be believed, the qualitative impact of economic change was obvious to contemporaries. The impression was of Prometheus Unbound, of extraordinary opportunities offered by technological change, whether the report in the *Darlington Pamphlet* of 1772 that in Nottingham, 'an ingenious mechanic has just invented a machine with which a girl of ten years of age may spin several threads' or the controversy in the *Leeds Intelligencer* six years earlier aroused by proposals to link the North and Irish seas by a Calder–Mersey canal. In 1750 a visitor from Derbyshire reported, 'what a great deal of good the cotton spinning does at their town and Youlgreave. He says it would be very hard to maintain the poor about them if it was not for that business.'[4] As one of the most crucial social changes in the second half of the century was the increase in population from around 6 million in England in 1760 to 8.6 million by 1791, an increase that was due more to rising birth than to falling death rates, the economic context of that change is not without importance, even though demographic shifts are notoriously difficult to probe. A sense of opportunity encouraging earlier marriages was more important than medical improvements or reductions in the severity of diseases. Other aspects of the economy ˜also changed greatly, including the transportation of people, goods and messages. On 19 June 1773 *Jackson's Oxford Journal* reported:

> The difference in the number of stage coaches, etc. travelling on the Western road, within these few years, is not a little remarkable. About ten years ago there only passed through Salisbury in the course of a week, to and from London and Exeter, six stage coaches, which carried six passengers each, making in the whole (if full) 36 passengers. At present there constantly pass, between the above places, in the same space of time, 24 stage coaches, carrying six passengers each and 28 stage chaises, carrying three each making in the whole, if full, 228 passengers.

This sense of change was very notable in the second half of the century and developments in transportation not only had specific economic consequences, but also helped to integrate the country. The provision of new facilities was important because it was combined with rising demand for them and the ability of some to afford their costs. It is instructive to compare the roads of England with the splendid highways of Languedoc which were used far less. Naturally only a small minority travelled in high-speed coaches on the new turnpike roads. The majority of the population, for whom travel for work, whether long-term or seasonal, was no novelty, mostly benefited little from the changes. However, the greater ease of communication helped to unify the elite, facilitating education, socialising and travel for business or political reasons. London newspapers were sent to the provinces in increasing numbers, postal services improved considerably, to the benefit of the expanding banking system as well as to the letter writer, that central character in two recent and rapidly developing literary forms, the novel and the magazine.

The anglicanisation of the Scottish, Welsh and Irish elites was a marked feature of the period, one that was helped by education in English schools, intermarriage, service in the armed forces (which was especially important in Scotland), and a determination to take advantage of the opportunities offered by the British state that makes any discussion in terms of English cultural imperialism somewhat misleading. At the same time that a strong sense of locality remained deeply engrained in the popular consciousness, a striking feature of certainly English public life, notably so in comparison with the situation elsewhere in Europe, was the relative absence of a regional politico-social consciousness. There were of course exceptions, the agitation over the cider tax in 1763 displaying a regional aspect.[5] However, the national political consciousness which can be seen at work in the political campaigns discussed by Harry Dickinson, also reflected institutional and constitutional arrangements. By European standards England was, for a country of its size and population, relatively centralised: there were no regional parliaments and no internal customs. Weights and measures, and legal inheritance practices varied comparatively little. A mid-century French visitor wrote: 'Arrival in England seems to announce liberty. The towns are not shut, nothing constricts trade, travellers are not asked where they go or whence they came and there are no internal customs.'[6]

On the British scale, Wales had long been joined, constitutionally and institutionally, with England, but Ireland remained separate and her constitutional and economic relationship with the territories under the Westminster Parliament became increasingly contentious.[7] Scotland witnessed both the '45 and a more gradual integration with England. The '45, a Scottish Jacobite uprising, was a dramatic consequence of the Glorious Revolution of 1688 and the Hanoverian succession. It was followed in late 1745 by an invasion of England, the logical consequence of the Act of Union of 1707, for Scotland had lost its independent political destiny. The '45 inspired fear and hatred, the Earl of Chesterfield writing to a fellow office-holder, 'that damned beggarly rebellious people provoke me'.[8] It erupted upon a defenceless nation. A loyal Scottish peer, Lord Glenorchy, wrote to his daughter regretting that, like so many landowners, he had weakened his house in modernising it: 'I have often repented taking out the iron bars from the windows and sashing them, and taking away a great iron door, and weakening the house as to resistance by adding modern wings to it. If it had remained in the old castle way as it was before, I might have slept very sound in it, for their whole army could not have taken it without cannon.'[9]

And yet despite the construction or repair of forts by the government, there was no reversal of architectural fashion in Scotland or northern England. The '45 was a terrible shock, though contemporaries were as divided on its seriousness as later historians have been. On the same day, both writing from London, the Earl of Bath suggested that, 'discontented as the nation may be in some respects, I really think that very few mean to submit to the Pretender introduced by a French force amongst us', while the Duke of Newcastle's private secretary, Andrew Stone, noted, 'the undertaking, in its present appearance seems (as it is the fashion to call it,) rash and desperate: But I cannot think it is altogether to be despised. We are so naked of troops, that, if a body of men was to be flung over, no one can say what may be the consequences.' Three months later, with the rebels passing Lancaster, George Grenville unsurprisingly wrote, 'nor do people trouble their heads much at present about Prussia and Saxony'.[10]

The ministerial response to the '45 was a sweeping attack on traditional Highland government, including the abolition of hereditable jurisdictions. In May 1746 Thomas Sherlock, the influential Bishop of Salisbury, warned that there had been laws passed on the matter before, 'but never executed, and perhaps the main thing to be provided for, is we secure an execution of the *Kings* laws in the country; which is at present under the absolute *will* of the lairds.'[11] The ministerial programme was not completely successful, but it indicated the determination of the British ministry to introduce radical changes when faced with a local elite with which it was unable to develop a working relationship. A specific view of civic peace and civil society was enforced by troops and legislation. Though the process varied in its effectiveness, much of Scottish society was increasingly pulled towards England. This was least true of Scottish religion and law, where national distinctiveness was legally established, and most true of national politics and business. Scottish lobbying increasingly focused on London,

George Chalmers writing to George Grenville in 1769:

> We are to make an application to parliament this winter for several matters regarding the linen manufacture which is a staple in this part of the kingdom. . . . I have much personal interest in one branch of the application viz the laying of an additional duty on foreign diapers or table linen having an estate here surrounding Dunfermline which manufactures more of that species than any other place in Great Britain or Ireland. . . . The principal manufacturers assure me that they are in a condition to supply a great part of the English consumption if they have proper encouragement and have no doubt but the laying on of a small additional duty on foreign diapers will at least double or triple the value of the manufacturers of this place in a year or two after the law may be passed. I shall . . . send you sometime before the Houses meet a state in print of what they propose to apply for.[12]

Change was not confined to the Highlands. The government of the British state became generally more sophisticated, although to an uneven extent. It is easy to stress elements of continuity and to criticise the corruption and incompetence latent in unmeritocratic appointments to bureaucratic structures riddled by patronage and self-assessment in taxation. The professionalism of the Excise service has been much praised lately, but Sir James Lowther, MP for Cumberland, wrote to his Whitehaven agent in December 1739 that John Hill MP, a Commissioner of Customs, 'as he finds Sir Robert [Walpole] looks upon me as a hearty friend he would have me to dispose of things in Cumberland both in Customs and Excise. At this rate are things managed in every part of the revenue. It is suffered to go on very often to the prejudice of the public, to gratify the friends of great men.' Four years later he added, 'everybody agrees that they must regulate the duties as the Revenue is dwindling away by frauds'. In 1763 George Grenville, then first minister, was told 'that Mr Pelham has allowed Lord Galloway to recommend all the little Custom House offices in the shire of Wigtown and the district of Burghs within it whilst the members who served for them were chosen by him and supported the measures of the government.' However,

British administration, though far smaller, was not obviously worse than that of the continental states and much of it was efficient and inexpensive given the circumstances of the period. It also did improve over the century. In the field of public finance it proved capable of shouldering, albeit not without difficulty, the burden of several lengthy wars. In part this was a reflection of the strength of the economy, but financial confidence in the growing stability of government helped to ensure a willingness to lend money to successive ministries at rates that were considerably lower than those obtained by Britain's rivals. The Duke of Newcastle, then First Lord of the Treasury, noted in 1757 that there appeared to be no difficulty in meeting the new commitment to provide greater military support to Prussia: 'towards that I have already been offered near six millions . . . and all this money will be borrowed (if necessary) something under 3½ per cent; when France gives 11 per cent and cannot fill the subscriptions.' By the last years of the Seven Years War (1756–63) government credit was not so strong, in large part because of the major expansion of the national debt that had already taken place, as in every other war Britain fought. The economic consequences of such heavy government borrowing were not entirely beneficial, but in Britain the same level of borrowing could be financed at lower cost to the state than in France, and this led to lower interest rates.

It was not only in public finance that the British government system was strong. In addition, the structure of colonial administration and commercial regulation received considerable attention, and the period witnessed much administrative reform and government activity, whether with the navy, or at the Treasury where North and, more especially, Pitt the Younger were very responsive to a climate of reform.[13] It is mistaken to argue that eighteenth-century ministries were always opposed to considering change. 'Let sleeping dogs lie' does not describe the typical late-eighteenth-century administration, for officials and politicians were often willing to act in accordance with the principles of state-directed action. This was especially the case in response to crises. Just as the administrative and judicial system in the Scottish Highlands was remodelled after the '45, so the size of the national debt at the end of the Seven Years War led to an attempt at financial retrenchment and reorganisation, which exacerbated relations with the American colonies and the cider-producing counties in the west of England. Similarly the crisis of the American war, with its attendant problems in Britain, especially Ireland, led to the powerful impetus behind post-war reform initiatives which were particularly important in colonial, commercial and financial matters and, though less successfully so, in British domestic politics. Similarly, work at the local level, on Justices of the Peace, law-enforcement, urban communities, and prison administration, has stressed the significance of planning and policy, showing change as much as continuity.

In this perspective the arguments centred on the existence of a Church–State and of ideological conservatism appear remote, and it is here that the case for an 'open society', in the sense of a society willing to allow the discussion and explanation of policy, can be made most forcefully. Local politics, administration and economic developments involved public as well as private discussion. The importance of parliamentary legislation on local matters, such as turnpikes, and of local subscriptions as a means of raising funds helped to further public discussion and local organisation. An example of this is the committee which met at Worcester in 1785–6 to oppose a proposed bill for erecting locks and weirs on the Severn and imposing a toll on trade on the river.

In arguing for the existence of an 'open society', it is not necessary to advance dubious suggestions that public opinion, however defined, explained policy. It is wrong to present public discussion as in some sense outside the political system, for the press and the amorphous pressures, interests and opinions understood by the term public opinion were part of the political process itself. Propaganda, the expression of opinion in an attempt to persuade, was not simply the recourse of opposition groups. In Britain, as on the continent, governments adopted the medium of print to serve their purposes and used to that end the particular forms that were available, including the sponsored press. If the direct political influence of the press was limited, it was nevertheless of significance from the point of view of the 'open society' because it offered the possibility of pluralism of opinion and of public debates that the argument of ideological coherence and homogeneity leaves little room for.

The terms of public debate were not always welcome. In 1763 Lord Strange, an independent MP for Lancashire, who was the county's Lord Lieutenant as well as being the heir to the Earl of Derby, criticised the London petition over the cider tax, 'spoke violently against the city of London, called the Common Council an Assembly of Shopkeepers, said that they wanted to raise themselves into a legislative body'. In a society where rank was generally seen as a definition of merit, snobbery and social exclusiveness were widespread. In 1744 the Duke of Bedford, on becoming First Lord of the Admiralty, insisted that another Admiralty Lord, John Phillipson MP, 'who has been a clerk', resign 'as not of quality enough'. In 1769 Lord North mocked a petitioning movement in Oxford: 'I believe the account in the papers is literally true, and that a scout of Christ-Church, and a shoe-black, of Trinity College were the two most active persons in the business after the baronet himself.' On 29 May 1773 the *Westminster Journal* reported: 'Last week some persons of fortune, in the county of Norfolk, riding together, overtook a poor lad, whom they humorously agreed to hunt, and whipping the boy forwards, made him run near four miles, when he dropped down with the fatigue, and his humane pursuers, after the sport was over, generously gave him 2s!' An unsympathetic sense of the poor as a problem was clearly presented in the discussion of many reforming proposals, for example in a report from a Dublin official in 1774:

Our police has undergone a great improvement lately by the establishment of a receptacle for the miserable vagrants who infested the streets of this metropolis. The great work of cleansing Madrid was not more necessary, nor in appearance more difficult to be effected; but by some humane and resolute people applying themselves seriously to the task, the streets of Dublin are now as exempt from that shocking nuisance as those of London and a man may get back to his home with the same quantity of silver in his pocket as he carries out of it.[14]

In such a situation it was not surprising that the opinion of 'the gentlemen of the greatest weight and property'[15] was

regarded as of particular weight. However, it would be misleading to suggest that deference was universal or that the
widespread desire for order prevented disorder, especially
from those who felt that their traditional way of life was under
threat. The seriousness of criticism of and opposition to the
existing order is a matter of debate. In some cases it was clearly
a matter of polemical points within a well-established
framework. The Berkshire by-election of 1776 led to criticism
of the 6th Earl of Craven, who dominated the county in alliance
with the 4th Earl of Abingdon, both supporters of the Opposition, for allegedly telling a county meeting: 'I will have it
known there is respect due to a Lord'. The argument that a
wealthy peer was overriding the gentry was part of the established currency of political debate. Lord Strange might in 1763
propose that the Commons should sit on the anniversary of
Charles I's execution, affirming that the words in the statute
enacting the day as the anniversary of a martyrdom that
'neither Parliament nor people can judge the King' were
'contrary to the constitution' but only 36 people voted for the
motion. Furthermore only 103 opposed it[16] and the issue did
not become a *cause célèbre*. The old agenda of seventeenth-
and early eighteenth-century disputes over dynasticism had
disappeared, attenuating religio-ideological divisions. *Felix
Farley's Bristol Journal* could suggest on 23 November 1788: 'In
a town in the North of England, on the Revolution day, a party
met to drink health to the *old cause and family* – they were in
number thirty, and we suppose comprehend *all* of that opinion
in the three kingdoms'.

There were also signs of unease. In 1742 Sherlock wrote to
the Lord Chancellor, the Earl of Hardwicke:

> your Lordship's observation on the present state of the clergy
> is very just; but it is a melancholy truth: and what is still
> worse, there is but little hope of finding a remedy for this
> evil. Discipline is in a manner lost; and the episcopal
> authority with respect to the behaviour and conduct of the
> clergy is become so feeble, that many are of opinion, that
> there is no other way to cover the weakness of it, but not to
> make use of it. This is a matter that deserves serious
> consideration, when the times will permit, and there shall

arise a disposition to take care of the morals and religion of the people.

The situation appeared little better in the secular sphere. In 1748 George II expressed the fear that the Dutch 'spirit of sedition' would spread to England and in 1763 Elizabeth Montagu, the wife of an independent MP, was shocked by the extent of critical sentiment in London:

The daemon of discontent is murmuring and whispering in well bred society, and bowling and scolding among the mob. Every species of abuse comes forth in print or pamphlet, and all the garretteer scriblers are treating the characters of great persons with a scurrility nothing but shameless vice could utter. I do not wonder the wretches sunk in infamy and poverty should be guilty of these outrages, but I'm surprised their works should be bought up in the manner they are . . . all mankind are philosophers and pride themselves in having a contempt for rank and order and imagine they show themselves wise in ridiculing whatever gives distinction and dignity to kings and other magistrates, not considering that these chains of opinion are less galling than those of law, and that the great beast the multitude must be bound by something. Alexander the Great was treated with contempt by a certain philosopher in a tub, but in this enlightened age the man who made the tub would use him with the same scorn.[17]

It was not only in London that workers displayed opinions. That year an official reported from Dublin,

The Lords Justices have at the request of the Earl of Hillsborough ordered a company of foot to the town of Lisburn for the preservation of the public peace. His Lordship was insulted or ill treated by a mob of weavers in that town . . . they pulled him about and squeezed him for near two hours, and tore his cloths, and compelled him to take an oath to be true to the interest of the weavers before they would let him go. His Lordship went thither to protect one Williamson against whom the weavers had vowed vengeance for having revealed some frauds practised in the linen manufacture, and in order by his personal appearance and weight to preserve the peace of the country . . . the true foundation of this, as well as other riots that have happened in this part of the kingdom is, and a melancholy considera- tion it is, that so total a disregard for all law, and decency, for government and magistracy prevail, that any three or four ill-intentioned men have it in their power to raise these disturbances by misrepresentations and evil suggestions, at the same time that nine in ten of the rioters are ignorant of the cause of their rising. I do not find that any one person concerned in this riot has been apprehended.

Elizabeth Montagu was depressed about Newcastle the fol- lowing year, 'There is an universal dejection among honest people. The public papers, absurd as they are, have made deep impressions', while the policing of the London mob gave Lord North concern. In 1773 the Cornish tinners 'rose in such numbers that it was not in the power of any civil police to quell them'. They seized grain and were fired on by troops. If a stability or strife antithesis is advanced such disturbances and discontent might appear threatening to the existing social order, but such an antithesis is arguably of only limited applicability. The extent to which popular disorder was in- tended to elicit favourable government action in defence of a shared moral order can be debated, but it is clear that indi- viduals and groups were prepared to break the law without intending any necessary rejection of the principles and practices of the social order. Similarly, the response of the landed elite was not uniformly hostile. In Cornwall in 1773 military assist- ance was sought, but measures were also taken to relieve poverty and reduce the price of grain, while one landowner blamed much on exploitation of the tinners by the smelters, 'thus is the face of the poor ground by those who so quickly and I fear unjustly get immense fortunes'. The great Norfolk landowner, the Marquess of Townshend, was sent a reassuring letter by a JP about the effects of the 1790 food shortage:

not the smallest appearance of tumult or dissatisfaction has broke out in any of the parishes near us; I have had many complaints but all in a regular submissive manner. The insurrection at Aylsham and Norwich proceeded almost entirely from the neglect of the gentlemen in that part of the country, we cannot be surprised that people should murmur when they are starving and find no probability of assistance, but I am well convinced that force is totally needless if a method is adopted to relieve their distresses, which surely is fair and reasonable if they represent such distress in a proper way without threats'.[18]

However, society was certainly more violent than a stress on the literature of politeness and social manners might imply; indeed such literature, like the codes of behaviour developed in assemblies and spas, was often intended to wean people from their unruly and often violent temperaments and tendencies. The genteel culture with its stress on harmony propagated with such care for fashionable circles and leisure towns, such as Bath, was not the same as the civic culture of most towns, where traditional rivalries and new disputes gave rise to a more divided and political society.

Lawlessness was particularly marked in remote areas. Rural violence was common in much of Ireland. The Whiteboys of the 1760s used nocturnal terror to resist the enclosure of commons. The middlemen who were crucial to a rentier rural society, as agents and tithe proctors, were attacked while fences were destroyed and cattle maimed. In England the level of violence was generally lower, though not always so. The *Newcastle Courant* of 28 May 1743 reported: 'Yesterday Mr. William Aynsley, Water Bailiff, with near 20 men on horseback, well armed, set out for Bellingham, in order to take possession of an estate which the country people by force of arms, have deprived the right owner of, and murdered a bailiff the beginning of this month.' In 1773 an effort to serve writs on two Cardiganshire JPs was forestalled when the server was forced to eat them before being beaten viciously and thrown into a river, feigning death. Another warrant was served on them only with the aid of a pistol. And yet in lawlessness and crime it would be wrong to make a contrast between town and country. The polite world of civilised urban spaces, of the assembly rooms and the circulating library, the subscription concert and the newspaper, coexisted with grime, squalor, misery and disorder. It would also be wrong to describe the period as one characterised by the rise of a 'modern' consumer society, driven by a desire for profit and a wish for new products and services linked by a world of print that could create and encourage fashions and a cult of novelty, if that led to a neglect of the continual importance of customary methods of production, consumption and service. It is too easy to suggest that modern or enlightened ideas banished those that owed more to the world of superstition, driving them down the social pyramid and marginalising them geographically. The great popularity of quack medical cures and almanacs should induce caution about such a triumphalist notion, as should the revival of astrology and millenarianism towards the end of the century. On 4 February 1744 the *Newcastle Courant* carried a report from Edinburgh: 'we learn that a great many people, who have little sense and great many deal of superstition, are in a prodigious panic, on consulting their almanacs, when they find Easter Sunday happens on Lady-day, grounding their fear on the prophecy: When our Lord falls in our lady's lap, England beware of a great mishap.' The London earthquakes six years later were located by most commentators in a scheme of divine punishment. An informed account of comets in 1758 closed with the fraternal advice, 'let not however any specious part of reason prevent our concern at such phaenomena, but rather put us in mind of the end and final conclusion of all things and but it induce us to pay a more than common homage at the foot stool of the throne of our good Almighty God, who with a rod or touch or breath can hurl us with fury and terrible destruction to all eternity', a very immediate portrayal of divine power.[19]

Criticism of 'popular superstition' carries with it the danger of overlooking identical or similar if more fashionable superstition at a more exalted level. A major problem is posed by the relationship of urban to rural change. Most of the institutions, individuals and practices that appear to represent what could be described as the British Enlightenment were urban. The extent to which their example was followed in the towns, let alone elsewhere, is unclear. The works of such Scots as Ferguson, Hume, Hutcheson, Robertson and Adam Smith enjoyed an international reputation and there has been considerable scholarly interest in the Scottish Enlightenment. Nevertheless, it has been suggested recently that 'such Enlightenment as existed in eighteenth-century Scotland was confined to a tiny minority who lived surrounded by a narrow minded nationalism and a bigoted puritanism'. And yet contemporaries did note differences between town and country, the Earl of Rochford, Secretary of State for the Southern Department, writing to the Earl of Grantham, the envoy in Madrid, that George III's visit to the fleet at Portsmouth in 1773 'exceeded our expectation . . . an immensity of people, happy beyond measure at seeing their sovereign. Every inn and village gave proofs of their joy, and the metropolis, if it has any feeling at all must be ashamed at having been so long defective in manifesting their loyalty to the best of sovereigns.'[20]

A contrast of urban change and rural conservatism would be misleading if it ignored urban conservatism, rural change and the multifaceted nature of the relationship between town and country. The pedlar hawking his wares round the hamlets, the newsman on his rounds, selling patent medicines and other products as well as distributing newspapers, played important intermediary roles, as did the country people who flocked to towns for markets and fairs. Many links, both between town and country and between different regions, were traditional, for example the relationships of transhumance, and permanent or temporary migration, but others developed or expanded during the period, helped by improving communications. Migration played an important role in eroding barriers, though many migrants congregated together and it is not clear how sustained were the links of permanent migrants with their areas of origin. A pamphlet of 1756 noted: 'I have heard many judicious farmers and country gentlemen say, that were it not for the great supplies of labouring people we annually receive from Scotland and Ireland, we should not have hands in England sufficient to reap our harvest.'[21] Migration was not, of course, new. Many of the social features that were to be associated with economic transformation were already common. Far from Britain being a rural elysium, lacking a Boucher to depict plenty and langourous calm, but all too soon to be ravaged by industrialisation, the rural world had already in the fifteenth and sixteenth centuries witnessed massive disruptions of land and labour. Neither enclosure, sweeping changes in land use, rural proletarianisation nor the social and economic changes wrought by industrialisation, technological change and the rise and decline of specific areas and economic activities were new.

Change and stress were part of the socio-economic fabric of the British *ancien régime* and no more incompatible with it than was popular political consciousness and activity. To demonstrate the existence of change and disorder no more qualifies the existence or stability of such a *régime* than it explains its alleged collapse in the early nineteenth century. In the political and government fields it is possible to argue that change brought fresh strength in the shape of administrative improvements and the ideological and political consolidation that was cause and still more consequence of the defeat of Jacobitism and the collapse of Toryism as a separate political identity.

Indeed the period 1742–89 is given a degree of cohesion by this move towards ideological consolidation. The 1740s saw both the most serious crisis faced by the eighteenth-century British state and the ending of Jacobitism as a viable military or political option. This was an unintended consequence of the fall of Walpole. Whereas Fleury, the leading French minister, in 1741 was not really interested in the idea of an invasion of Britain in support of the Jacobites, by 1742 his control was weakened and the anti-French zeal of the ministry that succeeded that of Walpole increased French interest in the idea of action against Britain. Carteret, the most influential member of the new administration, was distrusted by the French and in July 1742 Amelot, the French foreign minister, expressed strong interest in the means by which trouble could be created within Britain, though he was sceptical about Jacobite schemes.[22] The French were driven into supporting the Jacobites by the change in British policy in 1742. Carteret hoped that Britain would defeat France and that the latter would therefore be unable to mount an invasion. Certainly the dispatch of British troops to the Austrian Netherlands in 1742 made it unlikely that the French, with most of their forces committed in Germany, would be able to prepare an invasion force near Dunkirk. By 1744 the military situation had altered, but this was not predicted. The domestic position in 1742 was also reasonably propitious for the government. The opposition had been fragmented by the ratting of some of its leaders who joined the 'Old Corps' of ministerial Whigs, without insisting either that the policies they had supported when in opposition be implemented or that opposition leaders be taken into office. Over the next five years the opposition fractured on a number of occasions as divisions arose over the issue of supporting the ministry, a subject discussed by Ian Christie. Several prominent critics of the 'Old Corps', including William Pitt the Elder in 1746, proved eager to accept office. Whereas the fall of Walpole was followed by a more vigorous pursuit of an aggressive foreign policy, there was no comparable change in domestic policy. The ambitious legislative programme of the late 1710s was not resurrected. This arguably contributed something to making the volatile political atmosphere of 1742–46 less serious as a cause of tension in the localities.

However, the taking of Hanoverian troops into British pay was very unpopular, and it would be inappropriate to exaggerate the popularity of the Hanoverian regime. In 1745 Robert Trevor, envoy at The Hague, wrote to a fellow diplomat concerning the dispatch of Dutch troops in Britain: 'My private letters represent their presence as but too necessary; and it is apprehended by some good, sensible Whigs, that the indifference, and lukewarmness of the many is more dangerous than the activity of the few'.[23] The Jacobites who had claimed that Britain was ready to rise in revolution were to be proved wrong in 1745, but equally the Hanoverian regime was revealed as having a very narrow base. As with Bohemia, claimed and initially successfully invaded by Charles Albert of Bavaria in 1741 in the face of lukewarm support for the Habsburgs, the vagaries of military and political luck proved decisive in Britain too. Recent work on 1688 has arrived at a similar conclusion, though one clear distinction emerges. Whereas the Royal Navy was eager to fight in 1744–5, in 1688 the attitude of many captains was ambivalent and several supported William. If the role of chance is stressed it is plausible to present support of the Stuarts not as nostalgic folly, but as a considered response reflecting traditional loyalties, a coherent ideology and the awareness that they might be restored. Rather than simply a dying loyalty, Jacobitism was sustained by the activities of post-Revolution rulers and governments and by the prospect of foreign assistance. Jacobite propaganda referred to the former frequently. An anonymous undated work of late 1745 entitled *A Letter to the Archbishop of York: Humbly offering to his Grace's Solution some doubts and scruples suggested by his late speech to the Grand meeting of the County of York, called to subscribe an association for supporting the German Government in England* defended Charles Edward's troops from attacks upon their conduct, attacked 'the immoderate increase of national debts and taxes, lavished away to support' and aggrandise Hanover and claimed that religion was not flourishing in Britain.

> I love the Religion and Liberties of my country . . . did the Excise Scheme, the Number and Rigour of Penal Laws and Standing armys, the swarms of Placemen and pensioners, and the venality of Parliaments threaten no danger to the Liberty of the Nation? Whether Deism and Infidelity, Luxury and perjury, and Prophaneness of all sorts have not grown to an enormous height, and found not only impunity, but encouragement from this mild administration? Whether the most sacred offices, and highest Dignities of the Church have not been set to sale: or bestowed more with respect to Party-interest, than to real merit and fitness? Whether to offer but one instance out of many, your brother of Winchester does not well deserve something else than the first benefice in England, when by his Plain account of the Sacrament, and his measures of submission to Sovereign Powers, he has attempted to Burlesque the most sacred institution of Christianity, and a distinguishing doctrine of the Church.[24]

Such attitudes were mocked by Henry Fielding who claimed that, 'the Jacobites have always imputed scorching summers, hard winters, bad harvests, famine pestilence, etc. to the Revolution'.[25] But there is little doubt that the Stuart cause both sustained and benefited from a widespread moral repugnance towards the Hanoverian regime in church and state. If this produced little in the way of direct action, that was in accordance with the general nature of early modern English political activity. Work on the outbreak of the English Civil War in the provinces has stressed the hesitation with which the people resorted to violence. Most of England did not rise in 1688. Prudence complemented traditions of political activity that offered only a restricted role for violence, namely riots for essentially limited objects. Changes of regime, as opposed to ministerial reshuffles and upheavals in Court and Parliament, arose from invasion and from the different political traditions of the Celtic kingdoms, especially the readiness to resort to violence in Scotland. The Civil War owed much to developments in Scotland and Ireland and, in particular, to the failure to repel the Scottish invasion in the Bishop's War. The Whigs proved unwilling to rise at the time of the Exclusion Crisis while James II, as Duke of York, crucially kept Scotland quiet. James survived the Argyle and Monmouth rising in 1685 but fell to a foreign invasion in 1688. The Tories would not rise in 1714 and Scotland played the central role in the '15 and the '45. It was not surprising that after the suppression of the latter the Whigs remodelled Highland society.

Thus the Stuart cause was not unique in finding that most of England did not rise in its support, neither is that proof that its support there was scanty. However, this failure helped to cause the collapse of the movement, though not of sympathy for the Stuarts. Its immediate effect was the retreat of Charles Edward and the consequent failure of the '45. A move to the defensive did not generally prove the basis of a successful rebellion in this period. Its longer term effect was to destroy the international credibility of the movement and thus lessen the chance of mounting another invasion. The pretender, 'James III', had been told frequently by British supporters in the 1720s and 1730s that the Stuart cause depended on foreign support. Depending on one's assessment the '45 nearly proved them wrong, or proved them correct, because the French did not invade and success eluded Charles Edward. The period after Culloden supported the assessments made in the 1720s and 1730s. Thus Britain's relations with other powers were important for the success of the Stuart cause. The Stuarts suffered the fate of most exiles. Without a foreign base, comparable to Scotland in 1640 or the United Provinces in 1688, their options were limited, their position, both domestically and diplomatically, circumscribed. The absence of a second restoration did not mean, however, that the Stuart cause was without reason or consequence. The Jacobite critique of the Hanoverian regime, particularly of the direction of foreign policy for Hanoverian ends, was well founded.

From the collapse of Jacobitism until the 1790s Britain was essentially politically stable. This followed a protracted period when, though to varying degrees, there had been serious instability linked to profound differences over dynastic and religious issues. A stress on Jacobitism and a reconsideration of the nature of stability so that attention is focused on viable challenges to the established structure of authority rather than on opposition to particular ministries and government policies therefore offers a different chronology of eighteenth-century stability. Rather than seeing the early decades of the century simply as a period of rising stability, attention can also be directed to the continued threat posed by Jacobitism. Conversely, the seriousness of the challenge offered to George III and his ministries by opposition agitation in the first three decades of his reign (1760–89), especially in the 1760s, can be qualified, especially in so far as England was concerned. Political stability in the late eighteenth century did not preclude constitutional disputes, as in the 1760s, 1782–4 and 1788–9, ministerial instability, in the same periods, and extra-parliamentary action, some of it radical. Indeed in some respects it could be seen as a condition of it. The destruction of the principal external threat had a comparable effect in Britain and British North America. In the latter the conquest of Canada in the Seven Years War, in marked contrast to the result of previous conflicts, was arguably a necessary precondition of the breakdown of relations between Britain and many, though by no means all, of the colonists. Chance played a role in the loss of America. To a considerable extent the difficulty of retaining the link was ignored or underrated, first politically and then militarily. A pamphlet of 1756 urging import of iron from America, rather than Sweden, faced the objection that: 'it would occasion a vast increase of people and wealth, and consequently of power in those countries that in time might become rivals to their mother country, prejudice her interests, and become at last independent of her. But however plausible this objection may appear, there can be no just foundation for it, since ... it will be always in our power to subject them by our fleets, and still more by refusing them supplies of many of the necessaries of life.'[26] The course of the American Revolution revealed the error of this claim, but most political disputes and wars in this period ended in compromise. Though a crushing of the Revolution was unlikely, the achievement of a position that would encourage the revolutionaries to accept a compromise settlement was by no means impossible.

It might appear implausible to suggest that Wilkesite Britain was fundamentally stable, in light of the difficulty of forming a lasting ministry and the extent of extra-parliamentary political action, but the radicalism of the period scarcely prefigured that of the 1790s. All politicians, and the majority of those who thought about politics and society, wished to make the existing system work better or, in their eyes, more properly, rather than to introduce change. This shared objective did not prevent discord, in part because of the absence of general agreement over several major constitutional issues,[27] but largely because discord was and is compatible with a stable political system. A degree of ambivalence, albeit a diminished one, towards the notion of a loyal opposition and legitimate opposition tactics helped to blind many contemporaries to this. The search for office, the furtherance or prevention of policies, and economic problems and anxieties all played a part in the discord of the 1760s, though at the level of high politics much of this was due to a traditional theme, the difficulties resulting from the accession of a new monarch. Thanks in part to the press and to the determined popularisation of the cause of the opposition by Wilkes, which is discussed by Harry Dickinson, high politics was increasingly less of a distinct political sphere. However, discontent over the actions of a new monarch was less politically destabilising than the belief that he had no right to rule, because of the claims of another dynasty, as had been the case with the Jacobite challenge to Georges I and II. However imperfectly, the extent of popular representation through and participation in the electoral system helped to lead to a broad popular acceptance of the Hanoverian regime.

In April 1761 the Earl of Chesterfield, a veteran Whig, wrote to George III's favourite and soon to be first minister, the Earl of Bute: 'Parties are now abolished, and the King is King of his united and unanimous people, and enjoys their confidence and love to such a degree, that were I not as fully convinced as I am of his Majesty's heart, and the moderation of his will, I should tremble for the liberties of my country.'[28] George Lyttelton wrote soon after George's accession that 'the general disposition of the times [was] to let nobody complain or be discontented' though Elizabeth Montagu added a warning: 'Parliament . . . there will not be a division on any question such is the unanimity of all parties. The young king seems to endeavour to please every one, and he may do so for a time, but as he cannot have places for all who desire and think they deserve them, discontents will arise.'[29]

Initial reports were of harmony, the appearance of Tories at Court and royal declarations of political impartiality. The old division between Whigs and Tories and the proscription of the latter were both widely seen as things of the past. This political honeymoon did not last. Accessions could be deceptive as with the temporary replacement of Walpole by Compton in 1727 and the concurrent appearance of Tory leaders at Court. In 1760 the appearance of Tories was not deceptive, but the continuity in the ministry was. George III acted in a manner that he considered constitutional. He was no Gustavus III of Sweden who, in 1772, restored royal powers by overturning the constitution in a coup; neither did George's actions resemble the administrative and political changes introduced in France in the so-called Maupeou revolution of 1771. However, George's determination to be served by ministers in whom he had confidence and who he could rely on to support his views was very disruptive, because chance, the circumstances of 1761–2 and, arguably, royal and ministerial stubbornness, ensured that this led him to break with his grandfather's ministers. The Earl of Bath, an experienced politician, reflected in June 1762:

I fear he will have a very troublesome reign; those who have lately turned out, or resigned as they call it, in my opinion were suffered to stay in too long, and get too great a power in Parliament but if we have a little good fortune abroad, and obtain a good peace, and show that we are determined to pursue steadily right and popular measures at home and above all that the king appears to be resolute and steadfast, I think it may still do, and numbers may be persuaded to stick by a young king rather than an old minister. We were very lately, I think, going into an aristocracy or what is worse a king governed by one set of men, and his people by nothing but corruption.[30]

Bath was correct to identify chance factors. Bute proved a broken reed, unwilling and arguably unable psychologically to cope with the stress of contention. George did not find a satisfactory first minister until Lord North of whom the Duke of Richmond, a leading opposition peer, said and wrote in 1771; 'I had a great objection to him, and that is that he is a single man, no body. That as such I thought he ought not to be the minister of this country, for that as such a man did not depend upon the opinion of the world for his consequence but merely upon the king's pleasure, he could not follow his own opinions or those of the nation, and must be in too literal a sense the *servant* of the crown.'[31] The early 1770s witnessed a quieter political world and government success in the general election of 1774. North in turn was brought down in 1782 by circumstances, the inability to achieve through war or negotiation a satisfactory solution of the American Revolution. The different way the American developments could have led British politics is suggested by a letter of 1777 from Sir George Savile, the opposition MP for Yorkshire who had described American resistance as 'justifiable rebellion' in 1775, to the Marquis of Rockingham: 'We are not only Patriots *out of place*, but Patriots *out of the opinion of the public*. The repeated successes *hollow* as *I* think them, and the more *ruinous* if they are *real*, have fixed or converted 99 in 100. The cause itself wears away by rapid degrees from a question of right and wrong between *subjects*, to a war between us and a foreign nation, in which Justice is never heard, because love of one's country, which is a more favourite virtue, is on the other side. I see marks of this every where and in all ranks.'[32] Pitt the Younger's most serious political crisis before his fall, the Regency Crisis of 1788–9, arose from the unexpected, apparently permanent, incapacitating ill health of George III[33] and the likelihood of a regency under the hostile George,

Prince of Wales. Political clamour could be seen off if the ministry was united and certain of royal support, for these generally assured secure parliamentary backing. The popularity of peace further helped the Bute ministry to surmount its biggest problem, the negotiation and parliamentary defence of an acceptable compromise peace. In September 1763 Bute's successor, George Grenville, replied to a letter from Robert Waller MP; 'I agree entirely with you that the real difficulties lie in the exhausted state of the public revenues and not in the clamour of opposition of any individuals whatsoever.' Bath was similarly hopeful:

> when the angry folks of the West, have tried what they can do about cider, and find the Parliament will never consent to the repealing of a law, solemnly passed, only because a little unreasonable clamour has been raised against it, by a corner of the kingdom, (for that would be allowing a mob to be a fourth part of the Legislature) then I say they will sit down quietly and be contented to pay the duty, with some alterations in the manner of collecting it; and the manifestation of a large majority in both houses, will cool any future contentions from the opposers.[34]

Grenville was convinced that the greatest threat to the ministry was the belief that it was unstable,[35] which owed much to speculation over royal intentions. The disintegration of the old party divisions had thrown these intentions into greater prominence, which would have occurred irrespective of George's views. The impossibility of creating a dominant stable political grouping without active royal support was to be made readily apparent. The absence of party divisions placed a greater responsibility upon the monarch in his choice of leading politicians to favour.

Elite and extra-parliamentary politics were often related. Aside from specific links between the two spheres, there was also a transmission of ideas, which led Elizabeth Montagu to remark in 1762: 'What orators say in fine words and old ministers in soft words is repeated in Billingsgate phrase . . . by the mob!' However, it would be foolish to endow extra-parliamentary political action and thought with a false coherence, consistency and level of effectiveness. The Duke of

Richmond commented on the weakness of opposition sentiment in Sussex in 1769, 'from the natural indolence of men who
do not feel the immediate effects of oppression. From all these
causes, there was a supineness that of itself would not stir.'[36]

Richmond also wrote that he was against appearing factious
but, despite their general hostility to what was presented as
factionalism, political commentators were aware that disagreement was an integral part of the political system. In the words
of one pamphlet of 1755, 'If there ever was any one governing
principle of this great universe, I think, we may pronounce it is
the spirit of opposition.' George Lyttelton preferred a
meteorological image: 'our climate is not subject to such
furious wars of the elements as that of the Continent. Its
disorders are more frequent, but then they are not so violent.
Britannia is like a nervous lady, seldom well long together, but
not dangerously ill. This comparison I hope will hold with
regard to our politics as well as our weather.'[37]

This sense, that debate and disagreement were an integral
part of the political system, may have led at times to a certain
imperviousness in the face of criticism but also to a sense that
they were not necessarily in practice seditious or factious.
Rather than being a rigid oligarchical regime, constitutionally
protected by the defence of parliamentary sovereignty, one
could suggest a political structure that was more open to
discussion and debate than constitutional arrangements might
suggest. The impact of such discussion would clearly be far
from constant and the resilience of governments in the face of
unwelcome opinion should not be underrated. Any concentration on the clash of ideas and groups, however, risks detracting
attention from the degree of toleration and cooperation that
did exist. Elizabeth Montagu wrote in the spring of 1763 that
'the safest road to power is opinion', and of 'those who should
wish to establish authority by opinion rather than force.'[38]
Clearly force had played a major role, not least in the expulsion
of James II and the suppression of Jacobitism. However, it
would be appropriate to conclude by noting that although much
commentary naturally related to political tension and disagree-
ments, the structure of politics and government, far from
precluding debate and discussion, expected them.

Government relied on cooperation and lacked both a substantial bureaucracy and a well-developed bureaucratic ethos. In politics, aside from the institutional framework of contention, elections and Parliament, the Court and ministerial context of elite politics was not one of uniform opinions and an absence of debate. It would therefore be wrong to suggest that the English *ancien régime* was stable if that is intended to imply an absence of debate and of new ideas and initiatives. Nevertheless, there was no permanent struggle between government and the world of extra-parliamentary politics, no rigid divide, no consistent and coherent challenge to the political system. After the defeat of Jacobitism, the state became more stable and this situation was sustained until the challenge of the 1790s.

1

English Society in the Eighteenth Century Revisited

ROY PORTER

SOCIAL history may be coming of age. Yet, if confirmation were needed of its 'kid sister' status, the fact that the task of surveying the spectrum of social, cultural, intellectual and literary developments in Georgian England has been consigned to a single essay in this volume is surely eloquent. Some historians, of course, would argue that the history of society ought to play second-fiddle, on the grounds that where the action really was, was elsewhere.

For a currently prominent interpretation of the period – that advanced by J. C. D. Clark – takes it for granted that, precisely because the political structure of Hanoverian England proved so strong and enduring, its *social* developments cannot amount to much. Clark has thus ended up writing a book which, though entitled *English Society, 1688–1832*, says next to nothing about most of the problems over which social historians sweat: family formation and the domestic economy, gender hierarchies and sexuality, wealth and property distribution, crime, work and labour relations, the interplay between elite and popular culture, town and country, and so forth.[1]

As the discussion below will show, I believe that Clark is largely correct – if for the wrong reasons – to emphasise 'continuity' rather than 'change' as the key to the Georgian polity. But his vision of 'English society' is unremittingly Olympian: beneath the ruling elite, hardly anyone gets mentioned.[2] Trevelyan once teasingly defined social history as history with the politics left out. If we follow Clark, might we not end up, by contrast, with a 'social history' from which society is omitted?

Clark offers a reading of English society which says little about the way most people lived, because he believes that they are, ultimately, historically unimportant. There is also a far more humdrum, though just as devastating, reason why Georgian society still suffers neglect. For the century has long been subject to creeping historiographical imperialism from both 'before' and 'beyond'. This effect is caught in a nutshell in the titles of two recent social history surveys. J. A. Sharpe's *Early Modern England. A Social History* runs from 1550 to 1760; Trevor May's *An Economic and Social History of Britain* covers developments from 1760 up to the present.[3] Of course, for practical purposes, the seamless fabric of history has to be cut up somewhere. But because the scissors severing 'early modern' from 'modern' so often cut around 1760 or 1780, early Georgian England often appears only as a 'conclusion' to what came 'before', and the later Georgian age seems but an overture to what followed. The result is that sight is lost of the features distinctive to the eighteenth century. Clark has argued in favour of a scholarly enclosure act which would fence the period from 1660 to 1832 as a single unit. This notion of what may be called the 'long eighteenth century' is welcome. To meet the chronology of this volume, however, the present contribution focuses heavily upon the late Georgian age.

In this brief chapter, I shall not attempt the impossible, a thumbnail survey of all the initiatives in social history pioneered in the 1980s, or a full bibliographical listing of recent research. I shall instead be drastically selective. I shall concentrate upon a few areas of society and consciousness in which recent research and debate have challenged entrenched orthodoxies. And I shall explore others in which the quarrying of fresh sources, and attention to hitherto neglected groups and activities, are at least making darkness visible. In devoting space to such topics, I have had to leave out others of fundamental importance – new studies on population, the poor, family structure, and so forth. I regret these omissions.

I   SOCIETY AND THE STATE

First, however, it is necessary to address the question of the relation between society and state, or, in other words, between social history and political history.

In his *English Society 1688–1832*, and his subsequent *Revolution and Rebellion*, Clark has contended that mainline English historiography – Whig, Liberal, Marxist, and radical alike – had misunderstood the nature of the post-Restoration English polity. This (Clark claimed) should rightly be termed an *ancien régime*, indeed, a 'confessional state', thereby underlining its kinship to Continental monarchies. It should not be regarded as the uniquely progressive precursor of the reformed Victorian state. Subsequent contributions to this volume fully evaluate Clark's revisionism on dynastic, constitutional, religious and political issues.

But a further premise made by Clark is crucial to our interpretation of Georgian social history. Clark argues that the post-1660 English *ancien régime* remained sturdily intact almost until the accession of Victoria. Even then, it was not toppled by pressures from 'outdoors' – those irresistible subterranean social forces beloved of 'progressive' and 'reductionist' historians: the Industrial Revolution, the rise of the middle classes, the overwhelming tide of reformist public opinion. Rather it was 'betrayed' from within, suddenly, between 1828 and 1832, by a dramatic (and, one must say, barely explicable) failure of nerve amongst the ruling class. Clark's 'long eighteenth century' thereby entails a contentious reading of the relations between society and state, or what Marxists would call structure and superstructure.

For it counters the interpretation, entrenched in the 'great tradition' of Whig, Marxist and progressive history alike, which argues that new forces welling up within society at large proved so powerful, as eventually to compel major changes in the constitution and the distribution of power. (Because, thanks to the Glorious Revolution, the state itself was relatively 'modern', traditional wisdom holds that these adjustments could be achieved relatively peacefully, by 'evolution', without the need for a 'French Revolution'.)

In putting this case, Clark's revisionism entails three assumptions which social historians cannot neglect: (a) that the authority of the *ancien régime* remained massive throughout the 'long eighteenth century'; (b) that the political nation proved highly successful in maintaining hegemony – cohesion rather than conflict characterised Georgian society; and (c) that the supposedly disruptive socio-economic developments so much touted by traditional historians were in reality of no great moment.

There is a certain broad truth in Clark's claims. Yet if his overall portrayal is salutary, it is often right for reasons other than those he adduces. Because Clark tacitly assents to his opponents' presupposition – that change in society threatens stability in the state – he ends up compelled to minimise the degree and significance of social ferment. Yet one need not adopt this premise. I wish to argue, against Clark, that certain of the dynamic movements which he plays down, were in reality powerful social catalysts. Yet their effect was to *consolidate* and *modernise* the ruling order, no less than to challenge it. In implicitly subscribing to a model which treats social change as self-evidently subversive of political order, Clark inadvertently pays homage to the Marxism he mocks.[4]

It would, first of all, be foolish to belittle the sheer strength of the Georgian state. We must never underestimate the independent, personal power of the monarch throughout the eighteenth century, the constitutional clout of the House of Lords and the peerage, and the authority of the Anglican Church.[5] Recent research has confirmed that the aristocracy actually strengthened itself during the century, through managerial politics both centrally and locally, and through economic astuteness.[6]

To explain the enduring supremacy of the *ancien régime*, Clark emphasises the lasting sway exercised by 'traditionalist' modes of authority: the divine right of kings, patriarchalism. He is, however, loth to give due attention to the crucial new sources of strength which Georgian government pioneered. Preoccupied with puncturing J. H. Plumb's account of Walpole's achievement of political stability, and riled that left-wing historians prejudicially label Georgian politics 'Old Corruption', Clark fails to do justice to major innovations in political management – the deployment of patronage, the consolidation of alliances, the manipulation of propaganda. It should be stressed, by contrast, that the 'old regime' could function so effectively precisely because it developed new methods enabling it to adapt to and govern a changing society.

Victorian historians assumed that because the Hanoverian administration was 'unreformed' – because, for instance, the bureaucracy operated a spoils system, rather than competitive entrance exams for Balliol boys – it must, by consequence, have been 'inefficient' and 'weak'. This assumption has been strongly challenged. Geoffrey Holmes in particular has drawn attention to the expanding number of government officials employed from the late seventeenth century, to meet the needs of war and finance. He has emphasised the considerable technical expertise of such bureaucrats, at precisely the moment when larger numbers of highly astute lawyers, brokers, financiers, land-agents, estate managers, and so forth, were emerging. Developing Holmes's analysis, Peter Earle has argued that the generations after 1660 witnessed the 'making of the English middle class'. London throbbed with an educated, go-ahead, money-making bourgeoisie well-equipped with financial, legal and other technical skills. Directly and indirectly, at Whitehall and in the City, the business services of many of these capable men were commandeered by the administration. Through such channels, social change positively strengthened the sinews of government.[7]

Furthermore, John Brewer has now definitively shown that, in response largely to the state's need for revenue to wage war on ever grander scales, the civil service not only continued to expand throughout the century, but, in many departments, grew more efficient and bureaucratic. Far from being absentee sinecurists, many office-holders, or at least their deputies, were diligent, talented, career-minded administrators.[8] The Excise above all became the crack revenue service. Great devotion was expected of excise officers; their work was closely supervised; and the comprehensive powers granted them, of entering and searching premises, and of initiating litigation, suggests that accusations that the Excise represented a new twist of governmental 'tyranny', a threat to English 'liberties', were not just Opposition rant.

Despite popular stereotypes, England became one of the most heavily taxed nations in Europe, and an increasing proportion of taxes were indirect, being levied upon commodities purchased by the populace at large.[9] Thus it was the burgeoning prosperity of the trading and labouring classes which enabled Georgian governments to pay their way – at a time when France was always on the brink of bankruptcy. In turn, those administrations in certain respects policed their subjects' lives more thoroughly. We may certainly speak, with Clark, of an English *ancien régime*. The reality which Clark largely ignores, however, is that this 'old regime' was remarkably adroit in devising new material means of perpetuating itself, through stimulating and harnessing socio-economic change.[10]

Clark contends, secondly, that received historiographical wisdom, for self-serving purposes, has given undue attention to socio-ideological divisions under the Hanoverians.[11] Axe-grinding historians have exaggerated the role of disruptive middle-class philosophical radicals and artisan revolutionaries. More recently, rural protesters have become the heroes of 'people's history'.[12] But Georgian England, counter-claims Clark, was a world in which ideological consensus (shared sentiment about social hierarchy and subordination, the duties of man, etc.) counted for more than conflict. Above all, Clark forefronts organised religion as the cement of the state. To an impressive degree, Sundays still saw 10,000 parishes kneeling in prayer. Constitutional wisdom regarded the indissoluble alliance of Church and State as the safeguard of the Protestant faith and an Englishman's liberties.

Clark's case is fundamentally important. But he does not substantiate it through detailed investigations of religious belief and behaviour. Indeed, nobody could properly evaluate it at present, because the profession and practice of piety amongst the people at large remains deplorably underresearched. Even in his study of London's bourgeoisie, Earle was able to discover remarkably little about their deepest religious convictions.[13] The bulk of Clark's evidence for social piety derives from sermons and apologetics; but he fails to travel the road from the printed page to persuasion, from doctrine to indoctrination. Before this case could be clinched, or refuted, historians must examine the Georgian religious temper using the techniques so successfully exploited for French popular beliefs, by Robert Darnton for instance, under the rubric of the 'social history of ideas'.[14]

Clark claims that historians have been premature in characterising the eighteenth century as 'secular'. The point is well made. Neither, however, should we minimise the fact that religious activity, observance, and maybe also conviction seem to have fallen dramatically in quantity and (if this can be gauged) in fervour, in the Georgian era. The effectiveness of organised religion in mobilising the politics of consent still awaits investigation. Detached study of 'Church and King' mobs would prove useful.

Nevertheless, Clark is right to ask us to look to areas of ideological accord and not just discord – though one may query whether attention to 'the survival of patriarchalism' is the best place to start. One such area of effective hegemony appears to have been the law. Few would deny the contention of radical historians that there were departments of the criminal law in which the Georgian parliaments passed increasingly oppressive legislation, targeted against traditional common rights, and geared to the protection of landed property and capital.

Yet, as Innes and Styles have carefully argued, it would be foolish to project a radically polarised, politicised divide between law-makers on the one hand, and law-breakers on the other, or to interpret criminality as largely socio-politically motivated. English common law cannot simply be characterised as an instrument of exploitative class rule, for it commanded the assent of the vast majority of the nation. Practically everyone owned something which the law protected, many property-owners of all ranks went to law, and ordinary parishioners and burgesses were often personally involved in law enforcement and administration, in their capacities as jurymen, constables, and the like. Loyalty to the law provided one key expression of ideological assent.[15]

Another lay in the emergence of a popular patriotism, most notably during the latter decades of the eighteenth century. As foreigners noted – and here was one way in which, despite Clark's desire to assimilate England to Continental *ancien régimes*, contemporaries thought the English exceptional – the English were fiercely chauvinistic. Provincials held not just local allegiances, but aspired to a larger national identity and purpose. Yet, as recent research has emphasised, the symbolic focus of English patriotism was not, in any straightforward sense, the person of the king, or even Parliament, but rather the nation. Patriotism was not principally the manipulation from above of mindless flag-wavers, but the articulation of a complex consciousness from below, with as much potential to be radical as reactionary, critical as chauvinistic.[16]

Investigations of the ferment of patriotic feeling are helping us to understand more – though much still remains obscure – about the role of informal organisations, such as clubs, and technologies of communication, for instance, popular songs, in organising consent. The Georgian age saw a vast increase in the publicising of what would today be called 'media events', such as processions and celebrations. Novel channels of opinion, above all, newspapers and periodicals, hooked up the reading public with the affairs of the kingdom. This did not instantly and automatically create a new, radicalised political nation, any more than the recent advent of 'citizens' band' radio ensured the victory of Militant Tendency. In that sense, Clark is right to warn us against unthinking intimations of subversion.

Yet he is mistaken to give such little attention to the press. Recent studies of newspapers and cartoons have argued that it would be wrong to regard the Georgian press primarily as an agent for inculcating party political allegiances. Nevertheless newspapers put and kept the reading – and listening – public in touch with the language of national politics, just as the reitera- tion of visual cartoon stereotypes of John Bull ranged against Nick Frog, the Russian Bear, and Jean Maigre helped create notions of nationhood almost subliminally.[17] Once again, as with his indifference to the sinews of the state, Clark has failed to investigate the social history of the modern 'technologies', through which the ideological cohesion he astutely stresses was articulated.[18]

The two main features of Clark's revisionism considered so far (the strength of the edifice of the state, and the effectiveness of hegemony) are ones with which historians of very diverse ideological biases can agree. After all, Perry Anderson's struc- turalist Marxist account of the survival of the old order in Britain analytically converges with Clark's interpretation, though its underlying animus could hardly be more different; emphasising the continued sway of the Crown, House of Lords, Church of England, Oxbridge etc., up to the present day,

Anderson might dismiss Clark's 'betrayal' of 1828–32 as but a blip.[19] But Clark's third tenet is one to which few historians outside his own persuasion could subscribe. It is his belief that no very profound transformation of English socio-economic life was taking place at the grassroots during the 'long eighteenth century'.

Clark makes his case in various ways. In part he proceeds through omission. As mentioned earlier, there is a bizarre verbal sleight of hand involved in calling a book *English Society 1688–1832*, devoting well over a hundred pages to religion and much the same amount of space to political theory, but saying almost nothing about the patterns of living of most of the inhabitants, and the ways these changed.

Clark moreover contends that progressive historians' favourite talk of such 'deep-seated changes' and 'underlying causes' as the 'rise of the bourgeoisie', the spirit of capitalism, or the emergence of class consciousness is reductionist, teleological, and mere verbiage. Above all, he aims to dispel the 'myth' of the 'industrial revolution' (as also that of the earlier 'scientific revolution').[20] This, he claims, is yet another misleading and ideologically-loaded myth bandied around by the progressives.

Clark is right to emphasise that crude notions of cataclysmic economic transformations arising from the 1760s, thanks to the technological breakthroughs introduced by Watt, Arkwright, Crompton and Cort, and culminating in the 'factory system', are no longer tenable. Crafts in particular has argued for a relatively smoother graph of evolutionary change in the eighteenth century, and has confirmed that economic growth was at its fastest not in the age of Watt but in the railway age.[21] Factories remained extremely localised, exceptions rather than the rule. As Maxine Berg has convincingly emphasised, 'industry' (itself hardly yet an abstraction, still primarily a personal attribute) remained small-scale, very commonly tied to the cottage, the workshop, and the putting-out system, and typically reliant upon man (and woman and child) power, topped up with water-power, wind-power, and horse-power, though very rarely with steam-power.

But Clark seems to assume that to challenge the appositeness of the term 'industrial revolution' is as good as to demonstrate the absence of massive socio-economic change. This does not follow. Dr Berg, who herself finds the concept of 'industrial revolution' unhelpful, nevertheless calls her period the 'age of manufactures', and stresses the vast expansion of a bewildering variety of trades. Though these were individually organised in small-scale units, cumulatively they produced a huge booster effect upon employment, output, wealth creation, the geographical distribution of population, and so forth.[23] Not least, economic acceleration, involving the integration of agrarian change (higher gross production, a surplus of rural labour which migrated into manufactures), a better transportation network, and infrastructural consolidation (credit, banks, etc.), had as its consequence a vast, sustained, and unprecedented rise in population.

England had a population of around 6 millions in 1760. By 1781 this had become 7.7 millions; 8.6 millions just a decade later, and an astonishing 9.8 millions by 1811. The *rate* of increase even continued to accelerate. Population 'revolution' or not, a new socio-economic order was emerging which, with hindsight, we can see possessed a seemingly unlimited potential for continued demographic and economic expansion: England had never previously been able to support more than about 5 million inhabitants without incurring biological disasters of the kind Malthus (wrongly, as it turned out) feared.[24]

The causes and consequences of an economic and demographic transformation massive enough to support what by 1820 amounted to a doubling of the population within sixty years were once taken as primarily the province of *economic* historians. But it is becoming clearer that social historians have a major contribution to make towards understanding them. Family structures and household ways were elastic enough to respond to rapid change, and to encourage its continuation.[25] The remainder of this chapter will explore certain facets of these weighty social changes.

II   A CONSUMER SOCIETY?

For J. C. D. Clark, the suggestion that the Georgian age witnessed the 'birth of a consumer society' amounts to yet another instance of Whig historians' vice of ransacking the past for anticipations of the present. Yet the question is surely worth airing. For the transformations of the 'age of manufactures' need explaining. How far was unparalleled economic and demographic growth made possible by a greater disposition and capacity amongst large sectors of the population to purchase more goods (and services)? How far was it home demand that fuelled industrialisation? And if so, may we then speak of the advent of a new 'consumerism', indicative of a new *mentalité*, and itself pregnant with noteworthy social consequences?[26]

The evidence, though imperfect, is suggestive. The fruits of computer-assisted research into inventories are now becoming available. Inventories were drawn up, for legal purposes, to record a person's belongings at death. For obvious reasons, inventories probably under-recorded such movable property. Analyses of their contents, from the mid-seventeenth century through into the eighteenth, show marked and sustained increases in the range, quantity and value of goods possessed by dying people of both sexes, from all social ranks, and from all regions. (The rate of growth was, however, uneven, seemingly being faster where communications and markets were most efficient.[27])

Around 1650, even middle-class households appear to have been rather sparsely furnished, commonly lacking many items which had become standard by 1730: table linen, curtains, rugs, mirrors, clocks and pictures. From the Restoration, shop-bought goods were replacing homemade ones, and cheap, basic and plain forms of wares were giving way to more costly, sophisticated items. Thus wooden and pewter tableware yielded to silver, earthenware beakers were superseded by glassware and china tea services (the introduction of hot drinks – tea, chocolate, coffee – made all the difference). Commercial and imperial expansion flooded the market with exotic items. Goods newly imported from Asia, such as cottons and japanned *papier mâché* furniture, found eager buyers.[28]

Inventories give only an imperfect glimpse, however, of all that people actually owned. Above all, they record only those relatively permanent things surrounding them at death. They tell us nothing about items acquired earlier, all those more ephemeral objects which wore out, broke, or became 'old-fashioned', to be thrown away and replaced, perhaps scores of times. For insights into this we have to turn to more personal and circumstantial evidence: diaries, account books, letters, the Jeremiads of preachers fulminating against vanity and luxury. These sources show that, alongside the items regularly recorded in inventories, people were also acquiring multitudes of other bits and pieces: newspapers and prints, knicknacks, ornaments, a wider choice of garments, items of adornment, baubles, bangles and books. The advent of newspapers, jam-packed with advertisements, encouraged a desire for novelty; the demands of fashion grew more pressing; and people developed habits of buying 'disposables', things to last for a season and be thrown away (the introduction of lighter, cheaper fabrics sped this process). McCracken has plausibly argued that in Tudor times the 'patina' of age was positively valued as an attribute of belongings, betokening solidity and tradition, whereas by the Georgian era, 'old' furniture was increasingly dismissed as outmoded.[29] All in all, the later the inventory, the more probable that it records a diminishing proportion of all the goods acquired during a lifetime. Though inventories register increasing ownership of material goods, they also probably under-represent the acceleration of consumption.

In any case, inventories peter out after around 1730; thereafter we must rely upon a diversity of less easily quantified sources to gauge what people bought and owned – sale catalogues, pocket books, newspaper advertisements, and contemporary commentaries, such as the remarks of foreign travellers. The development of consumer psychology and salesmanship, the opening of salerooms, the circulation of pattern books amongst such suppliers as cabinet-makers and milliners, the business acumen of entrepreneurs of prints and engravings such as Hogarth and Thomas Bewick – all these well-recorded developments tell interlocking stories of intensifying activity in the manufacture and marketing of domestic items.[30]

For instance, in mid-Stuart times, when they fell sick, the petty bourgeoisie swallowed medicines made up by the apothecary or concocted at home following the traditional recipes of 'kitchen physic'. This changed: by 1800, a deluge of brand-name patent and proprietary medicines had swept the market; they were being saturation-advertised in newspapers, and sold at prices such people could afford. 'Designer' medicine chests were on sale, stocked with over a hundred different drugs.[31] The culmination of these broad trends of domestic acquisitiveness was that orgy of investment in domestic objects in the Victorian age, recently explored by Asa Briggs.[32]

Domestic consumption thus increased, stimulating economic growth. How the genesis of these 'consuming passions' should be explained has, however, been fiercely disputed. Studies of social structure and wealth distribution seem to be confirming that a sizeable part – a growing aggregate number, and perhaps proportion, of the population – had surplus disposable income.[33] The growth of markets, shops, better communications, improved transportation, the increased publicity bombardment through the press, etc., certainly encouraged buying: by the late eighteenth century, there were at least 150,000 retail outlets in England. Fashion-stimulated emulation (keeping up with the Joneses) has traditionally been touted as the prime explanation. Couched in terms of crude psychological drives, it may, however, prove essentially circular (people acquired more because they grew acquisitive).[34]

To understand why people wanted to surround themselves with a proliferation of possessions, we surely need to know about the meanings things held for them, indeed, about what has been called 'the social life of things'. Particularly in a changing, fluid society, the acquisition of significant objects may be valuable in conferring a distinctive identity. The Georgian tradesman who bought a toby jug, a print of Wilkes, a commemorative plaque celebrating Wolfe's victory at Quebec, was using his array of artefacts to display his allegiances.[35] Simon Schama has emphasised how the Dutch, in their golden age, gloried in their world of objects – fairly mundane articles, though richly wrought – as proofs of success and as emblems of the moral qualities they prized. Thus keeping an abundance of food and drink signalled hospitality and generosity, lavishing large sums upon home furnishings marked their commitment to the family and to domestic pride. Peter Earle has begun to explore the English experience in these terms. Particularly revealing of the subjective and sen-

timental meanings of goods are the formulae used in gift-
giving, in exchanges of goods, and in wills (the 'second best
bed' syndrome).[36]

This naturally leads to consideration of the social implications of growing consumerism. The point was not lost on
contemporaries. Preachers denounced vanity, and no end of
moralists decried the folly of spending beyond one's means,
just as economic writers of the late seventeenth and early
eighteenth centuries routinely denounced internal consumption
('luxury') as ruinous: instead, production, saving, and export-
ing were lauded as the secrets of national success.[37] Radicals
like Cobbett later anathematised farmers who filled their
parlours with pianos. They were symptoms of a new breed of
hard-hearted capitalist proprietors who sacrificed labourers (no
longer allowed to live in, or accorded hospitality) to their own
comforts and pretensions.[38]

But there was another side to the argument. A new political
economy arose – teasingly in Bernard Mandeville, analytically
in Adam Smith and his successors – arguing that a high
consumption economy, linked to 'liberal rewards' for labour,
would not merely fuel economic expansion (which in turn
would prove socially cohesive), but would furthermore give
incentives for labouring men to abandon their traditionally
'feckless' attitudes towards industry ('Saint Monday') in favour
of greater work discipline. How working men decided their
preferences as to work and remuneration, freedom and leisure,
remains contested amongst historians. But early nineteenth-
century plebeian autobiographers – mainly, of course, self-
made 'improving' sorts – are notable for their eagerness to
display their own financial responsibility, linked to a new
'domesticity'; these developments deserve further analysis.[39]

Historical demographers, researchers into the village community, students of the domestic economy, and social historians alike have all been emphasising the overwhelming importance of the nuclear family as the *primum mobile* of early
modern society – not only as the instrument of property-
accumulation and dynastic-aggrandisement amongst the titled,
but vital throughout all reaches of society.[40] The material
reality of the family as the basic unit of production and
reproduction appears to have become reinforced by a new

ideology, the idealistic promotion of family life as an agency of moral sanctity and improvement. Moralists, educators and journalists made great play of the virtues of domesticity and parenthood in the second half of the eighteenth century and, especially perhaps, in the nineteenth.

Praise of conjugal reciprocity, and increasing attention to children and the responsibilities of child-care helped emplace such values amongst the upper orders.[41] 'Improving' authors such as Sarah Trimmer and Hannah More similarly aimed to impress working people with their family responsibilities, and to promote a domestic economy of thrift and savings. Whether or not such manoeuvres to moralise the masses were effective, the experience of massive disruption of life and labour (enclosure, rural proletarianisation, the decline of living-in amongst servants in husbandry and apprentices, mass migration to new factory towns, etc.) meant that labouring people had no option but to fall back on the resources of family life as their liferaft for survival.[42]

In the emergence of a viable industrial society, domestic ideals probably played a considerable normalising role. Amongst the upper orders, and spurred by the Evangelical revival, the elevation of home and family helped the campaign for the remoralisation of the dissolute, which spokesmen such as William Wilberforce believed was essential if their social leadership were to be maintained.[43] Lower down the social order, the strong, self-sufficient household guaranteed economic survival, conferred respectability, and perhaps even afforded a 'haven in a heartless world'.[44] Broods of infants, the wider household, and the domestic interior provided boundless objects for the 'home demand' that fuelled an expanding economy. The history of the family, the expansion of consumerism, and the social transition to a successful industrial society, were thus all intimately interlinked, and need to be studied as such.[45]

III GENDER

These issues in turn demand discussion of shifting gender roles, and of the sexual politics of a developing commercial society.

With very few exceptions,[46] the history of women in the eighteenth century was for long grossly neglected, beyond accounts of the charmed circles of *grandes dames* and literary blue stockings.[47] Rather paradoxically, this neglect was sanctioned by a superb pioneering work which appeared early in this century, Alice Clark's *The Working Life of Women in Seventeenth Century England* (1919).[48] Clark contended that the transition from feudalism to capitalism – in which, for her, the seventeenth century was crucial – resulted in a major flight of trades and occupations from the domestic hearth. With the consequent growth of workshops, professions, and eventually the factory system, women – who were inevitably tied to household labour – naturally became excluded from paid occupations (except menial ones such as service),[49] and were doomed to downgraded domesticity. Rendered essentially private, women began to vanish from the stage of history.

Subsequent research has confirmed certain aspects of Clark's broad argument: thus Snell has shown how, with the growing use of heavy tools such as the scythe, women were steadily squeezed from the better paid and more prestigious forms of agricultural employment, being left to glean, weed, or tend kitchen gardens.[50] But Clark's argument about 'exclusion' cannot stand as a whole. Her periodisation and interpretation of economic change are patently inadequate. After all, in the eighteenth century so many of the new and expanding work 'opportunities' still clustered around the home-based workshop. Women were extremely prominent in managing, or at least working in, shops, inns, the clothing trades, putting-out industries, and the service industries, all greatly expanding sectors.

We have, as yet, disappointingly few studies of the place of working women within the Georgian economy.[51] Women's history has, perhaps unfortunately, chosen to concentrate upon pioneer feminists and women writers, from Aphra Behn to Mary Wollstonecraft, leaving us better informed about what often unrepresentative women advocated than upon what the generality of women thought, felt and did.[52] (Though it is here worth noting, referring back to the previous section, that late eighteenth-century feminists themselves contributed to the pro-domesticity and pro-natalist consciousness there discussed.

Whereas post-Restoration feminists, such as Mary Astell, were sceptical about marriage and fearful of being housebound, seeking milieux beyond, within which women could be educated and independent, by the close of the eighteenth century the leading feminist, Mary Wollstonecraft, grounded her impassioned advocacy of the superiority of women precisely on their motherly virtues.)

A modified version of Alice Clark's thesis has, however, gained ground. This is the view that a growing sexual division of labour ('separate spheres') was eventuating from the mid-eighteenth century. Its effect was increasingly to exclude middle-class women from public life.[53] Contrary to Alice Clark's essentially economic argument, the motor of change here is seen to be socio-cultural.

As bourgeois 'new wealth' was growing more conspicuous – in law, manufacturing, banking and finance – it felt pressured to carve out for itself a distinctive identity, thereby setting it above mere 'trade' and the dirty work of the counter and workshop, and establishing respectable credentials. A new *haut bourgeois* gentility was sought, especially under the banners of evangelical and dissenting religion. One strategy for achieving this lay in defining the world of work as the prerogative of men, while 'elevating' (or, we might retrospectively say, 'demeaning') women into the role of the 'angel in the house', guardian of the moral purity and sanctity of 'home sweet home', the family, and the children. By virtue of not 'working', the wife and mother could be a paragon of charity and holiness, while parading as a conspicuous ornament to her husband's success and honour. This closeting of the female into an essentially domestic role spread down the social scale during the nineteenth century. Such enhanced differentiation of gender roles, it is further argued, in turn led to an increasing polarisation of imputed male and female sexuality.

The sexual double standard was, of course, of long standing.[54] Yet traditional wisdom about sexuality, both learned and popular, had argued that men and women were by nature erotically equally passionate (witness the folklore image of the lusty widow). After all, age-old gynaecological teaching claimed that it was impossible for conception to take place without simultaneous male and female orgasm.[55] All such ideas came under fire in the late Georgian period.

By the 1820s, investigations into reproductive biology had finally demonstrated that, amongst human beings, female sexual arousal was not necessary for conception; but for several decades prior to that, exhortations warning against the dangers of undue female sexual arousal – arguments both moral and medical in tenor – were already being advanced. Doctors were beginning to contend that, physiologically speaking, so delicate was the female nervous system that it rendered sexual arousal risky, even perilous to good health. 'Passionlessness' would soon be advocated as the sole way of preserving emotional equilibrium amongst the 'weaker vessels', ever excitable and prone to hysteria. It would not be very long before Dr William Acton would be defending respectable women from the 'vile aspersion' that they experienced sexual desire at all; more popularly, Victorian brides would soon be invited to lie back and think of England. The emergence of an influential strand of advice literature and moral opinion urging the 'desexualisation' of women was well adapted (so the argument runs) to meet the needs of the 'separate spheres' ideology as outlined above.[56]

There is some truth in this reading of the growing differentiation of the genders – culturally, socially and sexually – and of the 'privatisation' and 'desexualisation' of women in late Georgian England; but it is far from the whole story. For one thing, grave dangers lurk in making inferences about how women actually behaved from the evidence of how moral, religious and sexual advice books told women to conduct themselves. Anna Clark has pointed to a surge of neo-patriarchal writings, from the late eighteenth century, warning women of the moral dangers of trying to be 'independent' of men. Clark's inference is that such advice literature actually dictated and restricted women's lives. The reverse might equally be true: this flurry of writings could just as easily signal the response of anxious moralists to the unprecedented independence of young, unmarried women in a mobile, wage-labour industrial society. Abundant contemporary evidence supports this view.[57] In any case, Peter Gay in particular has drawn attention to the lively and unashamed eroticism displayed by many utterly respectable nineteenth-century women.[58] Feminist historians sometimes seem to be perversely eager to claim that women in earlier centuries allowed themselves to be utterly oppressed by 'patriarchy'. Evidence from the workplace, home, and not least from popular culture, suggests that Georgian women were far from being so feeble.[59]

IV   IDEOLOGY, *MENTALITÉ* AND SOCIAL CHANGE

Discussion of the redefinition of sexual identities in the Georgian era raises a further question: the dynamics of social change. I have discussed the suggestion that the late Georgian divergence of male and female gender norms helped to rationalise and ratify a growing sexual division of labour within propertied society ('separate spheres'), which was itself a response to the anxieties of an *arriviste* bourgeoisie, desperate to acquire moral authority and social prestige. One might rejoin that such a model involves too simplistic an assumption of how ideas are moulded to meet social needs – a view, as J. C. D. Clark would say, both 'functionalist' and 'reductionist'. Attitudes and actions are undoubtedly related: but surely attitudes are not 'simply' or 'merely' crude expressions of 'material interests' (class, group, gender, etc.)? – are not just suits of clothes slipped on and off to suit the occasion? In other words, one of the key problems facing socio-cultural history lies in explaining the nature of the symbiotic interplay between new ideas and changing practices.

I wish to exemplify this problem by examining an interlinked series of shifts in the management and experience of fundamental life events – above all, birth, child-rearing and death – which took place during the 'long eighteenth century'. To state the matter in very simple terms, people from all ranks of society came into the world, in the late seventeenth century, in the time-honoured way, with the ministrations of a midwife.[60] Such a woman was a trusted member of the local community; she would normally be mature and experienced, and blessed with a bishop's licence. But she would have had no formal medical training.

Giving birth was an elaborate ritual in which the mother would be surrounded by female members of her family and her women friends ('gossips'); men were rigidly excluded. It took place in a heated and darkened room (i.e. one made as 'womblike' as possible). Spiced up in the form of 'caudle', alcohol often flowed freely. After delivery, the newborn infant might well be swaddled (bandaging, it was believed, would strengthen weak bones), perhaps before being handed over to a wet-nurse, who would suckle it till weaning. Affluent mothers would probably lie-in for several weeks after giving birth, at which point the 'rite of passage' of giving birth would be terminated by 'churching', a religious ceremony of purification. Men were excluded from the whole procedure, except that, in the event of complications during labour, a male surgeon would have to be summoned.

Amongst the better-off and better educated social strata, childbirth was radically transformed during the eighteenth century. The traditional 'granny midwife' was typically re-placed by a male operator, the 'man-midwife' or *accoucheur* as some liked to call themselves. He claimed superior exper-tise. As a properly qualified medical practitioner, often armed with a degree from Edinburgh University, his anatomical expertise allowed him to be confident that he could let nature perform the work for him in the case of normal childbirths: despite the claims of numerous modern feminist historians, leading man-midwives such as William Hunter prided them-selves upon being *less* aggressively interventionist than the traditional midwife.[61] Yet, at the same time, he also possessed (unlike the midwife) surgical instruments, above all, the new forceps, for use in case of emergency.

This new-style childbirth was no longer an enclosed, women-only rite. Fashionable eighteenth-century women increasingly had their husbands present. They gave birth in rooms into which daylight and fresh air were admitted. Their babies would not be swaddled: according to the new theory, allowing free-dom to their limbs would strengthen their bones and encourage healthy development. Increasingly, ladies also made a point of breast-feeding their own babies: surely mother's milk was best and would encourage good mother-baby bonding.[62]

In its childbirth and infant-rearing practices, the eighteenth century thus witnessed a sharp break with the customs of centuries – one which surely had a noteworthy knock-on effect in respect of the attention, affection, and freedom given to children growing up within such families: Plumb has thus written of the 'new world of children in the eighteenth century'.[63] How then do we explain it? Certain feminists have claimed that midwives were elbowed out of obstetrical practice by the new upstart male profession.[64] Assuredly, such a displacement occurred, but this reading offers no explanation as to why so many families *chose* to adopt the services of the new male operators. 'Fashion' may be invoked, but, beyond a certain point, it is a circular explanation. Neither is there any sign that husbands forced male practitioners upon unwilling wives (most opposition to the man-midwife came from men, not women). In any case, none of these arguments about 'men's work' and 'women's work' accounts for the further adoption of all the other associated practices (the abandonment of swaddling, the adoption of maternal breast-feeding, etc.).

What seems abundantly clear is that the new 'childbirth package' gained a purchase in educated society because it agreed with other prestigious values that polite and progressive society was embracing: the appeal to modern science, to reason in place of tradition, to notions of what was 'natural', to familial and specifically maternal affection (the suckling mother). The switch from 'peasant' midwife to graduate *accoucheur*, from 'custom' (wet-nursing) to 'nature' (the maternal breast), from 'superstition' (swaddling protects the bones) to 'science' (activity promotes sturdiness) – all these harmonised perfectly with the complacent confidence felt by many educated Georgians that they were living in an age escaping from ignorance into information, from vulgar superstition into science, from the benighted past into the progressive future – indeed, that they themselves were pioneering the process. The transition from the dimmed birthing chamber into birth by daylight wonderfully epitomises the very notion of 'enlightenment' so many espoused.[65]

Peter Gay has argued that one key feature of the Enlightenment's 'recovery of nerve' lay in the growing adoption of scientific medical and health procedures (inoculation is a good instance) which resulted in a healthier population.[66] By way of parallel, one could, given enough space, explore a similar transformation in the way 'men of reason' finally departed from life. The old Christian deathbed drama, in which the dying person stage-managed a dramatic exit from this vale of tears, denying the Devil and all his works and calling upon God, grew less common. Polite society instead came to prefer more peaceful departures, akin to falling asleep (increasingly aided by generous doses of opiates). Scions of the Enlightenment such as David Hume publicly paraded their repudiation of what Christians had always considered a rightful terror of oblivion.[67]

Here surely we see the Enlightenment in action, as applied to the fundamental realities of life – here perhaps is that historiographical Loch Ness monster, the 'English Enlightenment'. Yet it would obviously itself be simplistic to stop short with the portrayal of the triumph of light over darkness, or of an ideology of 'reason'. We must look at the *social* uses, the ritual meanings, of beliefs. We must be sensitive to the class origins and functions of different belief-systems. Peter Burke and others have drawn attention to the protracted hostilities waged between patrician and plebeian values in the early modern world.[68] Muchembled has pointed to the imposition of 'social control' from above.[69] Perhaps carrying such a view to its limits, Michel Foucault has suggested that, in respect of the people at large, 'Enlightenment' might be better seen as a programme not for 'emancipation' but for 'incarceration'.[70] Yet, as Burke suggests, surely correctly, the strategy most prominent in England was a form of secessionism by the genteel and the would-be genteel.[71] Polite culture evolved a repertoire of moves designed to differentiate itself from, and elevate itself over, the life-styles and beliefs of the masses.[72] In other words, it is not sufficient to interpret the Enlightenment merely in terms of the progress of disembodied ideas. It was part of the cultural and social history of the times, being functional to social differentiation and identity.

Psycho-historians have claimed that changes in child-rearing patterns change the world. That is possible, though I am not here advancing that claim. I am contending, however, that some of the changes which find no space in J. C. D. Clark's vision of *English Society* were in their own way momentous, and are now, belatedly, becoming the subject of proper historical scrutiny.

V SOURCES

This leads, finally, to a brief remark about sources. Great archival riches exist that have only recently begun to be systematically exploited: inventories are a good case in point. And well-thumbed records are now being put to new uses. Thus the ledgers of the Old Poor Law will tell us not only of the annals of poverty and its administration – a field in which much dated and outdated interpretation remains to be replaced; they can also, as Mary Fissell has demonstrated, be fed into computers to yield insights into the people's health and health-care choices.[73] Yet the siren songs of advanced software packages must not blind us to the value of more traditional 'literary' evidence and 'impressionistic' methods. Thus, to revert to 'consumerism', alongside the quantification of belongings, which can be done upon the basis of inventories, we also need an integrated 'qualitative' history, derived from diaries, letters, journals, wills, etc. – one that will tell us what such possessions meant to their owners.[74]

Historians must not be afraid of 'artistic' sources and 'fiction'. It would be a pity if the preciosities of post-modernist deconstructionist literary theories, with their cavalier denial of all 'extra-textual' life, and their dismissal of 'historicity' as the opium of the historians, were to lead researchers to fight shy of poems, plays and pictures.[75] Roger Lonsdale's admirable *New Oxford Book of Eighteenth Century Verse* has demonstrated how much more there is to Georgian poetry than Swift and satire, Pope and pastoral. Lonsdale's selection shows how deeply concerned were Georgian poets with commenting upon their own society.[76] Luckily, historians such as W. A. Speck continue to relish investigating history as refracted through the spyglass of fiction;[77] and literary historians such as John Barrell and Ronald Paulson have illuminated the ways in which writing and painting engaged in a cultural dialogue which, properly interpreted, can tell us both about society's cultural expectations, and equally of their transgression.[78] G. S. Rousseau has indicated the same for the relations between science, medicine, literature and society.[79]

Admittedly, such sources pose profound difficulties. Folklore, folksong and proverbs remain shockingly neglected by

social historians, not least because the evidential and inter-
pretative problems surrounding them are so great. Blame for
this may be laid at the feet of their Victorian collectors who
were such energetic Bowdlerisers and 'improvers' (themselves
'reformers' of popular culture, in the manner mentioned
above).[80] Recent attempts to use folksong as a resource for
social history highlight these problems.[81] The anonymity of
such materials heightens the difficulty of using them. Yet
knowledge of authorship does not resolve it. For we must also
take full account of their 'conventionality'. Thus one shortcom-
ing of recent attempts to use Georgian political cartoons as
'documents' of social history lies in a failure to make proper
allowance for – or, put more positively, a failure to exploit – the
symbols and stereotypes through which such works of art are
habitually expressed. Understanding the languages of the im-
agination will tell us much about the conventional codes of
society.[82] The better we grasp the ironies encrusting so many
sources for eighteenth-century social history, the better will be
our insight into the society itself.

2
The British Economy in Transition, 1742–1789

WILLIAM J. HAUSMAN

I THE INDUSTRIAL REVOLUTION

TWENTY-FIVE years ago, R. M. Hartwell began an article on Britain's industrial revolution by citing J. H. Clapham's earlier metaphor (1910) comparing the subject to a 'thrice squeezed orange' with an 'astonishing amount of juice in it'.[1] Hartwell noted that in the meantime study of the topic had been increasing rather than waning, and judging by the continued interest in Britain's remarkable transformation, it seems to have been an orange with a sufficient amount of juice to have defied the law of diminishing returns. This is perhaps appropriate for events which have been described as marking 'the most fundamental transformation of human life in the history of the world recorded in written documents'.[2] Furthermore, because poverty and backwardness remain a persistent problem in the world, the study of Britain's (or, sometimes more appropriately, England's) economy in the eighteenth and early nineteenth centuries retains a particular fascination for economic historians.

There is no question that major structural changes took place in the British economy between the early eighteenth century and the middle of the nineteenth century, and there is little disagreement that these changes were ultimately 'revolutionary'.[3] Yet the specific chronology, dimensions, causal forces and social impact of the industrial revolution remain the subject of vigorous debate.

Regarding chronology, Michael Flinn has noted that the dates of the industrial revolution have been pushed 'from pillar to post'.[4] The French were the first to use the term in the early nineteenth century when writing about the mechanisation of industry then in progress, and it appears in Marx's *Capital*; but it was Arnold Toynbee's *Lectures on the Industrial Revolution in England*, published in 1884, which firmly placed the term in the lexicon of the English language.[5] Toynbee wrote of an England on the 'eve' of the industrial revolution in 1760, but he dated the transformation somewhat later, from 'the end of the eighteenth and beginning of the nineteenth centuries'.[6] Historians such as H. L. Beales and T. S. Ashton argued that the period of transition should be extended to run from 1760 or 1750 into the middle of the nineteenth century, or beyond.[7] Charles Wilson felt that the social and economic changes which were to transform Britain were 'only just beginning' in the 1760s, and J. H. Plumb wrote of the parallel existence of two worlds, the old and the new, between 1760 and 1790.[8] W. W. Rostow has more boldly and more precisely dated the revolution ('take-off' in his terminology) in the period 1783–1802.[9] Phyllis Deane and W. A. Cole found a turning point, based primarily on trends in overseas trade statistics, in the 1740s, but argued that the revolution did not become 'effective' until the last twenty years of the century.[10] C. K. Harley recently has revised downward estimates of the growth of industrial production between 1770 and 1815, consequently de-emphasising the magnitude of the transition during this period. He saw overall industrial progress as being more gradual over the course of the eighteenth century, with acceleration coming only after the conclusion of the Napoleonic wars.[11] The choice of timing often depends on the historian's conception of the definition or dimensions of the industrial revolution.

According to Toynbee the essence of the industrial revolution was the 'substitution of competition for the medieval regulations which had previously controlled the production and distribution of wealth'.[12] Since Toynbee, the numerous historians of the period have pursued one of three broad definitional strategies. These emphasise changes in either economic organisation, technology, or, more recently, aggregate macroeconomic indicators, although elements of all three often enter into a particular historian's definition.

Phyllis Deane focused on the characteristics of economic

organisation. She identified seven related organisational changes: the application of science and empirical knowledge to production for the market, specialisation of economic activity directed to ever larger national and international markets, urbanisation, the enlargement and depersonalisation of the unit of production, movement from production of primary products to manufactured products, more intensive and extensive use of capital resources as a substitute for human effort, and the creation of new social and occupational classes defined by their relationship to capital rather than land.[13] According to Deane, these fundamental changes occurred in the century after 1750.

Douglass North more recently has argued, as had others before him, that continuous technological change was the paramount defining characteristic of the industrial revolution, but he stressed that better specification of property rights was the determining force behind this change. In his model increasing market size induced greater specialisation and division of labour, which initially increased transaction costs. Organisational changes (principally, increased supervision and central monitoring of inputs and outputs) were devised to reduce these transaction costs, which had the consequence of lowering the cost of innovating at the same time that increasing market size and better-specified property rights were raising the rate of return on innovating. North rejected the notion that there was a radical break with the past during the eighteenth century; rather he saw it as the culmination of a series of prior events and argued that the real revolution did not come until the last half of the nineteenth century, when technical change was more closely related to breakthroughs in basic science.[14]

Virtually all historians identify technical change as one of the most salient features of the industrial revolution. Some focus almost exclusively on technical change, the subsequent adoption of machinery, and the spread of factory production as the essential characteristics of the revolution: 'The use of machinery, even if not in itself a sufficient definition or explanation of the industrial revolution, remains at any rate the leading fact, in relation to which every other fact in that great historical process must be studied.'[15] David Landes believed that the heart of the industrial revolution could be found in a series of interrelated technological changes that yielded an unprecedented increase in productivity, ultimately leading to a higher standard of living.[16] And according to François Crouzet the process 'was first and foremost a technical revolution'.[17] To these historians, such changes were initiated during the last half of the eighteenth century, although most recognised that it was not until the middle of the nineteenth century that the factory system became dominant.

Most historians who focus on technology as the driving force in the revolution emphasise the dramatic changes that took place in a relatively small number of industries. Primary among these was, of course, the cotton industry. Eric Hobsbawm stated the proposition most dramatically and succinctly: 'Whoever says Industrial Revolution says cotton.'[18] In W. W. Rostow's scheme, with its emphasis on unbalanced growth, the cotton industry was the initial 'leading sector' in the transformation.[19] This emphasis is quite understandable. Technological developments in cotton production were dramatic and visible; no other industry grew as rapidly as cotton during the late eighteenth century; and regions where cotton production was concentrated, such as Lancashire, were the first to acquire the full range of features characteristic of the new wave of industry.[20] Other historians believe that the cotton industry has been forced to accept too heavy a burden. Rondo Cameron recently has argued that an industry which employed less than 5 per cent of the non-agricultural workforce and produced only 10 per cent of total industrial output as late as 1841, however impressive its achievement, could not alone have generated an industrial revolution. He argued that the coal, iron and engineering industries, with related developments in the application of steam power, were more important in the long run than cotton.[21]

A final group of historians emphasises macroeconomic indicators in the search for a definition of the industrial revolution. Much of this work was stimulated by Phyllis Deane and W. A. Cole's grand attempt to tell the story of British economic development in quantitative terms.[22] In their chapter on the 'eighteenth-century origins' of growth, they assembled a vast array of statistics on population, trade, agriculture and industrial production. The culmination of this endeavour was a conjectured index of real output, from which they perceived the dual turning points of the 1740s and 1780s.

According to Hartwell, the essential feature of the industrial revolution was 'the sustained increase in the rate of growth of total and per capita output'.[23] The critical aspect was an increase in per capita output, since this represented an increase in human productivity and was the basis for higher living standards. Using this as a standard Hartwell argued that by taking the long view, comprising the entire period from 1700 to 1900, there obviously was a radical shift in the structure of the economy leading to higher per capita growth rates, but he failed to identify a fundamental 'turning point'. He argued, however, that 'central influence can be attributed to the great technical breakthroughs in industry of the period 1760–1800; . . . which allowed the acceleration of economic growth.'[24]

The most substantive revisions of Deane and Cole's sectoral and aggregate output figures have been made by N. F. R. Crafts.[25] The revisions for the later eighteenth and early nineteenth centuries indicate slower overall growth, thus reducing the importance of the decades following 1780 as representing a fundamental transformation. Crafts pointed out that as late as 1840, 'when Britain had an employment structure quite unlike the rest of Europe, . . . much of the industrial activity of the economy remained small-scale, little affected by the use of steam power and characterised neither by high productivity nor comparative advantage.'[26]

Joel Mokyr has put this type of analysis in perspective. He accepted the notion that in aggregate terms it is difficult to find a turning point in the eighteenth century, but he used a simple mathematical example to explain why this should not be surprising. The dynamic industries were initially small relative to total economic activity. If the economy can be divided into two sectors, a small but dynamic sector producing 10 per cent of total output, and a large traditional sector growing one-fourth as fast (conditions similar to those in Britain during this period), then it would take over seventy years for the two sectors to attain equality in terms of shares of total output, and aggregate output growth would appear to be unspectacular.[27] This serves as a trenchant reminder not to underestimate the changes occurring in the British economy in the last half of the eighteenth century even though they may be difficult to identify in the aggregate statistics. It is also appropriate to repeat Michael Flinn's admonition that in the enthusiasm for quantification it is important that non-measurable factors do not get pushed into the background or totally forgotten, and, finally, to reiterate T. S. Ashton's point that the revolution was industrial, social *and* intellectual.[28]

If questions regarding the timing and definition of the industrial revolution have generated debate among historians, the determination of causal forces is even more controversial. Was it initiated by shifts in demand or supply? Was it generated spontaneously from within the economic system or was there some external shock that set the process in motion? Was balanced or unbalanced growth the key? If these questions were ever answered to historians' satisfaction, then perhaps the whole world would be developed, or at least we would know why it was not. One thing is clear. It was a complicated process and no monocausal explanation will suffice. Neither are all-inclusive lists of forces making for growth likely to generate much enthusiasm. In a devastating, if rather cynical, methodological essay Peter Mathias observed:

> The spectrum of mono-causal, or the ingredients of multi-causal, explanation has been all embracing, including: a favourable natural resource position, population movements, social structure and a flexible social process, the growth of internal demand (particularly the rising demand of 'middling' income groups), a commercialized and progressive agriculture, a developing tradition of rural-based industries, foreign trade and colonies, the availability of capital, a native genius for inventing, or innovating or entrepreneurship, Protestant Nonconformity, a government system favouring intervention and *laissez-faire* in the most suitable mixture at different times, a legal process encouraging the efficiency of competition and a market economy, scientific knowledge and scientific attitudes, psychological drives and motivations. . . . educational innovations, and other dimensions of the concept of 'human capital'.[29]

That effectively sums up the literature. With each historian selecting a particular prime mover or blend of interacting forces, as many views (perhaps more) as there are historians are conceivable. But as one economic historian has warned, 'Those who seek definitive answers should not venture into economic history.'[30] And the subject of economic development is of such importance that the search for underlying causes will not be abandoned. If there is any consensus in terms of explaining long-run success, it is that technological progress, broadly defined and not limited to the more spectacular innovations of the period, must remain at the centre of any discussion of the industrial revolution.[31]

The discussion up to now has ranged rather broadly over time, but it is necessary to place the events of the years 1742–89 in context. Few would doubt that developments prior to the middle of the eighteenth century set the stage for the transformation to come. It is even more certain that the full force of the industrial revolution was not felt until the middle decades of the nineteenth century. Developments with lasting consequences, however, were concentrated in the years between 1742 and 1789: 'No one would deny that the period which began around the middle of the eighteenth century was a period in which important and far-reaching changes took place in the characteristic tempo of economic life in Britain, and that these constituted a transformation that was, in a sense, the prototype of the transition from pre-industrial to industrial forms of economic organisation which is everywhere a necessary condition of modern economic development.'[32]

II STRUCTURAL CHANGE AND AGGREGATE GROWTH

One of the most immediately striking features of the period 1742–89 was the acceleration in the rate of growth of population that began around the beginning of the period. The population of England and Wales increased from roughly 5.95 million to 8.2 million over those years; that of Scotland from about 1.25 million in 1751 to 1.6 million in 1801. The population of England, which had been expanding (irregularly) at a rate of 1.2 per cent per decade from 1660–1740, more than quintupled its growth rate to 6.5 per cent per decade from 1740–90.[33] In earlier times such a rate of increase would have led inexorably to diminishing returns in agriculture, decreased living standards, and a slackening or reversal of population growth – the infamous Malthusian trap. This period differed, however, in that living standards did not decline appreciably (although real wages probably stagnated or fell), and the rate of growth of population was sustained into the next century.

The work of the Cambridge Group for the History of Population and Social Structure, culminating in the publication of E. A. Wrigley and R. S. Schofield's *The Population History of England, 1541–1871* in 1981, has enhanced considerably both the factual basis and the understanding of the process of population growth. Wrigley and Schofield determined, for example, that almost three-quarters of the increase in population growth could be attributed to an increase in the fertility rate as opposed to a decline in the death rate, with earlier marriage playing a key role in the expansion of fertility. When they moved from demographic reconstruction to interpretation, however, Wrigley and Schofield entered a more controversial debate on the relationship between economic development and population growth. In their model, fertility responded endogenously to economic forces, whereas mortality fluctuations remained primarily exogenous, that is, they were not responsive to economic change. The key relationship ran from real wages to fertility, with rising real wages associated with an increase in fertility, although they acknowledged the existence of a disturbingly long and variable lag of up to half a century.[34] The last half of the eighteenth century was fortunate in that mortality crises were limited, except for two years in the 1760s and three years in the early 1780s, when mortality rates were more than 10 per cent above trend.[35] Although either of these incidents could have signalled the beginning of another Malthusian cycle, they did not. What ultimately broke the Malthusian trap and allowed population to continue increasing into the nineteenth century was 'the complete disappearance of the positive link between population size and food prices'.[36] The agricultural sector this time responded vigorously and by the end of the century had managed to increase food production at a rate close to population growth. In addition, Britain was able to draw increasingly on agricultural supplies from the rest of the world, at least partly because of developments in the commercial and industrial sectors of the economy.

Wrigley and Schofield have not settled the debate on the links between economic development and population growth (or vice versa); the direction of causality in this case may be impossible to determine. While both their methods of reconstruction and their model have been criticised, one of their sternest critics conceded, 'The basic framework of English population growth set up by Wrigley and Schofield . . . will surely stand the test of time.'[37]

Along with increased population growth came an increase in the growth of output in the economy. The achievement in aggregate output growth was offset by the increase in population growth, so that in per capita terms the results between 1740 and 1790 were far from spectacular. In fact, per capita output and income growth rates probably declined for much of the period. Table 2.1 contains Crafts' estimates of growth rates by sector and aggregated.[38]

TABLE 2.1   Growth rates in real national output (% per annum)

	1700–60	1760–80	1780–1801
Agriculture	0.60	0.13	0.75
Industry	0.71	1.51	2.11
Commerce	0.69	0.70	1.32
Rent and services	0.38	0.69	0.97
Government and defence	1.91	1.29	2.11
National output	0.69	0.70	1.32
National output per head	0.31	0.01	0.35

A noteworthy feature of these new estimates is the decline in the rate of growth of agricultural output which occurred from 1760–80. This was counterbalanced by an increase in the rate of growth of industry in the same period. Perhaps most striking is the finding that the rate of growth of national output did not change appreciably during the first eighty years of the century, although the periodisation chosen by Crafts conceals some fluctuation in the first sixty years of the century. After 1780, virtually all sectors of the economy exhibited an increase in the rate of growth of output, leading to a revival in the growth of output per capita. Growth rates over the whole period, however, remained modest compared with those achieved in the nineteenth century.

The clear implication of these new estimates of sectoral growth rates is to emphasise the gradualness of the process. No dramatic breakthrough can be identified in the aggregate figures. Yet, according to Crafts: 'By the end of the eighteenth century it is clear that a substantial "structural" change was also taking place. The relative importance of industry and commerce in output and employment was increasing and that of agriculture was falling.'[39] The proportion of the male labour force in agriculture fell from roughly 60% in 1700 to 53% in 1760, and further to 40% in 1800, while that in industry rose from around 19% in 1700 to 24% in 1760, and to 30% in 1800.[40] Thus the 'triumph' of the British economy at the end of the eighteenth century 'lay in employing a lot of people in industry and relatively few in agriculture rather than in achieving outstanding productivity levels or growth rates in industry taken as a whole'.[41]

There were other structural shifts in the economy, towards both investment and overseas trade, each of which has been cited as a fundamental cause underlying Britain's transformation. Charles Feinstein has provided estimates of capital formation back to 1761.[42] His figures show a rather abrupt increase in gross investment as a share of total product (using Deane and Cole's output figures) from 8–9% during 1760–80 to 12% in 1780–90, a level that then was maintained into the 1830s. Crafts, applying his higher estimates of national income for the earlier eighteenth century, postulates a more gradual increase in the share of investment, rising from 4% of national income in 1700 to 6% in 1760, 7% in 1780, 8% in 1801, and not reaching 12% until 1831.[43] Although these patterns might provide some evidence for Rostow's take-off thesis (or for Ashton's emphasis on the declining cost of capital), Jeffrey Williamson points out that these gross investment figures were quite small for an economy experiencing such rapid population growth: 'The rise in the investment rate was barely sufficient, more or less, to take care of the capital widening associated with the surge in labor force growth generated by the demographic transition.'[44] Once again, the lack of spectacular achievement for the period is emphasised. In addition, Feinstein's sectoral investment figures for the period 1761–90 indicate that the largest single user of capital was agriculture, which invested nearly a third of the total. Industry and trade, transport, and residential and social equally shared the remainder. Barely 6 per cent of the total was investment in machinery and equipment, items normally associated with industrialisation. This pattern of investment was quite different from that which was to occur in the nineteenth century.[45]

Over the course of the eighteenth century British foreign trade grew faster than both population and the economy as a whole, thus increasing its weight (albeit modestly) in the economy and leading some historians to posit trade as the engine of eighteenth-century growth. Growth in trade, however, was not smooth. Exports, imports and re-exports were at one time or another expanding quite rapidly, but setbacks and rather abrupt shifts in the pattern of trade occurred, especially during war. One inclusive measure of foreign trade (net imports plus domestic exports) was growing less than 1% per year from 1700–40, accelerated to about 2% per year from 1740–70, and after a dip in the late 1770s, reached nearly 5% per year in the last two decades of the century.[46] The pattern of exports, perhaps more relevant to the industrial sector of the economy, behaved quite differently. Exports were growing rapidly in the early years of the century, at nearly 3% per year, slowed to about 1% per year from 1714–44, rose again to their previous level from 1744–60, actually declined from 1760–81, and then expanded rapidly at over 5% per year from 1781–1800.[47] Within the context of these fluctuations, exports increased as a share of national income from about 8 to slightly over 10 per cent over the course of the century.

Foreign trade played a critical role in Deane and Cole's explanation of the mechanics of eighteenth-century British growth: 'There can, of course, be no doubt of the central importance of overseas trade in the expansion of the economy during this period.'[48] Yet the role was complex and somewhat peculiar. The key stimulus to growth was not an autonomous increase in the demand for British goods in the rest of the world (which would have led to higher export prices relative to import prices, precisely the opposite of which in fact occurred when trade was expanding most rapidly). Rather Deane and Cole find the impetus as coming from the expansion of the domestic economy, the consequent rise in demand for *imports*, and the feedback effects this had on trading partners, especially in the colonial dependencies towards which trade was increasingly directed. They argued that 'the expansion of the British export trade was limited by the purchasing power of Britain's customers, and that this in its turn was limited by what they could earn from exports to Britain'.[49] Thus, the vicissitudes in purchasing power of her colonial customers, especially southern and West Indian planters, limited the growth of British exports in the eighteenth century. When the planters prospered, so also did British exporters. Cole more recently has moderated this view, allowing a somewhat greater, but far from deterministic, role for the autonomous expansion of overseas demand: 'both the evidence which so far has been collected and a little common sense might lead us to conclude that the impulses which promoted the expansion of Britain's trade in the eighteenth century came first from one side, then the other, and that in the long run both home and overseas demand were essential to the growth process.'[50] Many economic historians would argue that even this moderate view suffers from a problem shared by all demand-side explanations of economic growth in that to be effective in raising incomes such a process depends critically on the existence of unemployed or underemployed resources in the economy.

Although there was little change in the proportion of total industrial output that was exported between 1745 and 1790, exports were more important for some industries than others. In 1700 British exports went predominantly to Europe, and woollens comprised 70 per cent of total exports. Exports of woollens and worsteds grew slowly over the first half of the century and their share of total exports declined to 47 per cent by the 1750s and to 42 per cent by the 1770s. Cotton exports started from a very low base in the mid-eighteenth century, but it was one of the few industries (along with non-ferrous metals and manufactures) to continue expanding in the 1760s and 1770s. Cotton goods, however, comprised only 2 per cent of total exports in the early 1770s. Between 1783 and 1792, there was a broad-based expansion in exports, which now were directed primarily to North America and the West Indies. Cotton exports were the fastest growing component of the total, but they remained small in the aggregate. In addition, as late as 1789 only 23 per cent of cotton goods were exported, suggesting the fundamental importance of home demand to this critical industry.

Total imports into Britain increased by just under 120 per cent between 1700 and 1773. Imports of manufactured goods (over half of which were linens) increased by only 17 per cent over these years, raw material imports about kept pace with the overall increase, but the importation of foodstuffs more than tripled. Spectacular percentage increases occurred in the importation of grain (which previously had been exported), tea, rice, sugar (the largest single import by value), spirits, and to a lesser extent, coffee. The rising importance of the colonial trade is evident in the nature of these products. Imports from America increased by nearly four and a half times between 1700 and 1773, far outpacing activity in other areas. Imports from the British Isles tripled, those from the East Indies increased by two and a half times, and those from northwest Europe actually declined.[51]

The foreign trade sector contributed to economic development between 1742 and 1789, making it possible by the end of the period for Britain to import critical food and raw material supplies and providing markets for the output of British industry, but it was never more than a sputtering engine of growth and not alone sufficient to generate development. As Crouzet has noted: 'Only in the mid-19th century did Britain become a full-fledged export economy.'[52]

The impact on living standards of the aggregate changes discussed thus far is problematic. As already shown, real national output per head was growing modestly up to 1760, stagnated for the next twenty years, and then resumed its modest growth (Table 2.1), all within the context of rapid population growth after around 1740. This did not translate immediately into higher living standards for the bulk of the population. The evidence on real wage rates is mixed, partly because there is no aggregate index for Britain as a whole. It appears that real wages in southern England fell substantially between 1750 and 1790 and did not turn upward until around 1800.[53] This pessimistic view has been confirmed recently by L. D. Schwarz, who found a decline in real wages of around 50 per cent for certain London occupations.[54] On the other hand, Gilboy found that real wages were rising in the north.[55] In a recent study of several industrial occupations in North Stafford-shire, E. H. Hunt and F. W. Botham found that real wages rose from 20 to 60 per cent over the same time period (1750–90). They attributed this increase in real wages to the changing industrial structure of the region. Moreover, they noted that in the 1760s most of Britain's high-wage counties were in the Southeast, whereas by the 1790s eight out of the eleven highest wage counties were in the North and Midlands. The proximity to industrialisation, they argued, was associated with expand-ing opportunities and rising real wages.[56] Considerable work needs to be done before generalisations for all of Britain can be made, although the evidence may indicate that real wages, while not likely to have risen overall, probably did not fall by as much as the pessimists have asserted. Feinstein's figures on real consumption per capita from 1761–90 indicate little movement in that figure.[57] It is also quite conceivable that incomes grew while real wages were falling because the pressure of popula-tion growth on living standards caused more people to seek employment and those already working to work longer, more regularly, and harder.[58]

The years from 1742 to 1789 were difficult yet ultimately successful. Britain began the period with an income per head that already was high compared with underdeveloped econo-mies (but not much different from her chief rival, France). Productive potential grew as a result of increased supplies of factors of production, with only a modest contribution from increased productivity. Perhaps most important, population pressure this time led to both harder work (a mixed blessing) and to innovations which successfully offset diminishing re-turns. This response paved the way for the greater success of the following century.

III AGRICULTURE

The agricultural sector was declining relative to the economy as a whole. Still, in 1789 more people were employed in agriculture than in industry, a greater proportion of national income was generated in agriculture than in industry, agriculture remained the largest single outlet for private investment, and those who stayed and worked the land were becoming more productive.

Evaluation of progress in agriculture is seriously hampered by lack of aggregate output statistics, and all discussions are necessarily conjectural. E. L. Jones, however, cites a figure of 61 per cent for total output growth between 1700 and 1800.[59] The gains occurred because of an increase in the supply of factors of production (including a modest expansion of labour and land under cultivation, with a more substantial increase in capital), greater intensity of land use (which translated into higher output per acre), improved factor productivity, organisational changes (including greater regional specialisation), and the diffusion of new crops (especially grasses and legumes) and mixed farming.[60] Recent historians have demolished the older notion of an agricultural revolution occurring simultaneously with an industrial revolution. Agricultural output per capita probably stagnated over the whole period from 1740 to 1790.[61] Michael Turner has contended that Deane and Cole's figure of 10 per cent for yield improvement during the eighteenth century may have been too low, but argued that most of the increase came before 1770 and that grain yields stagnated subsequently.[62] Whereas productivity improvements made before the middle of the eighteenth century may have set the stage for the population explosion of the last half of the century, one historian has gone so far as to argue that 'the main productivity gains of eighteenth-century agriculture were made by extending techniques pioneered, and more than merely pioneered, before 1700, within a set of institutions also brought into being then.'[63]

One development that was not new in the eighteenth century was the enclosure of open fields, commons and waste land. What was new about the enclosure movement beginning in the middle of the eighteenth century was that it was brought about by parliamentary action rather than private agreement. According to Turner it is not obvious why this change occurred.[64] Jones speculated that one category of owners, tithe owners, may have benefited particularly from this form of enclosure. Tithes were costly to collect, tithe owners were not asked to bear the costs of enclosure, and they received a higher proportion of the enclosed land than they had traditionally received in tithes. A problem with this explanation is that their representation in Parliament was not fundamentally different in the eighteenth century from what it had been earlier.[65] Two external factors that are widely agreed to have stimulated the movement were the increase in agricultural prices and lower interest rates after mid century.

Just over 70 per cent of England already had been enclosed through private arrangements by 1700.[66] Turner estimated that slightly over 20 per cent of England was enclosed by parliamentary act. These enclosures occurred in two waves, one concentrated in the years 1755–80, the other beginning in 1790 and lasting into the nineteenth century. Almost 40 per cent of the total number of enclosure acts were passed during 1755–80, with an intense movement in the last half of the 1770s. Parliamentary enclosures differed both spatially and temporally. Much of England outside the Midlands had been enclosed before the eighteenth century. By 1790 the process had been completed on the heavier soils of Northamptonshire, Warwickshire and Leicestershire, as well as in the lowlands of Scotland, yet the process had hardly begun in East Anglia or the highlands of Scotland.[67]

The question remains, why did this new wave of parliamentary enclosure arise when it did and what effects did it have? It may have been partly a response to agricultural stress due to increased population pressure, partly a response to increased opportunities. According to Turner, contemporaries were certain of the benefits. Landlords could and did raise rents, but tenants also benefited from productivity improvements in grain yields (from 10–25 per cent after enclosure), which freed land for other uses. It allowed greater flexibility and made farmers more responsive to market forces. Farming in severalty allowed farmers to grow a greater variety of crops and permitted a reduction in fallow acreage. It enhanced the speed with which new crops could be diffused, permitted an extension of animal production (and its important by-product, manure), and allowed a quick adjustment in the mix between crops and livestock, all of which led to increased productivity.[68]

In previous times, rising agricultural prices would have led to significantly lower living standards. R. V. Jackson has estimated that after falling for the previous eighty years, real agricultural prices rose substantially (by 7.7 per cent per decade) from 1740 to 1790. This was a period in which real wage rates probably stagnated or fell in much of Britain but also one in which real national income per head rose modestly. The composition of consumption moved away from agricultural products (with the prospect that diets might have worsened) and towards industrial products, a movement consistent with relative price changes.[69] Additional work (focusing on actual dietary trends) must be undertaken before any firm generalisations about the overall standard of living of the greatly expanded population of 1790 can be made.

IV INDUSTRY AND TRANSPORT

Changes initiated in industry in the middle decades of the eighteenth century set the stage for the much more impressive developments that were to follow. The era witnessed technological improvements (not all of which were dramatic) and output expansion in a wide array of industries: non-ferrous metals such as copper and brass; traditional consumer goods such as beer, candles, glass, paper and soap; and newer consumer items represented by common pottery and the Birmingham toy trades. Developments, however, in a small number of industries – cotton textiles, iron and coal – are regarded as exceptional.

Crafts has estimated value added (revenues minus raw material costs) by major industrial sector for several benchmark years. The figures for 1770 and 1801 are presented in Table 2.2.[70]

These figures lead to several observations. The more traditional woollen textile industry remained important throughout the eighteenth century, but its rate of growth was relatively

TABLE 2.2   Value added in industry (£m current and % of total)

	1770			1801	
Wool	7.0	(30.6)	Wool	10.1	(18.7)
Leather	5.1	(22.3)	Building	9.3	(17.2)
Building	2.4	(10.5)	Cotton	9.2	(17.0)
Linen	1.9	(8.3)	Leather	8.4	(15.5)
Iron	1.5	(6.6)	Iron	4.0	(7.4)
Beer	1.3	(5.7)	Coal	2.7	(5.0)
Silk	1.0	(4.4)	Linen	2.6	(4.8)
Coal	0.9	(4.4)	Beer	2.5	(4.6)
Cotton	0.6	(2.6)	Silk	2.0	(3.7)
Candles	0.5	(2.2)	Candles	1.0	(1.8)
Soap	0.3	(1.3)	Copper	0.9	(1.7)
Copper	0.2	(0.9)	Soap	0.8	(1.5)
Paper	0.1	(0.4)	Paper	0.6	(1.1)
Total	22.9		Total	54.1	

slow. Although woollen textile production had been rather widespread in the early eighteenth century, the rise of new centres of production came at the expense of decline in others. By the end of the century Yorkshire and Lancashire were in the ascendancy, Norfolk was barely holding its own, and areas such as Colchester, Suffolk, Worcester, Dorset and Exeter had seen decline.[71] Along with wool the biggest relative declines were in the linen, silk and leather industries. The cotton textile industry was the fastest growing of all up to 1801, although it began from a low base. In the 1780s alone cotton production expanded by nearly 13 per cent, a rate of growth not achieved by any other industry in any decade of the eighteenth century.[72] Both the iron and coal industries grew rapidly but without achieving a substantial shift in their share of value added. Not all the rapidly growing industries were technically advanced. The building industry stagnated technologically but most likely benefited from the demand of the ever-rising population for additional housing. Finally, when examining the textile industry as a whole, it is clear that what was happening, at least in the last third of the eighteenth century, was a major structural shift *within* the industry. The share of all textiles in value added declined only slightly, from 45.9 per cent of the total in 1770 to 44.2 per cent in 1801.

The story of the cotton textile industry has been told often. It originated in the sixteenth century when Walloon and Dutch immigrants settled in Norwich and began the manufacture of fustians, a mixture of linen warp and cotton weft. Towards the end of the sixteenth century the industry moved into Lancashire where it competed for resources with the established woollen industry. By the late seventeenth century the practice of printing fustians, and later calicoes, with bright-coloured patterns had established a market niche so effectively that the silk and woollen interests felt threatened and succeeded in getting Parliament in the early eighteenth century to ban the sale of English calicoes. The restrictions were not effective, and since production for export also was exempted, the industry continued to expand modestly.[73] By the 1740s retained cotton imports had reached £2 million per year. Still, compared with the woollen industry, the cotton textile industry remained relatively small and equally backward. It was then that the 'wave of gadgets' (the felicitious phrase of Ashton's schoolboy) descended on the industry and transformed it into one of the most dynamic industries of the late eighteenth century.

The innovations 'came in a sequence of challenge and response, in which the speed-up of one stage of the manufacturing process placed a heavy strain on the factors of production of one or more other stages and called forth innovations to correct the imbalance.'[74] The earliest inventions were intended for wool rather than cotton. Kay's flying shuttle, patented in 1733 but not adopted until mid century when it was applied to cotton, greatly exacerbated an existing imbalance between weaving and spinning. The response was Hargreaves' spinning jenny (1764), originally containing eight spindles, but increasing to 80 by 1784; Arkwright's water frame (1769), which for the first time produced a yarn strong enough to produce an all-cotton cloth and stimulated the movement from home production to factory production in spinning; and Crompton's mule (1779), which finally reversed the previous imbalance between weaving and spinning. Cartwright's power loom (1789) was a response to this, but it was not immediately successful and not until the nineteenth century were effective power looms adopted. One result of these mechanical innovations was a tremendous increase in the productivity of labour in the industry. By 1812 one spinner could produce the same amount of (a higher quality) yarn that would have consumed the labour of two hundred workers before the invention of the spinning jenny. By the late 1780s retained cotton imports had reached £25 million per year.[75]

In spite of these impressive achievements, it would not be appropriate to exaggerate the importance of this single industry in the process of industrialisation and modernisation, especially before 1789. The forward and backward linkages created may have been modest:

> The fact is that its connections with other important British industries were not large enough to set off powerful secondary repercussions. . . . The principal raw material was entirely imported. . . . It was a long time before cotton manufacture began to use much coal [water being the main source of power]. The industry was localized so that it did not create a spreading demand for new transport and building facilities. . . . It was not until the second quarter of the nineteenth century that a textile-machinery industry developed on any scale.[76]

Maxine Berg, while appreciating the connection between the cotton industry and new forms of industrial organisation, nonetheless emphasised the continuities with the past. Even the most advanced Arkwright-type spinning mills remained fully integrated with the small jenny and mule shops and with the putting-out system of weaving. In 1789 there were 40 per cent more jenny spindles in operation than water frame and mule spindles combined.[77] Large-scale production was only just beginning. The cotton textile industry remained a dynamic, but still small and rather isolated, component of the economy as a whole.

Whilst changes in the cotton textile industry were mainly mechanical and labour saving and only later led to the demise of the putting-out system in favour of factory production, changes in the iron industry were mainly chemical and led to advances in both quantity and quality of output, but did not immediately conserve labour. Unlike cotton textiles, iron had always been produced in a factory setting.[78] In addition, there were important interconnections between iron, coal, steam power and transport innovations that made the iron industry a powerful force for change in the last half of the eighteenth century. Up to 1750, iron had been produced in furnaces using charcoal as a fuel. The industry stagnated in the early decades of the century and both the number of furnaces and average output per furnace remained stable. Aggregate annual output was around 27,000 tons in 1720–4 and was the same in 1745–9.[79] The fundamental turning point in the industry came in the 1750s. Although Abraham Darby had been smelting iron with coke at Coalbrookdale since 1709, cost and quality considerations prevented its widespread adoption. With an increase in charcoal costs beginning in the 1750s, the substitution of coke for charcoal occurred rapidly. C. K. Hyde has estimated that by the late 1750s the total cost of smelting with coke had fallen below the variable cost of producing charcoal pig iron.[80] The adoption of the improved Boulton and Watt steam engine after 1775, which provided sufficient power to secure an adequate blast, gave both industries a substantial boost. By 1789 the iron industry was producing around 80,000 tons annually, seven-eighths of which was smelted with coke in furnaces that were three times the size of those in the 1750s.[81] The adoption of the 'potting process' (so called because of the use of pots containing a lime flux through which carbon and sulphur impurities were removed from the metal) in the wrought iron sector in the 1760s and 1770s stimulated the smelting sector by increasing demand for the intermediate product, but it was not until Cort's invention of the puddling process in 1784 (which was not adopted until the 1790s) that production techniques in wrought and bar iron were revolutionised.[82] These changes would have meant little if there had not been an increase in the demand for the product. Iron came to be used extensively in construction work – buildings, factories and bridges (the first being an iron bridge over the Severn in 1779), which provided an expanding market for the now-cheaper iron.

The iron industry was fundamentally different from the cotton textile industry in that it created a derived demand for domestic raw materials – iron ore, limestone and coal. The relationship between the iron industry and the coal industry was especially important. At the beginning of the century the main use of coal was for domestic heating and the Northeast was the dominant producing region, contributing over 40 per cent of total output of around 3 million tons. Total output expanded to 5.2 million tons by 1750, to 8.8 million tons by 1775, and to 15 million tons by 1800. Output had been expanding by just over 1 per cent per annum to 1750 but doubled its rate of growth from then to the end of the century. The fastest growing regions after 1750 were Lancashire and South Wales, which increased their share of total output at the expense of the Northeast (which had fallen to 30 per cent by 1800).[83] The growth of iron production centred in Staffordshire and South Wales greatly stimulated the demand for coal in those districts. From virtually nothing in 1750, the iron industry was consuming about 12 per cent of total coal output by 1800.[84] There were no dramatic technical breakthroughs in the mining of coal in the last half of the eighteenth century (the application of steam power having already occurred), but the increased level of production was brought forth from deeper mines at a roughly constant real cost through mundane advances in draining, ventilation, lighting, hauling and winding.[85] The dramatic change in the industry was associated with the declining cost of transport, which brought down the price of coal to the domestic and industrial consumer.

Transportation in the eighteenth century was crucial because few traded goods were produced where they were consumed and raw materials were not always conveniently situated. Transport costs thus comprised a substantial portion of the final price of virtually every processed good. An inefficient transport sector hinders development by limiting the market, and improvements can have far-reaching effects. Britain had always relied on its excellent coastwise shipping to move commodities. This had been especially important for the development of its major commercial centre, London. Inland transportation, however, depended on good (at least passable) roads. According to Pawson, the road network in the early eighteenth century remained 'strangely medieval' and was inadequate to handle the strains put on it by an expanding economy.[86] The emergence and diffusion of the turnpike trust (a local administrative device), whose use peaked in the years 1750–70, led to the creation of a coherent, well-ordered, and fairly intensive road network by 1770. This succeeded in reducing travel times (e.g. from ten days in mid century to four in 1776 for a summer journey from Edinburgh to London[87]), but remained inadequate for bulky, low-value goods, such as coal. The need to move coal stimulated the other major transport innovation of the era, the canal.

In 1755 a group of Liverpool merchants was sufficiently concerned about the high cost of transporting coal to the city by turnpike that they proposed building a waterway to circumvent the problem. Completed in 1757, the Sankey Brook Navigation led to an immediate reduction in the price of household coal from St Helens. The existence of the canal also led to the growth of coal-consuming industries in Lancashire, Merseyside and north Cheshire, which in turn stimulated production in the St Helens coal field.[88]

The greatest of all the early canal builders was the Duke of Bridgewater, a coal producer rather than consumer. In order to exploit his fields, one of which lay a mere six miles from the centre of Manchester, he petitioned Parliament to build a canal, which was completed in 1763 (the Worsley). He later extended navigations to the south and west, which allowed him to exploit his coal fields fully.[89] The financial success of these early canals led to successive waves of canal building (with peaks in the 1770s and 1790s) in other coal fields and for other purposes that lasted into the nineteenth century. The coal canals, however, had the greatest economic impact. They lowered the cost of coal to consumers both directly (by as much as 50 per cent) and indirectly, by allowing production to be relocated to lower-cost sites:

They did this in part by stimulating increased output, and in part by widening the market areas which enjoyed the lowest coal prices. These areas were predominantly inland, adjacent to coalfields but previously denied an effective supply of coal by the barrier of transport costs. Since they also contained the raw materials and other components of an industrial base, the removal of the transport constraint led to observable surges in their industrial growth.[90]

Perhaps more important, these canals formed an integral

part of the self-reinforcing iron–coal–steam engine-transport nexus, which was a powerful force in this transitional phase of Britain's economic development.

There was another structural change, definitively located in the period 1742–89, which had a wide-ranging impact on economic activity but still is not fully understood. Technical advance comes through the discovery (and subsequent adoption) of new and better ways of doing things. Inventive activity is at the heart of technical change, and patents issued provide a reasonable measure of inventive activity. Historians previously have noted a marked increase in patents issued during the eighteenth century. Richard Sullivan recently has applied sophisticated quantitative techniques to patent data in order to pinpoint significant turning points. He found that the trend in number of patents issued permanently shifted upward in 1757 (increasing from a rate of growth of 0.5 per cent per annum from 1661–1756 to 3.6 per cent from 1756–1851) and that the trend in number of patents per capita did likewise in 1762. Furthermore, the fluctuations around the trend decreased significantly after those dates, indicating more consistent inventive activity.[91] Why this fundamental change should have occurred during the midst of the Seven Years War is a mystery. There was no institutional change in the method of patenting that can explain the change, neither is there evidence of a fundamental change in the propensity to patent inventions. This is a topic worthy of further exploration.

V PUBLIC FINANCE

'Of the non-economic factors that shaped Britain's economic destinies in the eighteenth century, the most potent was war.'[92] Whether or not one agrees with the assertion that war was a non-economic factor, the wars of the eighteenth century did have a substantial economic impact. Referring back to Table 2.1, it can be seen that government and defence was the most rapidly growing sector of the economy over the whole of the century. Whether this was ultimately beneficial to the economy is questionable, for the impact of war was felt in diverse ways, some of which stimulated development and others which inhibited it. It is certain that warfare during the eighteenth century was an extraordinarily expensive activity, disrupted commerce, and led to substantial debt accumulation. That Britain successfully met the financial challenges of warfare represented an impressive achievement, something that cannot be said for her major opponent.

In 1720 after the close of the Baltic and Spanish war, the national debt of Britain stood at £54 million.[93] During Walpole's administration, this gradually had been whittled down to £47 million by the eve of the War of Austrian Succession. This conflict, which also witnessed the brief invasion of England by Prince Charles Edward in 1745, was a relatively modest affair by eighteenth-century standards. The war cost of just over £4 million per year was financed by increased taxation and additional borrowing. At the close of the war in 1748, the national debt had risen to £76 million. The next encounter was to be much more costly.

Annual peacetime expenditures in the early 1750s had amounted to roughly £6–7 million, nearly half of which were interest payments on the accumulated debt. After war broke out in 1756, expenditures escalated until they reached over £20 million in 1762. In the end the war cost over £80 million and the national debt rose to £129 million in 1763. Annual peacetime expenditures in the late 1760s and early 1770s settled back to £9–10 million, nearly half of which again were interest payments on the debt.

The American War of Independence proved to be equally costly to Britain, and this time there were no spoils of victory to enjoy. Government expenditures reached nearly £30 million in 1782, and the national debt stood at just under £240 million at the close of war in 1785. Normal peacetime expenditures again ratcheted upward, to £15–16 million annually between 1785 and 1789, before the final great conflict with France sent expenditures skyrocketing again.

By any measure these figures were staggering. The national debt in 1785 was nearly two and a half times as large as national income in that year. The sums raised by government in the 1760s amounted to twice the amount of total gross domestic fixed capital investment and half again as much as total investment.[94] If even a portion of sums spent on war in this period had been diverted to domestic investment, capital formation would have been much higher and economic growth in the eighteenth century may have been much more rapid than it was, especially in the 1760s and 1770s. Jeffrey Williamson's argument that the 'crowding out' of private investment during the French Wars inhibited growth in the late eighteenth and early nineteenth centuries could be applied equally to the wars of the mid eighteenth century.[95]

One of the legacies of the accumulating debt was the creation of a system of taxation to secure it. Indirect taxation (customs and excise duties) was increasingly relied upon to finance the burden of debt. Between 1698 and 1701, 31% of total revenues were raised by the land tax, 32% by customs duties, and 27% by excises. By 1786–9 the land tax comprised only 18% of total revenues, customs duties 24%, and excises 43%. Indirect taxes not only raised the prices of many goods, but the system represented a fairly massive transfer of resources from the common consumer to the relatively few and generally wealthy holders of the national debt. Because population also was growing, it did not represent a massive increase in real taxes per capita up to 1789, but because of the relatively slow rate of growth in per capita output, it meant that there was an increase in the share of per capita output collected in taxes (from 16% in 1715 to 23% by 1785).[96] The ultimate impact of this system of taxation depends upon 'one's judgement about the relative constraints being imposed upon the economy from problems of accumulation and investment on the one side, or from limitations in effective demand in the mass market on the other'.[97] If a shortage of savings or difficulty mobilising savings were critical problems, then the regressive tax system in Britain may have produced some economic benefit. But if the problem was a lack of effective demand, then the tax system was perverse. Whichever it was, the longer-range significance of debt accumulation almost certainly overshadowed any short-term stimulus given to a limited number of sectors of the economy due to war.

VI CONCLUSION

By 1789 Britain was in the midst of a transformation that would have been visible to an increasing number of citizens (as it was not to Adam Smith in 1776). Several new industries had grown up and others had expanded, new opportunities for employment in different settings existed, new products were available to more consumers, and new means of transportation emerged. These changes, however, were not yet felt in the standard of living of the average citizen, and some (such as the nascent movement to factory production) initially met with resistance. The material payoff for the vast majority of the population was not to come for another century at least. But without the inventiveness, the risks taken, and the forces put in motion in the middle decades of the eighteenth century, the great transformation might not have occurred when and where it did. In the words of Toynbee: 'It is well that the beaten ways of the world get trodden into mud: we are thus forced to seek new paths and pick out new lines of life.'[98]

3
Scotland and Ireland 1742–1789

BRUCE P. LENMAN

There is an insoluble difficulty involved in writing about two complex national groups such as the Scots and the Irish within an Anglocentric frame of values which would reduce their histories in the later eighteenth century to mere footnotes to a metropolitan saga. Nevertheless, attention will here be focused on appropriate aspects of their relationship with the metropolitan authority, not because that was necessarily the most important aspect of their eighteenth-century histories, but because such a theme can be treated within the available space without gross over-compression. What follows is therefore not an attempt to give a balanced mini-summary of Scottish and Irish history in this era, but an attempt to set the development of the relationship between these two nations and the central government of the British world-state against the relevant Scottish and Irish background.

The central authority in the British world-state after the Glorious Revolution of 1688 was the king in his Westminster parliament. This marked a sharp breach with the theory of late Stuart absolutism, which had stressed the king's sovereign majesty as the unifying element in his multi-realm monarchy. Inevitably, therefore, the Revolution introduced potentially destructive core–periphery conflicts into this Atlantic monarchy. The principle of absolutism was not eliminated. Rather was it carefully preserved as a pretension of the Westminster politicians, of whom the king was the most important. In practice, the Glorious Revolution in England marked a sharp check to the scope of central government and for over a century its main impact in that kingdom was to confirm the right and power of local elites to rule their own county societies without undue interference. England was in theory an Anglican church-state, so there was an implicit assumption that those elites were well-disposed towards the existing order in church and state. In dealing with the other two nations in the British Isles, the behaviour of the central power was deeply affected by its perception of the political attitudes of their ruling aristocracies. As a result, there was much more concern, at the start of this period, with the possibility of disaffection in Scotland than there was fear of rebellion in Ireland, and there is no better illustration of this fact than the Irish viceroyalty of Lord Chesterfield.

That viceroyalty has to be seen against a European back-ground dominated by the fact that Britain had by 1744 become involved in three overlapping wars. The maritime war with Spain which broke out in 1739 did not carry any very serious implications for the security of the British Isles. Spanish troops had invaded Scotland in 1719 when a desperate Cardinal Alberoni had tried to save his sinking ministry by playing the Jacobite card against George I, whose warships were des-troying the ambitions of the new Bourbon dynasty in Spain to recreate a Spanish empire in the western Mediterranean. The invasion had turned into a total fiasco which was not likely to be repeated even when the maritime war with Spain had added to it a continental conflict geared to the claims of Philip V of Spain to the Austrian succession, and his wife's territorial ambitions in Italy for her son Don Philip.[1] However, the Spanish alliance with France sealed by the treaty of Fontainebleau in 1743, and the confrontation between the British and French governments which culminated in a formal declaration of war in the spring of 1744, did create a most dangerous situation in which a major European power had both the incentive and the military and naval power to consider intervention in the British home archipelago.

Chesterfield's accession to office after a long period of opposition which had made him obnoxious to King George II was itself a symptom of crisis. Since 1742 the unhappy coalition of Carteret and the Pelham brothers had plunged deeper and deeper into deadlock, and in 1744 an attempt was made to revitalise it by adding to Carteret, now Earl Granville, and former Walpole supporters such as the Pelhams and Lord Hardwicke, Hanoverian Tories like Lord Gower, ambiguous Tories like Sir John Hynde Cotton, and Whig malcontents of whom Chesterfield was one. 'The Broad Bottom' was precipitated by foreign policy failure, but it turned out to be a forcing bed for domestic faction. Significantly, Chesterfield, whose Irish appointment both gave him nominal cabinet rank and kept him clear of the monarch, made no effort to head for Dublin. Instead, he was despatched as ambassador to The Hague where it was hoped that his diplomatic talents might confirm the Dutch as active allies in the grand alliance against France which lay at the core of the Whig 'old system' of diplomacy. Ireland as such featured in his correspondence with the Duke of Newcastle not at all, with the solitary exception of his insistence that the next Irish bishopric go to his own domestic chaplain. Rightly concluding that the refusal of George II to confirm his nomination was yet another example of that monarch's desire to snub most of the ministry, Chesterfield warned Newcastle in March 1745 that he would return to London only to resign his Irish post on the ground that:

If my recommendation to the dirtiest Bishopric in Ireland (independently of its name) is not to prevail, it can only be because it is mine. An indignity by which I am distinguish'd from all my predecessors, and to which I shall upon no account submit; and I think it but fair to give your Grace and our friends notice that, upon this foot I will not be Lord Lieutenant of Ireland one hour after my arrival in London.[2]

There was nothing particularly outrageous about a man resigning as Lord Lieutenant of Ireland before he even reached the island, because no great cosmic crisis was likely to arise if a given Lord Lieutenant dropped dead in post, let alone resigned before occupying it. The country was peaceful and most Lords Lieutenant made little difference for good or ill. For example, the third Duke of Devonshire, a great English nobleman who held that office between 1737 and 1744, is usually reckoned a successful incumbent (one of the key criteria for 'success' appears to have been a willingness to spend lavishly on wines served at vice-regal receptions), but his reign was marked, quite fortuitously, by the famine of 1739–40, usually deemed the worst of the eighteenth century, and one where there was unusually heavy mortality from the typhus-like fevers which subsequently ravaged a weakened population. Smallpox, typhus and tuberculosis were endemic in Ireland, and the famine would probably have occurred under any conceivable regime.[3]

The Irish countryside was as peaceful as any in Europe in the first two-thirds of the eighteenth century. It was, for example, as peaceful as that of Scotland, where the Leveller's Revolt in Galloway in the 1720s (a protest against the creation of vast drystone-dyked enclosures as part of a general expansion of cattle grazing at the expense of arable), was very much the exception that proves the rule. The Irish equivalent of this was the hougher movement in Connacht in 1711–12. Not only was this an exceptional episode, but it was recognised as such by the Dublin administration, which whilst demanding effective action against those houghing (or hamstringing) cattle, made it clear that it expected the letter of the law to be respected, and that it would tolerate no steps beyond the normal framework of the Common Law to deal with the problem.[4]

Broadly speaking, the English elites of the mid-eighteenth century felt more at home with similar levels of society in Ireland than they did with the elites and institutions of contemporary Scotland. After all, there had been a tradition of several centuries of parallel development in the Kingdom of England and the Lordship of Ireland before the Reformation, and the Revolution Settlement in Ireland had ensured that the all-purpose aristocratic ruling class of eighteenth-century Ireland would be Anglican and loyal to the British connection, as it had to be if political chaos and strategic insecurity were not to haunt the British monarchy. To an English observer, a parade of condescension about Irish university education was in no way automatic, as Lord Chesterfield demonstrated in 1749, long after he had laid down his Irish office without ceasing to maintain an extensive correspondence with the many friends he had made there. Writing to the Reverend Doctor Madden, mainly about the affairs of those incorrigible encouragers of Improvement, the Dublin Society, Chesterfield remarked casually that:

I hope the University of Dublin, that enjoys a share of your premiums, deserves them. Our two universities, at least, will do it no hurt, unless by their examples, for I cannot believe that their present reputations will invite people in Ireland to send their sons there. The one (Cambridge) is sunk into the lowest obscurity; and the existence of Oxford would not be known, if it were not for the treasonable spirit publicly avowed, and often exerted there.[5]

The mention of treason is a reference to the expression of Jacobite sentiments, which may well have been the university's way of registering its rage and frustration at the high-handed behaviour of successive Whig administrations after 1714, but which no Westminster office-holder was prepared to treat lightly, for a Jacobite restoration would have meant at the very least a dramatic turnover in the ranks of the holders of office and power. Upper-class Jacobites scarcely existed in an Ireland where the bulk of the aristocracy regarded the Revolution Settlement as the supreme guarantee of their estates. Despite the absence of a police force, and the habit the British government had developed of withdrawing the bulk of the troops on the Irish Establishment whenever a war or crisis broke out elsewhere (a habit partially justified by the fact that most of these regiments were in fact English, and were being hidden in Ireland during peacetime to spare the executive criticism from economically-minded members of the British legislature), the Dublin executive just assumed that the traditional ruling classes could and should keep order in the Irish countryside. When Chesterfield was urging the admission of various Irish noblemen to the Irish Privy Council in 1746 he pressed the case, among others, of the Earl of Kerry, whom he described as 'a kind of sovereign in the wild county of Kerry; a very honest man, and very zealous for his Majesty's Government'.[6] That the earl ran Kerry in no way perturbed the Lord Lieutenant: that was what the earl was supposed to do. When he and other members of the aristocracy could be relied upon to do their duty, it did not matter that the Irish forts were falling down, that the militia was disgracefully neglected, or that there were very few troops in the country. Internal revolt was unthinkable. The idea that the Irish peasantry regarded their resident nobility as 'aliens', or were anxious to rebel against heretic overlordship was, as the Lord Lieutenant had the wit to see, inherently unlikely. Despite the fact that 'my good subjects here' were in his view as frightened as they were zealous for the cause of King George when they heard of the Jacobite rebellion in Scotland, Chesterfield also correctly assumed that the late seventeenth-century wars had taught the French that Ireland had little choice but to follow whatever dynastic decision was reached in Britain, so they were likely to concentrate their efforts on the larger isle.[7]

This assumption reinforced the naturally relaxed style which made him so popular in Ireland. So far from following the bad example of London and closing Roman Catholic chapels in Dublin, he encouraged their use during the Jacobite rebellion by firmly guarding them against Protestant mobs, and he would much have preferred to replace the violently anti-Roman Catholic oaths of supremacy and abjuration by a simple oath of allegiance which was not theologically offensive to that communion.[8] Yet when we look at the way Chesterfield responded to the crisis in Scotland in 1745-6, we see the unacceptable face of that mirror of urbanity. Towards Scots Chesterfield was an indiscriminate bigot with a strong tendency towards genocide. His urbane purr turned into a screech of fear and hate, as in his letter to the Duke of Newcastle, written from Dublin Castle in March 1746, in which he denied that the Scots rebels had any right to be treated as enemies. Chesterfield thought that they should be regarded as common felons and that a price should be offered for their heads. The egregiously francophile Lord Lieutenant was happy to deem French troops in the Jacobite army 'fair enemies', but for their Scots opponents he had as little time as he had for their Scots allies, saying to Newcastle that:

> I would likewise order all the *loyal Highlanders* under your Loudons and Campbells into garrison in Newcastle, Berwick, and other towns in England, and employ only English and Hessians in subduing the Highlands. I would also forbid provisions of any kind being sent upon any pretence whatsoever (unless directly to the Duke's army) into Scotland, and I would starve the loyal with the disloyal, if the former thought proper to remain with the latter.[9]

Given that Scotland had come close to a major subsistence crisis in 1742; had only just contrived to avert a general dearth by importing cereal and organising measures to minimise non-essential use of scarce grain whilst providing emergency relief for the most vulnerable sections of society in several regions; and was still suffering acute privation in peripheral regions such as the Highlands in 1745–6, Chesterfield's ideas were draconian. So was his practice. In the same letter he said that Major-General John Campbell of Mamore, the future fourth Duke of Argyll, who was commanding the Argyll Militia, had appealed to him for food from Ireland to supply his men in the campaign against the Jacobites. Chesterfield not only refused flatly to allow Irish supplies to reach General Campbell, but he also made it clear that he regretted that the general and his levies were receiving provisions from Liverpool and Milford Haven: greater love hath no man than to sacrifice his friends for his cause.

The underlying reason for the venomous Scottophobia of so polished a product of the English social and political establishment was that there existed a strong tradition of active Jacobitism among the Scottish nobility and lairds. The Westminster politicians, of whom Chesterfield was one, had a skewed perception of how pervasive that tradition was, mainly because they had been badly shaken by the fact that as late as 1745 a few thousand Jacobite Scots had reached Derby after repeatedly demonstrating how incompetent and unpopular the British government was even on its home ground. Jacobite sentiment was in fact on the wane in Scotland, and had been declining there amongst the elites for a long period. At the time of the war of the Revolution in 1688–90, there had been little or no active military support for the Jacobite cause amongst the Scots magnates. By the time of the abortive Franco-Jacobite invasion of 1708 there had been a great deal of support for the invasion plan (which might well have succeeded in its cautiously limited aims had it been executed), as the very large number of Jacobite nobles shipped to London in April and May 1708 'like hoggs to market' to face charges of complicity in the Jacobite conspiracy, testified. The whole episode made less impact than expected because of a characteristically devious ploy by the Duke of Hamilton, who had been far more involved with the Jacobites than the ministers of Queen Anne were aware, and who cut a deal with the power-obsessed Whigs at Westminster whereby he secured his own liberty and that of the other Scots nobles in exchange for selling their votes to the Whigs in the forthcoming election for sixteen Scots representative peers in the House of Lords.[10] By the time of the 1715 rising, which was by far the most formidable of the series, not least because of the existence of significant potential support in England, it was clear that, particularly north of the Forth, there was massive support for the Jacobites at all levels of Scottish society, and it had required a heroic effort of dishonesty and obstruction on the part of the Scottish social and legal establishment to minimise the price of failure for the Scots upper classes. However, the total mismanagement of the rising, and its consequent failure, deeply undermined Jacobite morale and sentiment in Scotland. The rapidity with which the government crushed the ill-conceived Hispano-Jacobite mini-invasion of 1719 undoubtedly accelerated the process of Jacobite decline, and until the British government became involved in hostilities with France there was no serious prospect of a Jacobite revival, as the exiled Old Pretender knew full well. That was why he regularly urged his few crypto-Jacobite Tory supporters in Westminster to vote for measures likely to embroil Britain and France.[11]

The '45 was never a national rising like the '15 was, at least to the north of the river Forth. It was more a coup by a small minority who exploited two things. One was the usual disgraceful neglect of home defence by the administration of the day. Both French intelligence projections and informed British sources agreed that on the eve of the '45 there were probably less than 5000 troops in Britain, and the king and some of his ministers, due to their Continental obsessions, remained reluctant to recall regiments from Flanders at an amazingly late stage in the rising. The other was the widespread apathy towards Westminster administrations which were widely and rightly seen as systematically undermining the much-vaunted 'Revolution Principles' on which their authority ultimately was supposed to rest. The only peers who joined the Young Pretender in Scotland tended to be marginal ones either positively bankrupt or very likely to become bankrupt in the foreseeable future. No magnate of substance rallied to him. It was important that there did exist a hard core of committed Jacobites in the laird class, often men much influenced by non-juring Episcopal clergymen of passionately Jacobite conviction. Equally, the long era of Walpole's ascendancy in Westminster had left behind a bitter harvest of frustration amongst crypto-Jacobites such as Simon Fraser, Lord Lovat, who was corrupt enough to cut a deal with the Hanoverians, but who could not, in his own opinion, ever get past the Cerberus who guarded the gate to Walpolean patronage in Scotland – the Argyll interest's man of business, Duncan Forbes of Culloden. There were also loyal hereditary Whigs like Ludovick Grant of Grant who repaid the Westminster government during the rising for the decades in which it had stonily refused to grant him his relatively mild and reasonable professional ambition of a judgeship in the Court of Session. Grant of Grant did nothing against the government. He simply refused to make any more unrequited sacrifices for it, and that was enough gravely to weaken the Hanoverian position in Strathspey and the Central Highlands.[12] Men like Chesterfield or the Duke of Cumberland were incapable of seeing the reality of the Scottish situation, and preferred to take refuge in genocidal fantasy, not least because acknowledging massive general apathy towards their regime, which its shrewder members like Henry Pelham could recognise, privately, would have been even more impossible for their pride to swallow.

By no means all prominent spokesmen for the Hanoverian dynasty in England were so purblind. Even when he was busy churning out lurid anti-Stuart propaganda in the thirty-three numbers of his weekly newspaper *The True Patriot*, which began publication in London on 5 November 1745, the novelist Henry Fielding was a great deal more perceptive about the Scottish situation than leading figures in the political group with which he had long been associated, such as Lord Chesterfield. The very first number of the weekly contained, understandably enough, an article entitled 'Observations on the Present Rebellion' which appealed to its readership against what Fielding called 'that indiscriminate Censure which some over-hot Men are at this Season too apt to vent on the whole Body of the

Scottish Nation'. Fielding suggested that a moment's examination of the facts would make it apparent that the bulk of the
Jacobite army was drawn from:

> the savage Inhabitants of Wilds and Mountains, who are
> almost a distinct Body from the rest of their Country. Some
> Thousands of them are Outlaws, Robbers, and Cutthroats,
> who live in a constant State of War, or rather Robbery, with
> the civilized Part of Scotland. The Estates of this Part have
> always been pillaged by the Thefts of these Ruffians, by
> whom they are now openly plundered.
>
> And how greatly it is to the Honour of the Nobility and
> Gentry of North Britain, that they have rather chosen to
> submit to this Alternative than join or countenance a Rebel-
> lion, which hath hitherto been carried on in their Country
> with such a Torrent of Success. This is a fact so true, that
> except Outlaws and one or two profligate younger Brothers,
> there is not a single Man of any Name in the Kingdom, who
> hath given Sanction to the Pretender's Cause.

It was all good stirring stuff, even if it gave a distinctly
over-simplified version of the facts of Scottish life, and it did
contain more than just a grain of truth: there was very little
support amongst the Scottish aristocracy for the cause of the
Young Pretender. Fielding was on even safer ground when he
pointed out the way in which the 'Scotch Clergy' had prayed for
King George in the midst of his triumphant enemies. Fielding is
here, of course, referring to the clergy of the Kirk by Law
Established, with its Presbyterian form of government, and he
was particularly impressed by the way the Synod of Glasgow,
ten days after the Jacobite triumph at the battle of Prestonpans,
had presented a warmly loyal address to their Hanoverian
monarch.[13] There existed a very solid basis for a loyally
Hanoverian social and political ascendancy in Scotland after
the defeat of the Jacobites had totally discredited their already
fading career. It is, however, understandable that the rulers of
Hanoverian Britain were not amongst the first to appreciate
this fact, not least because it would have required an understanding of the Jacobite mind which they could hardly be
expected to display.

Irish Jacobitism, which was well-represented in the tiny group of close followers with whom Prince Charles had landed in Moidart in the late summer of 1745, had been effectively the creed of exiled aristocrats for more than two generations. After Culloden, Scots Jacobitism went the same way, with the important qualification that many of the aristocratic Scots exiles were extremely anxious to jump off what they knew full well to be a permanently immobilised bandwagon. In the Highlands, disillusionment over the failure of French assistance to materialise during the rebellion meant that it would have been impossible to raise even convinced Jacobites for another unsupported venture. The immediate military strategy pursued by government in the Highlands after 1746 showed no grasp of these facts, but rather a natural and prudent desire to insure against Jacobite resurgence. After a disarming act had in theory banned all persons, with few exceptions, from carrying arms in the Highlands after the first day of November 1716, the government had built four new garrison posts at Inversnaid in Stirlingshire, and at three Invernessshire sites; Kiliwhimen, Ruthven-in-Badenoch, and Bernera. All were essentially barracks for regular troops employed on gendarmerie duty to maintain rural order. Incapable of serious defence, especially against artillery, they had all fallen easy prey to Jacobite forces, as had some of the few artillery forts in the area, like Fort Augustus (raised only a few hundred yards from Kiliwhimen). After the '45 large sums were ploughed not only into reconstructing the fallen forts but also into creating a vast new Fort George, not situated like the old one on the castle hill of Inverness, but on the peninsula of Ardersier Point some miles to the northeast, where there arose over the years one of the greatest and most sophisticated artillery forts in Europe, destined never to hear a shot fired in anger.[14] Though the effective forfeiture of extensive Jacobite landed estates and the placing of the bulk of them eventually under the Commissioners for the Forfeited Annexed Estates, who were charged to encourage Protestantism, Loyalty and Industry on the properties, was no doubt essential, if only as evidence of government determination, the overall impact of this and other measures such as a stricter disarming act and penal legislation against Highland dress, music and the Gaelic language was probably only slightly to accelerate changes which would have occurred anyhow. Equally, the many ambitious schemes floated in the next half-century for dramatically changing the Highland economy into a far more dynamic mode capable of generating Lowland levels of prosperity for the population simply broke on the reefs of reality.[15]

What really mattered in the later years of the reign of George II was the integration of the peripheral elites of the British Isles into the oligarchical system run by the predominantly Court Whigs of the ruling ascendancy. In a sense, this process was determined by two sets of factors: the willingness of the periphery to integrate, of which there was little doubt in either Scotland or Ireland after 1746; and the openness of that central ascendancy to penetration from the peripheral elites. Here the deep divisions amongst historians of the English aristocracy in the eighteenth century need not prove as grave a barrier to analysis as might at first sight be feared. The difference between the relatively closed oligarchy of some and the much more open aristocracy of others seems to be very much a question of defining the level of landownership qualifying for admission to what was essentially a landed ruling class, however much some of its members supplemented their riches from mineral or urban revenues. There is also a dispute about how this aristocracy compared with other European aristocracies, a dispute which in the current context is confusing rather than illuminating.[16] What seems generally acknowledged is that it was much easier to join the lower ranks of the landed class of eighteenth-century England than it was to rise rapidly in rank and influence within it. Equally, there is no dispute that in absolute terms the English peerage, the core of power and privilege, was small. In 1700 there were 163 English peers. By the start of 1800 there were 257, of which 113 held peerages granted since 1780, and wiseacres were cracking jokes about their origins. In fact, of those 113, most already had noble connections, and 25 were promotions from the English peerage, 7 from the Scots peerage, and 17 from the Irish peerage. The beginnings of a pan-British peerage can be seen here, though it clearly came slowly.[17] That slowness is unimportant compared with the direction of development, especially when two other factors are considered. One is the fact that the

Hanoverian aristocracy of Ireland had the consolation of extensive practical autonomy as well as access to the English political scene, and the other is that the Scots aristocracy was in no position to argue about the terms of association after 1746, indeed many of them were anxious to recover estates lost through decades of arguing about what they or their ancestors had seen as unsatisfactory terms.

The process of integrating the Scottish aristocracy into a British political context had in fact been well advanced before the Act of Union of 1707. The huge standing army created by William III to fight his Continental war against Louis XIV was always treated as a coherent British force, even though a nominal Scottish establishment survived for another few decades. Many Scots peers held commissions in that force, and virtually all of them were predictably strong supporters of the Act of Union in the Scots Parliament.[18] Between 1714 and 1763 upper-class Highland Scots still tended to go in disproportionate numbers into commissioned service with foreign states; either Catholic powers if their family was Jacobite, or the United Provinces (Netherlands), where there had long been a Scots Brigade in the service of the republic. Lowland Scots were, however, as successful as they could expect to be in relative terms in this period in securing commissions in the British army. There was, of course, a very strong tradition of military service among the often large families of the lairds. The extreme example is the Agnew family. Sir James Agnew of Lochnaw, the third baronet, had eight sons, all of whom became professional soldiers as did most of the many sons of the cadet branch of the family, the Agnews of Lochryan. That the Lochnaw family came from Galloway, of which its head was hereditary sheriff, did it no harm in the British army in Flanders in 1742, for there was a Galloway group of officers including the Commander-in-Chief, the Earl of Stair. It was no accident that in the years of peace between 1715 and 1739, when the army was a small force of some twenty cavalry and forty infantry regiments plus the household troops, out of 94 new appointments to the rank of colonel 19 were Scots, whilst in the years of expansion between 1739 and 1763, of 199 such appointments 47 were Scots, making a total of 78 Scots out of 374 since 1715 – roughly the proportion which matched Scotland's share of the population of Great Britain. Given the violent prejudice shown by George I and George II against the slightest taint of Jacobitism in a family, this was a more impressive achievement than it looks.[19]

That the Whig nobility and gentry of Scotland had been assimilating to the Union state since 1707 is hardly surprising, but it is important to note that the Jacobite aristocracy was coming to terms with the House of Hanover by the 1750s. By the end of that decade the Earl Marischal, the Scottish friend of Frederick the Great of Prussia, had received his pardon, and the 1760s saw him buy back much of his forfeited estates. By the end of the 1770s General Simon Fraser of Lovat, the son of the Lord Lovat executed for treason after the '45, had had his forfeited estates returned for outstanding service to the Hanoverian dynasty, not least in the conquest of French Canada. At lower social levels, in those professional and commercial fields which were to be of more and more significance with the passage of time and the changing distribution of wealth, there had been equally striking developments, of which the medical profession provides a good example. As early as the reigns of William III and Queen Anne, Scots medical men like John Arbuthnot, William Cockburn (who became Swift's doctor), David Hamilton and George How were well-established in London. However, with the great expansion in Scottish medical education, especially in the middle decades of the eighteenth century when Edinburgh University in particular invested heavily in its medical school, the movement became a flood, and not just to the metropolis, for with 200 students in each year of medicine in Edinburgh alone, there were graduates to spare to colonise the English provinces.

By the reign of George III Scottish or Scottish-trained doctors dominated English medicine to the point that of the 90 graduate physicians practising in a sample of six English counties excluding Middlesex (and therefore London), at least 48 held MDs from Scottish universities, while of the remainder 6 were graduates of the Dutch University of Leiden, and 5 more were products of other Continental institutions.[20] London still remained the supreme place of opportunity for the British world. It is no accident that the dominant figure in its medical life earlier in the century had been the first medical baronet, Sir Hans Sloane. President of the Royal College of Physicians from 1719 to 1735, and a prince of collectors whose scholarly and scientific collections were to be the basis of those of the British Museum, Sloane was an Ulsterman and a staunch Revolution Whig. Irish talent, like Scottish, was drawn to London as to a magnet. A man could starve in the gutter there, but equally he could find not just one but several fields for his gifts, as the extraordinary career of Tobias Smollet demonstrates.

Born into a Dumbartonshire family which had been prominent in support of the Revolution (his grandfather had been knighted by King William in 1698), Smollet was apprenticed to William Stirling and John Gordon, well-known Glasgow surgeons. He reached London in the very severe winter of 1739–40, and used his connections to attain a naval commission which led to service in the ill-fated expedition to Carthagena in 1740–1. Marriage to the Jamaican heiress Anne Lassells meant that his venture into the Caribbean was far from profitless, but unlike Sloane, whose trip to those parts just before the Glorious Revolution in England had been the prelude to a medical conquest of London, Smollet returned to make a name as a man of letters rather than as a doctor. Best known for the novels which before his death in Italy in 1772 had given him a permanent place in the pantheon of English literature, he retained a strong sense of Scottish identity, expressed most movingly perhaps in his poem *The Tears of Scotland* written in 1746, whose tone is well set by the opening lines:

> Mourn, hapless Caledonia, mourn
> Thy banish'd peace, thy laurels torn!

This tone, allied to the way he wrote up the '45 in his *History of England*, led contemporaries to accuse him of being 'actuated by an attachment not the most loyal', but a closer reading of the poem suggests that he regarded the rebellion as a species of civil war whose essential tragedy was the way it led to the further destruction of Scottish autonomy and identity by vengeful London politicians. By the end of his active political life in the early 1760s Smollet was unpopular precisely because he was too enthusiastic by half about the government of the day. When in 1762 the Scot Lord Bute became first minister of state to George III, Smollet not only identified with him but also established a weekly journal, *The Briton*, which was dedicated to serving his patron's causes and image at a time when an unpopular peace was being negotiated. Here Smollet was destined to meet total defeat at the hands of an old friend, John Wilkes, whose creation of the ferociously anti-administration *North Briton* marked the opening of an extraordinary career as the spokesman for traditional English liberties and whose strident Scottophobia was rooted not in ignorance of that nation (for Wilkes had had close Scots friends), so much as in a conviction that Scots had become the hireling servants of a new wave of executive aggrandisement. In February 1763 Smollet acknowledged defeat by ceasing to publish his weekly. By June he had left for a long tour in France and Italy, defeated by English chauvinism and, be it said, perceptiveness.[21]

Ireland shared some of the patterns of career development characteristic of non-aristocratic Scots. From the two great comedies of George Farquar (*The Recruiting Officer* and *Beaux Stratagem*) produced in 1706–7, the last only two months before the author's tragic death, Irish talent produced nearly everything now remembered of the English comedy of manners in the eighteenth century and it came to London to do it. Arthur Murphy, Henry Fielding's first editor, continued the tradition when he turned to farce after 1756, and this whole Anglo-Irish comic tradition peaked in the 1770s with the work of Oliver Goldsmith, who had reached England penniless in 1756 after studying medicine in Edinburgh and travelling on the Continent, and Richard Brinsley Sheridan. One authority remarks that: 'Unfortunately for English comedy Sheridan became interested in politics and entered parliament in 1780 with the help of the Duchess of Devonshire and the expenditure of a thousand pounds.'[22] However, this is essentially unrealistic, for this particular format had somehow run out of further capacity to develop after Sheridan's *School for Scandal* produced in 1777. The same was not true of the Anglo-Irish political relationship, which was in fact full of vitality in this period.

Though the Declaratory Act of 1719 had asserted the absolute right of the Westminster parliament to legislate for Ireland, and the Tudor Poynings' Law seemed to give the English

Privy Council control over the legislative agenda of the Irish parliament, the Irish legislature, by the device of discussing heads of bills and by informal consultation between the two houses before presenting these to the Lord Lieutenant, had invested their joint heads of bills with real authority. Though subject to executive approval and revision, the Irish proposals carried political weight, and there was a political price to be paid for refusal because the Irish legislature had considerable control over the ability of the executive to raise adequate revenue in Ireland. Faced with stubborn opposition in the Irish parliament in 1723–5 English ministers had accepted the need for a system of local parliamentary undertakers which lasted until 1767. These men were Irish aristocrats with power over parliamentary boroughs. Though top jobs in church and state still very often went to Englishmen, the undertakers successfully asserted a right and need to control significant parts of Irish patronage, eventually including even such sensitive matters as military patronage. The older school of romantic historians who denounced the Irish parliament in the era from 1730 to 1760 as a spineless tool of a foreign executive were applying criteria at once anachronistic and unrealistic.[23]

The decision of the English ministry of the day and of its arrogant Lord Lieutenant, George fourth Viscount and later first Marquis Townshend, to break with this system by creating a Castle party immediately dependent on the Lord Lieutenant, who thereby became the dominant undertaker, in the first instance to push through a much-desired augmentation of the Irish military establishment, was a success only in the short term. Set up in 1768, the new system was inaugurated with an octennial act which for the first time set a limit to the duration of the Irish parliament other than the life of a sovereign. Though by-elections had always provided some sort of thermometer to test the temperature of the political nation, this new measure added to the volatility of Irish politics just before they entered a difficult phase. Earl Harcourt, the veteran English politician who consolidated the new system, was recalled in 1777 in the middle of an American war in which the Westminster government was to be discredited and humiliated. Its usual failure to provide domestic defence for the peripheral parts of the archipelago bred an Irish Protestant Volunteer movement which deprived it of its usual monopoly of organised force, and the presence in the Irish legislature of orators of the stature of Henry Flood and Henry Grattan, not to mention incorruptible practising 'Country' Whig noblemen like Grattan's patron Lord Charlemont, ensured that there would be a price to pay for defeat. The repeal of Poynings' Law and of the Declaratory Act was more symbolic than significant, for consultation rather than dictation had long been the norm in their exercise while the results of the lifting of all commercial restraints on Ireland were less dramatic than expected, partly due to the fact that many had been unenforceable and many had been suspended during the wars which in the second half of the century had become the usual rather than the exceptional state of affairs. The real challenge was to shape a new political structure for that British world to which all leading Irish politicians were genuinely loyal. The depression of 1783–4 nearly bred a mutually-damaging tariff war between Britain and Ireland, and the failure of a proposed commercial agreement in 1785 underlined the need for constructive action.[24]

The aftermath of the American Revolution had demonstrated the feasibility for Westminster of a policy of shrugging off a population which refused to accept association on Westminster's terms, a policy which had actually been advocated before the Revolution by the radical Anglican Dean Tucker. Ireland was not yet in this category. It was too close and too big. In 1760, when British North America had about 2,000,000 inhabitants, and England and Wales 6,500,000 to 6,750,000, Ireland had about 3,000,000 people. Scotland in 1775 may have had roughly 1,400,000 people, an increase of more than 10 per cent over the 1755 figure. With strong pre-industrial growth in the third quarter of the eighteenth century, Scotland was enjoying an increase in income per capita, and was to be able to plug successfully into the English industrial revolution in the fourth quarter. These changes did produce regional disasters, but they were confined to the Highlands. Ireland experienced the most rapid population growth in contemporary Europe, reaching approximately 5,500,000 population by 1800, and that with far greater areas of chronic poverty and endemic underdevelopment. What in Scotland was a minority problem was in Ireland the main problem.[25]

On top of all this, the fact was that the Irish nobility, a comparatively small group of a little over a hundred men at the start of this period, were the apex of an Anglican minority facing an overwhelmingly Roman Catholic population in most of the island outside Ulster, where there was a significant Protestant Dissenting element, mostly Presbyterian. Despite the existence of the penal laws against Catholics, relations between denominations had eased after the '45, and the era of the American Revolution had seen the removal of most of the social and economic disabilities of the Catholics by a series of Catholic relief measures. There were indeed formidable concentrations of economic wealth in Catholic hands by the late eighteenth century, but the Irish parliament had in 1784 firmly rejected Volunteer pressure for admission of Catholics to the political nation in any way. British politicians, despite the fact that their last effort to tighten control over Ireland had proven profoundly counter-productive by the time Lord Harcourt was being compelled to make big concessions to extract grudging support for the American war,[26] still automatically assumed that however bad a situation was it would be better if they could have more control over it, and the Catholic issue gave them a sense of their own enlightenment which only accentuated this assumption.

The chances of a constructive development balancing the need for both coordination and devolution of power within what was left of the British world were not high. During the American war the Carlisle Commission had in 1778, on the eve of French intervention, been authorised to make offers so sweeping as perhaps to have broken the immobilism of the Westminster elite, and the Scots MP George Johnstone, who served on the commission, called the doctrine of the absolute sovereignty of the Westminster parliament what it was: 'unintelligible jargon'. Irishmen repeatedly referred to the 1778 offers,[27] but Pitt the Younger was revitalising the political system defeated in America. He was prepared for a more equitable economic settlement with Ireland, but not for power-sharing, for he said he would never 'let them into a control on the executive government of the empire which must *completely* reside here'.[28] The Regency Crisis of 1789, which aborted when George III unexpectedly recovered his senses, is usually seen as

an occasion on which the Irish parliament showed its irresponsibility by offering the Prince of Wales full regal powers when
he was likely to be denied them by Pitt in England, but it can
equally be seen as evidence that Pitt, who held office as a
defender of the royal right to choose ministers, was prepared to
undermine monarchy and precipitate a massive crisis between
the two biggest British state units rather than surrender power
at Westminster. By 1789 Scotland was docile before the Westminster machine. Its politics, however assertive in detail, were
geared to graft, not representation.[29] In 1745 disaffected Scots
aristocrats had been the plague of the Westminster establishment. By 1789 their place as the bugbear of the metropolitan
elites of the British world had been taken by disobliging
aristocratic Irishmen.

4
The Changing Nature of Parliamentary Politics, 1742–1789

IAN R. CHRISTIE

I

IN THE years covered by this survey British politics underwent a major transformation. Up until the 1740s opposition still found its main focus in a Tory phalanx – one reduced to a situation of powerlessness and proscription, from which there seemed no escape unless through a radical change in the attitude of the reigning sovereign. Such a change, it appeared, might come about either through a political revolution entailing the return of the Stuarts or by a demise of the crown resulting in the accession of a well-disposed heir to the throne. First the former solution and then the latter claimed the attention of at least some Tories during the 1740s. During the next decade the advancing age of George II brightened the latter prospect – one factor contributing to the beginning of a transformation of politics during the 1750s. Well before 1760 the old rivalry of Whig and Tory which had dominated politics for a full two generations had virtually disappeared, the way was becoming open to new political alignments, and there followed a speedy transition into the age of personal parties characteristic of the reign of George III.

While the years 1754–7 appear as a major watershed separating two different political systems,[1] at least two other turning points can also be distinguished. At the outset, in the early 1740s, Walpole's fall signalled a break between two different styles of ministerial management of Parliament. Before 1742

Walpole's exclusion of rivals had created an exceedingly formidable opposition of Whig factions which irregularly recruited further support in Parliament from the more permanent opposition of the Tories. After 1742 the tendency was towards conciliation and comprehension of possible dissenters within the ministerial ranks – the practice sometimes referred to as 'Broad Bottom'. This process reached its apogee with the Pitt–Newcastle coalition of 1757, during which even the generally irreconcilable Tories were brought into some degree of association with the government and on the whole supported it – a development of primary importance since it completed the extinction of their separate identity as a party.

'Broad Bottom', however, like its opposite, 'Exclusion' was a condition fraught with an inherent instability, and the first decade of George III's reign was marked by its breakdown – not this time into a new Whig–Tory polarisation,[2] but into a system of personal parties, all of them in substance born out of the Whig political tradition of the previous reign, into which the remnants of early Hanoverian Toryism had been subsumed. Such polarisation in politics as did occur during the 1770s under the impact of the American War of Independence was more specific and less based on general principle, as was to be made clear by the confused party manoeuvres of the years 1782–4, which produced new alignments only in part derived from those of the 1770s.[3] Through the 1770s and the 1780s the style of politics remained much the same, until transformed once more by the internal political responses to the French Revolution and the Revolutionary war, during years which lie outside the scope of this volume.

II

In the 1740s and 1750s the Whigs were pre-eminently the party exercising a monopoly of royal favour and political power. But by 1742 Sir Robert Walpole's intolerance of rivals, and the natural emergence of challenges to his political ascendancy from ambitious politicians, had split parliamentary whiggery between a main stock, the 'Old Corps', and a number of dissident factions led by Lord Carteret, William Pulteney, Lord

Cobham, the Earl of Chesterfield and others, intent on forcing their way into office and a share of power.[4] The resulting instability made it clear that the policy of 'Exclusion' had to be reversed. Accordingly, as the Duke of Newcastle and his brother, Henry Pelham, began to emerge after 1743 as the new leaders of the Old Corps, so, during the early 1740s, one experiment after another took place to broaden the support of the administration in the two Houses of Parliament.

Among the factors affecting choice in this process of seeking pro-ministerial allies from among the disgruntled 'outs', was the difference in attitudes towards the Tories to be found among various groups of the Whig dissidents.

William Pulteney and, to a lesser degree, Lord Carteret (later Earl Granville) wished to perpetuate exclusive Whig control of power and patronage, and had no qualms about kicking aside the ladder of Tory votes by means of which they had destroyed Walpole's ascendancy. Since these anti-Tory prejudices chimed in with those of the leaders of the Old Corps, not surprisingly the first ministerial reshuffles after Walpole's retirement were based on a junction of these groups. Only minimal concessions were made to the Tories – their leading peer, Lord Gower, being appointed to the office of Lord Privy Seal.[5] It was on this basis that Carteret, whose mastery of the German language and espousal of German alliances endeared him to George II, became for a short while, as secretary of state, a dominating figure in the government. But his foreign policy, itself by no means successful, proved acceptable neither to his Old Corps colleagues nor to their following in the House of Commons, and by late 1744 the other ministers combined to force his resignation. Carteret's lack of success also made him vulnerable to a new form of attack from the Tories and dissident Whigs still in opposition, who now made jealousy of Hanover and allegations about the sacrifice of British to German interests a major issue in parliamentary argument.

The decision of Henry Pelham and his friends to jettison Carteret necessitated recruiting strength from elsewhere, and making more cordial connections with the other dissident groups led by Chesterfield, Cobham and the Duke of Bedford, men who believed that some degree of power-sharing with Tories was both desirable and necessary, and who, in reference to their general aim, came to be referred to as the 'Broad Bottom' Whigs: Bedford himself was the son-in-law of Lord Gower, and had long been accustomed to cooperation with Tories at the level of election politics in the Bedfordshire constituencies in which he had an interest. However, the leaders of the Old Corps were still hesitant about such cooperation – many of their followers resented the idea of having to share out government patronage with this new band of potential competitors for place – and although two or three positions were found for their leaders, concessions on policy were still not forthcoming. Chesterfield's hope that the Tories might be hopelessly split between a majority of moderates willing to accept the crumbs offered to them and a minority of irreconcilable Jacobites was not fulfilled.[6]

The consolidation of this 'Broad Bottom' administration in the face of royal hostility between the end of 1744 and the beginning of 1746 – a consummation confirmed when, by mass resignations, the Pelhams at the beginning of 1746 blocked an attempt by George II to float an alternative administration headed by Carteret and Bath – established a pattern of ministerial and parliamentary arrangements which was to endure until 1756. The ministry's position in the Commons was virtually unassailable.[7] But one consequence of all these manoeuvres was to leave the Tories isolated and unreconciled at a time when a prospect of foreign intervention in favour of the Stuart dynasty offered to some of them an irresistible temptation.

Historians have sometimes been inclined to view the phalanx of some 130–140 Tories in the House of Commons in the 1740s as simply a 'Country Party' finding much common ground with dissident Whigs in opposition to Walpolean dominance, standing armies, placemen, and ministerial exploitation of patronage for the purpose of maintaining support in Parliament and a monopoly of office and power. But more recent work has indicated that the Tory party had a distinct, separate identity, and its programme was not simply a 'country' one but was tailored to serve the party's objective of securing a lifting of the political proscription under which it had laboured since 1714 and thereby securing a share of power.[8] The Tory campaign against proscription and Whig dominance embraced various planks of policy: elimination of placemen and pensioners in the

Commons; 'free' (that is, uninfluenced) elections and repeal of the Septennial Act; a smaller standing army or complete reliance on the militia for defence in times of peace, and lower taxation; repeal of the Riot Act; avoidance of expensive military or diplomatic entanglements on the Continent, which were seen as involvements in Hanoverian not British interests; and full participation for Tory country gentlemen in local government by admission to the commissions of the peace.[9] As a permanent minority the Tories could not achieve legislative redress alone, and they found it impossible to secure support from dissident Whigs for the reversal of what they regarded as a Whig gerrymandering of the constitution to their detriment after 1714. Only Jacobites sometimes in public went further and blamed this perversion of constitutional forms on the autocratic instincts of the Hanoverian kings themselves.[10]

Some recent scholarship points to the conclusion that Jacobitism was more widely spread among the members of the Tory parliamentary party, and in the country at large, than has been generally allowed.[11] Its extent is naturally difficult to establish: treason inevitably works underground. There is no doubt that a small clique of party leaders were Jacobites and clearly involved in the preliminaries to the Rising in 1745.[12] Were these the only suspects, one could agree without reserve with those historians who have concluded that the Tory party in general was by the 1740s wholly loyal to the Hanoverian dynasty. But a closer survey of the Tories returned to Parliament at the general election of 1741 and during the next four years suggests that, out of a party membership of about 140, some 20 were prepared to be active plotters on behalf of the Stuarts, another 16, including some of their relations, were strongly sympathetic to the idea of a Stuart restoration, and at least 20 more (but the figure may be larger) would have welcomed such a restoration or at least regarded it with complaisance.[13]

In the next few years death winnowed the Tory party of its Jacobite leadership, defeats in the general election of 1747 constituted a severe rebuff, and the personal deterioration of the Young Pretender struck disillusionment into such Jacobites as remained. These developments helped significantly to pave the way for a positive Tory response to feelers from the Hanoverian heir to the throne which were more promising than any that had been forthcoming from that quarter in the 1730s. For a major feature of politics in the late 1740s was the attempt to organise an opposition centred upon the court of the Prince of Wales at Leicester House. Prince Frederick and his new chosen adviser, Viscount Perceval (later Lord Egmont), sought to establish a close and cordial alliance between their Whig friends and the Tories. In hindsight, owing to Frederick's premature death in early 1751, this development appears merely a fleeting episode in mid-century politics; but as it gathered pace in the years 1747–50 it seemed pregnant with significant possibilities. On points of policy Frederick was prepared to meet the Tories more than half-way, holding out the prospect of full participation in public life and in the distribution of patronage both locally and at the centre and an ending of the oppressive monopoly of office and power by their Whig rivals which had been for so long the fundamental cause of Tory resentment.[14] But, as one scholar has noted, neither the Prince nor the Leicester House entourage were prepared to swallow some key Tory demands, a reduction of the army, or a return to annual or triennial parliaments by a repeal of the Septennial Act. Possibly these princely reservations partly determined the somewhat lukewarm response of the Tory magnates, who promised general support for these objectives without committing themselves to a full coalition.[15]

Tory uncertainty about Frederick's good faith reduced the political impact of this alliance, and in any case the whole Leicester House opposition never attracted the numbers in the Commons to become a serious embarrassment to the Pelham administration. Its leaders recognised this limitation. Though differing on tactics, their general aim was not to seek power for the present but to prepare for the new reign, by keeping programmes and personalities before the attention of the informed minority of the public and of Parliament itself, and laying the ground for a smooth take-over after George II's death, ensuring that his ministers would have no time or opportunity to perpetuate their tenure of office and power as Walpole had done in 1727.[16] In Parliament the Pelhams meanwhile beat off casual attacks with ease. Much of the vulnerable ground on which they might be attacked had disappeared with the ending of the War of the Austrian Succession in 1748. More minor difficulties came to an end with the death of Frederick in March 1751 and the consequent collapse of the Opposition. From 1751 until 1754, when Henry Pelham died and disruptive forces within the government began to create new stresses, the Commons chamber was almost free of political incident.[17]

The renewal of political friction after 1754 was due not so much to the death of Pelham as to the initial disasters and later triumphs of British forces in the Seven Years War. The interaction of internal and external events promoted an eventual complete recasting of the political system. On Pelham's death his brother, the Duke of Newcastle, aspired to his role and was generally accepted as the head of the connection by the Whig Old Corps. His plan was by no means so pretentious as was suggested by some past historians.[18]

Newcastle's double problem was to keep an able front bench in the Commons and to avoid thrusting talented frondeurs into an opposition which under crisis conditions could become formidable. In the short term he succeeded: in the longer term he failed. The two leading personalities in the Commons were Henry Fox and William Pitt. Neither felt that their pretensions were sufficiently recognised. So far as Pitt was concerned there was nothing Newcastle could do: George II was adamantly opposed to receiving into the higher offices the former eloquent critic of Hanoverian entanglements. Fox he managed to keep for a time, bringing him into the cabinet at the end of 1754 and advancing him to a secretaryship of state in September 1755. But tensions over claims of influence and authority remained unresolved, and in October 1756, as the government came under increasing pressure over defeats in the Mediterranean and in America, Fox decided to resign. Meanwhile Pitt, after conducting a sort of guerrilla opposition from within the administration during 1755, sometimes in cooperation with Fox, had been ejected from his post, and sought new bases of political support. One proved to be Leicester House, where there was growing resentment and apprehension over the increasing influence in governing circles of Fox and his patron, the Duke of Cumberland. The other base was provided by the disgruntled and isolated Tory party.[19]

Without Fox's support in the Commons Newcastle had no option but to resign. His ministry was replaced by one headed by Pitt and the Duke of Devonshire. George II hotly resented the imposition upon him of Pitt as secretary of state, and from the viewpoints alike of royal approbation and of parliamentary support this administration displayed much of the character of a stopgap. On neither side was it secure. The king was likely – as he did – to take the first opportunity to dismiss Pitt. Pitt's parliamentary position depended upon the Old Corps majority in the Commons not being used against him, and to this extent he held office by the sufferance of Newcastle. His closest parliamentary links were with the Tories, although by his junction with Devonshire he had in effect compromised – for neither the first or the last time – the 'patriot' principles on which he had made his appeal to them.[20]

In the end it was the king's decision to get rid of Pitt which led to the final resolution of this unstable situation after an interregnum of eleven weeks during the spring of 1757. The detailed faction manoeuvres between March and June proved that the only viable combination on which a ministry could be securely based in the Commons would be one constructed on a Pitt–Newcastle alliance, with Fox brought to acquiesce by the bribe of the lucrative paymastership. Newcastle, with the united strength of the Old Corps still solidly behind him, successfully held in check the excessive pretensions of Pitt. Among other things this episode revealed that in an extreme political crisis of this nature the crown had only limited power to determine ministerial appointments or maintain any right of veto.[21]

The political crisis also confirmed a fact which had been becoming gradually more and more apparent since 1742, that the Tory party as a political force was impotent. The ministerial settlement had depended solely on the establishment of a balance of forces and interests between the Old Corps led by Newcastle and the personal connections of Pitt and Fox. With their junction in one great combination 'party' had become an irrelevance, and the pressures for the absorption of Toryism into a 'Whig' consensus became compelling.[22]

This absorption was to occur very rapidly in the years ahead. In some ways the ground had been long prepared, and Tory party identity was to a large degree an empty shell by the late 1750s, a fact symbolised by the gradual conversion of the 'Tory'

Monitor into a 'Whig' organ during the years 1756–65.[23] From the early 1750s onward the desire of Whig leaders to exploit Tory assistance in the pursuit of their ambitions or the defence of their interests reduced the degree of obstruction on their side, infiltrating into political rhetoric the idea that the Jacobitism that had made Toryism suspect was now dead and that no points of principle separated them from Whigs.[24]

This was not quite true. The Tories of the early 1750s still clung to the populist reforming policies they had adopted as a response to proscription after 1715. They paraded themselves as a constitutionalist party, concerned both to ensure the power of the crown was not abused by encroachments on freedom of elections and other English liberties, and also to preserve the crown against the machinations of aristocratic cliques. Circumstances after 1756 – increasing, though still limited cooperation with the Whig establishment and the growing obviousness of the fatuity of any other course – drove them to play down various of their distinctive policy commitments. As one historian has phrased it, they were forced to recognise, 'that no administration could satisfy the peculiar blend of monarchical, Anglican, anti-executive and radical attitudes which [they] had been able to nurture in the vacuum of political irresponsibility. Nor could any monarch.'[25] The course of the Seven Years War made clear that their anti-militarism (originally a Jacobite ploy to disarm the Hanoverian state) was unrealistic, at least while the war lasted; and when, from about 1755, administrations anxious to make acceptable concessions to them began to treat seriously the creation of an effective militia, they were brought face to face with the possible threat to aristocratic society of a policy of arming the people.[26]

After 1756 war and the prospects of conquest in the New World opened opportunities for profit among many Tory landowners and also London business men: straight conflict between Whig and Tory over foreign policy came to an end.[27] Legislative concessions in the Militia Act of 1757 and the Freeholders' Qualification Act of 1758 were supplemented by an increasing share of government patronage.[28] While these various developments whittled away causes of Whig–Tory polarisation, Tory involvement in successive political manoeuvres by the Whig politicians destroyed the rationale of their separate party identity. Having once backed Pitt in 1756 they were then left with no distinctive patriot platform from which to attack the Pitt–Devonshire ministry or the Pitt–Newcastle coalition of 1757.[29] Although there were still occasional attempts to rally Tories to vote as a block in the Commons,[30] there is little doubt that for numbers of others as well as for Sir Roger Newdigate, who avowed the fact,[31] an on-going process of assimilation had by 1760 produced a situation in which little Tory party affiliation or loyalty remained. The formal ending of proscription of Tories on the accession of George III – very much an initiative on the part of the king and of his favourite, the Earl of Bute, but with the general though covert approval of Pitt[32] – removed the last cement that held Tories together as a party. By the general election of 1761 in numbers of constituencies former Tory and former Whig interests were merged together and Tory distinctiveness had disappeared.[33]

This blending extended to fundamental points. In at least some areas of the country High Tory Anglicanism was no longer a line of demarcation, for Tory Anglicanism had been infected to some extent with deism.[34] On monarchy and the executive there was much common ground. On the one hand the idea of the 'Patriot King' preached by Bolingbroke and taken up by elements of the Whig opposition in the 1740s provided a conceptual capsule for divine right attitudes common to all politicians loyal to the Hanoverians.[35] On the other hand old Tory attitudes carried through into the 1760s did not imply unrestrained support for the royal executive: for instance, while, in general, a substantial block of the old Tories supported the ministry of 1763–5 led by George Grenville, over 40 of them voted against him on General Warrants, putting constitutional liberties before the authority of government.[36] Whig ideological prejudices were also being washed away. By 1760 political fundamentals had ceased to be a source of disquiet to the old Whig leader, Newcastle, when he contemplated the distasteful prospect of promoting Tories. He was oppressed by the much more prosaic consideration that there would be fewer places available for his old Whig friends.[37]

Thus when in 1765 George III gave renewed directions that Tories should be recruited to government without discrimination, but individually, and on 'Whig principles',[38] he was endorsing a development which was already in train by the time of his accession and which marked the disappearance altogether of the old party divisions. Other contemporaries echoed this. The prominent pamphleteer, John Douglas, writing in support of the new ethos of politics and government in 1761, remarked: 'A nation of *Whigs* we may now justly be called'.[39] About the same time Sir Roger Newdigate (Oxford University) saw himself and his friends as a 'Country' or constitutionalist party and repudiated the Tory label.[40] Similar reflections a few years later can be culled from the writings of Horace Walpole and Edmund Burke.[41]

For a few years after 1760 some men might still be referred to as Tories and the Cocoa Tree Club remained as a social meeting place for some of them, but the reality had gone. Of the MPs returned to Parliament in 1761 about 113 were identified by various political managers as Tories during the 1750s and 1760s.[42] Leaving aside the fact that in at least half a dozen of these cases the identifications are disputable and dubious,[43] this group was not only losing coherence and sense of identity, but was failing to attract new blood, and contained a high proportion of men who were elderly, disillusioned, indifferent to politics and inactive in the House of Commons. Nearly half of them were over fifty in 1761 and, as might be expected, there was a high mortality among them over the next few years. Substantially less than half of them – only just over forty – were fairly consistent supporters of the government after 1762, an almost insignificant leaven absorbed into the general body of 'Whig' supporters of the administrations which served George III. Almost as many of the remainder became associated with the parliamentary opposition.[44] A new structure of politics based on personal groupings had become fully established.

III

Unlike the politics of the period before about 1750, based on the existence of two fairly sharply defined parties, the dominant one being flanked by breakaway groups, the system that emerged during the 1760s was loose and shifting, affected in part by the personal rivalries of political leaders, in part by the changing preferences of George III for one set of ministers or another, as issues often of a personal nature influenced his relationships with one individual or another. The disappearance of the Whig–Tory polarity gave the king exceptional freedom of manoeuvre. Few historians would deny that at the outset of his reign his use of that freedom was not always wise or to his own best advantage. His search for ministers who would, firstly, be personally acceptable to him, and secondly, able to discharge the responsibilities of governing, was dogged by both bad luck and misjudgement. His advancement of Bute, first to a secretaryship of state and then to the treasury, has sometimes been treated as a 'royal whim',[45] but this explanation wholly fails to do justice to the admixture of misconceptions, misinformation, bad guidance, hero-worship, nervous apprehension, and lack of experience in judging character which lay behind it.[46] Neither were the frequent changes of ministry over the next few years, which the king deplored, merely to be attributed to his whim or hatred of party. George III had indeed arrived on the throne believing that the old Whig–Tory confrontation was an undesirable evil in politics and had set himself to destroy it – but at a moment when this destruction was already in train in the wake of the political crisis of 1756–7. What he set his face against after 1760 was not party division but the politics of faction, the rivalries of knots of politicians in Parliament banded together to pressure their way into office and a share of power and patronage incommensurate with their talents or their acceptability to him.[47]

Partisan political writing, uncritically absorbed into later Victorian historical scholarship, has left a degree of confusion of nomenclature which even now can create an embarrassment in the way of full understanding of the late eighteenth-century political system. An accurate rendering of the political spectrum of the 1760s and early 1770s would be a description in terms of Butean Whigs, Grenville Whigs, Bedford Whigs, Pittite Whigs, Newcastle (later Rockingham) Whigs, and Northite Whigs, and reference to the factions under the names of their leaders only, without any use of the word 'Whig' would be perfectly sufficient. There were contemporaries who saw this clearly enough.[48] But the perpetuation in historical labelling of the term 'Whigs' *tout court* for the opposition led successively by Rockingham, Portland and Charles Fox from 1766 to 1806 – a labelling which this opposition claimed for itself – carries with it an inherent tendency to distort understanding by suggesting that all the other politicians who were not members of this group and who were in varying ways associated with government were in some way not 'Whigs' but something else. To be tempted into this line of thinking is to be drawn into profound error and misunderstanding of the real nature of parliamentary politics after 1760.

A clear but limited 'descent' of Rockingham's party from Newcastle's 'Old Corps' has been carefully established by O'Gorman. But a more material point is that the Rockinghamites after 1766 had no peculiarly exclusive claim to be regarded as the heirs of the early Hanoverian Whig tradition. Roughly half of the Pelhamite–Rockingham connection as it stood in 1765–6 was absorbed into the ranks of supporters of the Chatham–Grafton administration after mid 1766 and numbers of these men remained ministerialist after 1768. Neither was this by any means the sum total of the 'Whig' backing of the king's ministers after that date: around 1770 supporters of North's ministry included at least 120 men who had entered the House of Commons at or before 1761 and were connected in some way with the Whig groups of the 1750s.[49]

This is not to say that the Rockinghamite party of the late 1760s and the 1770s was not a phenomenon of significance in late eighteenth-century British politics. Not only was it rather larger than the personal groups led during the 1760s by George Grenville and the Duke of Bedford – though not all that much larger, until the controversies over America attracted critics of the American War into its ranks, raising its numbers from a little over 40 in 1774 to over 80 after the general election of 1780. But it developed a distinctive ideology, on the basis of which it implicitly rejected George III's charge of faction and championed the role of party as such in politics.[50]

During the early 1760s, before this development, major confrontations in Parliament reflected faction rivalries and clashes of opinion about particular current issues.

The major parliamentary difficulty that embarrassed Grenville's administration (1763–5) arose over its use of general warrant procedures against its chief press critic, John Wilkes.[51] Oppositionists seized the opportunity to pose as champions of liberty and to denounce the ministers for committing an illegal act of power. Yet this campaign was in a real sense artificial and brought no substantial gain. Both Pitt and Newcastle had made just as flagrant use of general warrants on the assumption that their use was perfectly legal. Grenville's resistance to Opposition motions to declare the warrant illegal sprang not from any desire to establish or re-establish a measure of tyrannical power in the hands of the king's ministers – on the main issue he shared the Opposition's view – but from a sense of legal propriety, since the matter was then *sub judice*. Despite the narrow margin of 14 on this issue general confidence in his administration was not in jeopardy and his policy of retrenchment at the treasury won him wide popularity. At bottom it was incompatibility of personality that led to the king's replacing him.[52]

The Rockingham administration's tenure (1765–6) coincided with the emergence of more serious questions of principle. The Rockinghamites' expedient for dealing with the outburst of colonial defiance of parliamentary authority which greeted Grenville's Stamp Act was to abandon the tax but insist upon the principle of the supremacy of Parliament and to exploit trade regulations more effectively as an alternative, and it was hoped more acceptable, way of raising a revenue in America. In the heated parliamentary debates of early 1766 the ministers came under fire from both flanks. Pitt insisted that the Act had been contrary to a basic constitutional principle of no taxation without representation, although Parliament's right to impose indirect taxation remained inviolate, a view so eccentric as to arouse only derision in the two Houses of Parliament. Not so the campaign mounted by the ex-ministers responsible for the Stamp Act, with whom Bute, in his last notable piece of political activity, associated himself, pressing the view that the government would be selling out all parliamentary authority over the colonies by sacrificing the Act even if it secured the enactment of a legislative confirmation of its authority. On this issue the administration was at times run hard in both Houses of Parliament, and found itself embarrassed by the king's reluctance to influence court placemen, some of them associates of Bute, to vote for its policy against their convictions. The ministry carried its bills, but ministers' confidence in their capacity to fight off attacks in Parliament was severely shaken, the failure to recruit Pitt as an additional source of strength led to the resignation of one of the secretaries of state, the Duke of Grafton, and this was a major factor in the situation leading to the king's decision to bring Pitt and his friends into office in July 1766.[53]

When Parliament reassembled at the beginning of 1767 the new ministry headed by Pitt, now Earl of Chatham, faced not only the old opposition led by Grenville and Bedford but also new elements in the train of the Marquis of Rockingham and a remnant of the former administration and its connections. Criticism in Parliament fastened on the government's handling of American and East Indian affairs, and at one time opposition efforts in the House of Lords came near to defeating the ministers. But the various sections of the Opposition were divided between themselves by their rivalries and by attitudes on the American question, not least by their different past stands on the Stamp Act; and the Chatham ministry, despite the weakness due to the illness of its nominal head from January 1767 onwards, made the most of three advantages. One was the final consolidation of a 'party of the crown' which had been accreting ever since 1762 out of those elements of the Whig 'Old Corps' who felt more commitment to the king's government than to any particular political leader. The second was the accession of voting strength secured by Chatham's agreement to absorb into the government ranks a number of the former supporters of Lord Bute: most of these men in time became assimilated to the party of the crown.[54] The third was the determination of the king to uphold the government in every possible way, in order to prevent the return to office of Grenville, a preoccupation which governed his politics until Grenville's death in November 1770.[55]

Headed at first by Chatham and then by the duke of Grafton, and with gradual changes of personnel, which led up to the promotion of North to the treasury and the absorption of the following of the deceased Grenville, this administration proved its durability. By that fact it brought a new stability also to the Opposition, which came to be constituted almost exclusively and as it seemed permanently by the Rockingham party. These years saw the creation of a new ideological cleavage between Government and Opposition, based on the Rockinghamite commitment to the theory of the 'double cabinet' and government by 'secret influence'. This myth had no foundation in fact, but it was as impossible to disprove as it was to substantiate.[56] From about 1767 onwards it was to become as cardinal a theme of political argument as had been the Tory dogma of the 1720s and 1730s, that only corrupt elections, illegitimate crown influence and the gerrymandering of the constitution by the Septennial Act had denied them a majority in the Commons after 1715. The renewed political fracas over the return of John Wilkes to Parliament for Middlesex and his later expulsion from the House of Commons at the beginning of 1769[57] gave further edge to this opposition doctrine, brilliantly and skilfully expounded in Edmund Burke's *Thoughts on the Cause of the Present Discontents*, and it became the basis for an opposition policy of constitutional reform directed to the reduction of crown influence in parliamentary elections,[58] which echoed one aspect of the Tory programme of the previous reign.

However, this was not a creed which commanded much respect among the politicians or brought much political milage to the Opposition. As the administration gathered further solid support in Parliament with the absorption of the Bedford and Grenville factions and emerged in 1770–1 with the effective leadership in the Commons of Lord North, the Rockingham party, now isolated in opposition save for the erratic and occasional support of independent members and the few followers of Chatham, found itself increasingly impotent. After the general election of 1774 its numbers in the Commons had fallen to about 43,[59] and North and his colleagues appeared as secure in Parliament as Walpole had been at the height of his power.

The stances adopted by the Rockinghamite opposition on the questions of 'secret influence' and American taxation imposed their own peculiar twist upon parliamentary conflict over government policy during the 1770s. The administration faced two particular problems: India and North America.

In India the ultimate consequences of the Seven Years War had been to make the East India Company the ruling authority in Bengal and the paramount power in large areas of the Indian subcontinent, raising acute problems of political, commercial and financial stability both in India and in the business world of the City of London.[60] The logic of the situation pointed to the transfer to the government of full administrative and diplomatic responsibility for British interests in India. This was in any case probably impracticable for lack of the necessary qualified administrative cadres. But any such suggestion would have been political dynamite in the hands of the Opposition, for – as Rockingham pointed out – it would have held out the prospect of an enormous increase in the political patronage available to the crown, which, on Rockinghamite theory, would have been exploited with results fatal to the constitution by the irresponsible power-grabbing secret advisers supposed to be operating behind the scenes.[61] North avoided exposure to damaging parliamentary attack along these lines by the limited nature of his India Regulating Act of 1773, which created a more powerful and responsible directorate of the Company in London and gave both the directors and the government a rather larger degree of control (though as it soon proved, not enough) over the Company's servants in India. But his attempt to assist the Company's tea trade, by encouraging the vent in the American colonies, where the tea was subject to import duties, opened a Pandora's box of American discontent which decisively shaped parliamentary politics for the next few years.[62]

For by the end of 1773 the parliamentary Opposition had run out of steam and but for the development of an American crisis might for long have failed to regain it. The cause of 'Wilkes and Liberty', which it had taken under its wing in 1769–70, had brought in little in the way of political dividends,[63] and North had carefully avoided exposing himself to damaging attack on the Indian question. But the Boston Tea Party and its legislative sequel, with their ultimate consequence of an outbreak of hostilities between Britain and the thirteen North American colonies, raised new issues and gave edge to old ones, which produced a degree of polarisation in Parliament not seen since the fall of Walpole over thirty years before. On the one side the government became firmly committed to the maintenance of imperial unity and parliamentary supremacy throughout the empire. On the other the Rockinghamite opposition, with some aid from Chatham and his friends, deplored the pursuit of policies which led to war, attacked the ministry's competence in conducting it, called for a peace settlement under which it hoped American independence might be avoided at the cost of a virtual surrender in practice of all parliamentary authority, and linked the refusal to accept the virtual independence the colonies demanded with the Wilkite affair, identifying both as attacks on the traditional constitutional liberties of Englishmen organised and sustained by the 'secret cabal'.[64]

Compromise between the two sides in Parliament was impossible. More than once between 1779 and 1781 Lord North put out feelers to see whether it would be possible to detach a few of the opposition politicians – Grafton perhaps, or Charles Fox, or the Earl of Shelburne – or even to draw Rockingham and his friends into a war coalition. None of them would touch such a proposition. Rockingham made it clear in 1780 that he could only accept a royal invitation to take office on the basis of a clean sweep of the existing cabinet, full freedom to negotiate a peace even at the cost of independence for America (a conclusion which his party now regarded as unavoidable and essential), and full powers to bring forward legislation in the form of place bills to reduce the influence of the executive in the House of Commons – this last with the intention of preventing any further activities by the presumed 'secret cabal'.

None of these points were acceptable to George III. The first he saw as an invasion of his right as head of the executive government to choose the ministers; the second conflicted with his primary duty as he saw it to maintain the unity and integrity of the British empire. A reluctant North was pressed to stay in office until, at the beginning of 1782, it became clear that independent members of the House of Commons, hitherto supporting the king's government on principle, would, through conviction that the war must be given up, withdraw their support, and by abstentions if nothing else let through a motion of no-confidence in the administration. North resigned, and for the moment the Opposition was in a position to dictate both on policy and on the selection of new ministers.[65]

However, the Opposition was not a single united force. Rockingham, leader of its main component, with about 80 followers in the Commons, was obliged to turn for extra support to the Chathamite group, now led by the Earl of Shelburne, which was thus able to commandeer nearly half of the cabinet posts. In the new ministry the two secretaries of state, Fox and Shelburne, were at odds both over policy and their personal rivalry, the latter loth to concede complete American independence if it could be avoided. In these circumstances the king sought to use Shelburne to put a curb on Rockinghamite policies, and so fostered divisions within the administration. In the Commons the government's position was uncertain. It secured the passage of its bills, but during the remainder of the 1782 session no critical attack against it was mounted by the cohorts of court party men and personal adherents of the old ministers: for the time being these men abstained from parliamentary attendance.[66]

How long the cabinet would hold together under such circumstances was problematical, and it seems that the death of Rockingham at the beginning of July merely precipitated a breach about to come in any case over policy towards America.[67] When George III offered the treasury to Shelburne many of Rockingham's associates immediately resigned. Shelburne's administration thus stood on an even narrower parliamentary base than its predecessor, and as the beginning of the next parliamentary session approached, it became clear that the votes of the men who had supported North's ministry would be crucial. Some of these were natural 'court and administration' men, whose support for the king's government would be beyond doubt. But of more moment was the future behaviour of North's personal following and of those country gentlemen who preferred him to Shelburne. In this situation North's decision at the beginning of 1783, made against the king's wishes, to oppose the terms of the peace treaty negotiated by Shelburne just tipped the balance against the administration. Shelburne was obliged to resign.[68]

For the meanwhile only a combination of the parliamentary followers of North and the Rockinghamites, now led by Fox and the Duke of Portland, could guarantee a majority in the Commons. George III resisted this party diktat of the choice of ministers for as long as possible – both on principle and because of his contempt for Fox's person and politics – but after a six-weeks interregnum he was obliged to surrender. It was a

ministry founded largely on personal ambitions and resent-
ments – Rockinghamite resentment at being ousted the previous July and animus against Shelburne for, as they felt,
betraying them and the constitutional cause they were uphold-
ing; resentment by North of young William Pitt's proscription
of him, which might end his career in office, to which was
added hostility to Pitt's interest in parliamentary reform, and
also disapproval of the peace terms, which, however, neither
he nor Fox had any prospect of improving before the signature
of the definitive treaties at Paris in September 1783. George
III, like his grandfather in 1746, now experienced the fact that
if the sovereign fell out with too many of the politicians at once,
their weight in the House of Commons might inflict a reverse
with implications for the crown's presumed freedom of selection of ministers. But in the circumstances of 1783 this situation
was not irretrievable, and the king bided his time.[69]

Various considerations weighed in his favour. Unlike George
II in the mid 1740s (or himself in the early 1760s) he was not
trying to cling to a favourite who was unpopular and mistrusted
by the general run of the politicians. His defence of the
principle that the sovereign had a right to choose the ministers
corresponded with common understanding of the law and
custom of the constitution: to numbers of uncommitted men in
both Houses of Parliament there was something illegitimate in
the actions of particular groups of politicians forcing their way
into office against royal wishes by political manoeuvres in the
Commons. A number also were shocked at what they saw as a
degree of political cynicism and opportunism on the part of the
partners in the new coalition, especially of Fox. To join with
men whom he and his friends had for years been accusing of
involvement in an unconstitutional mode of government by
influence under the control of a secret cabal seemed irresponsible and disreputable.[70]

An implication of all these interlinked factors was that a
detached group of politicians, if one such could be found,
capable of manning an administration acceptable to the king,
untouched by these factors of unpopularity, and standing as
champions of a due, not excessive, power of the crown, against
which the constitutional balance now began to seem overset,
might be able, uniting the support of independents and of the

party of the court and administration, to secure a sufficient majority in the Commons to carry on the king's government. The younger Pitt already seemed to fit this role in the spring of 1783, but he judged the circumstances not yet ripe and for the time being declined to act; for the moment he, like the king, bided his time.[71]

This was not many months in arriving. The coalition ministry's bill for the further control of the affairs of the East India Company created a situation in which it was possible for the king, with Pitt's assistance, to destroy it. On two issues in particular the bill was highly vulnerable. A sufficiently large minority of the Proprietors in Leadenhall Street vehemently opposed the measure to give plausibility to the charge that the government was laying violent hands upon chartered rights. A proposal that a commission appointed by the government in Parliament should have full control over civil and military appointments in India and would thus vest the present ministers with a huge body of patronage appeared to be a new flagrant instance of cynical opportunism on the part of the coalition, the Foxite wing of which had been campaigning vigorously against 'corrupt influence' during the previous ten years, and a step which might fatally overbalance the political system in favour of one particular group of politicians. Public and parliamentary opinion consequently began to turn against the coalition. In the House of Lords a verbally-circulated message indicative of the king's displeasure with the bill – a step taken on Pitt's insistence – combined with growing suspicion about it among the peers, was sufficient to secure its defeat as a preliminary to the king's dismissal of the two secretaries of state, North and Fox. This step ensured the resignation of the rest of the ministry. An alternative administration was quickly patched up under the leadership of William Pitt.[72]

At the outset Pitt's administration faced a small but clear coalition majority in the House of Commons; but within three months this adverse force had been whittled away. Pitt's argument prevailed, that the Commons had no automatic right of veto over the king's choice of ministers if those ministers did nothing to deserve dismissal. When Fox's majority had sunk to one, the situation was resolved by a dissolution and a general election which reduced the Fox–North opposition groups to a helpless minority, rather below 200 strong in a House of 558 members and rarely able to field much more than half that number in divisions in the Commons.[73] During the next year or two parliamentary politics gradually fell into their customary pattern. On the one side were Pitt's personal friends and followers, a number of small supporting factions, and the court and administration party, backed by substantial numbers of independents who distrusted Fox and believed that in normal circumstances the king's ministers should receive the necessary support from the Commons. On the other was an Opposition composed of substantial remnants of parties excluded from office by the disfavour of George III and of a large part of the political class, driven to despair and inaction by their inability to cause serious embarrassment, save on rare occasions, to the government's conduct of business in Parliament. On much of the routine business of the session they offered no opposition at all, and the few occasions when the purposes of Pitt or of his colleagues were thwarted did nothing effective to shake their hold on office. Opposition confusion was confounded by the fact that, while old Rockinghamites still nursed the superstition about corruption and secret influence, to the significant North-ite phalanx this was meaningless nonsense in no way relevant to the parliamentary campaign against the government.[74] This pattern of politics was to endure until overturned as a consequence of the repercussions of the French Revolution in the years after 1789.[75]

5
Radicals and Reformers in the Age of Wilkes and Wyvill

H. T. DICKINSON

IN HANOVERIAN Britain the aristocratic elite clearly dominated both government and Parliament, but another political world existed at the same time that was not controlled by this narrow oligarchy. In this other political world large numbers of people, mainly but not exclusively drawn from the middling ranks of society, were able to act independently of the ruling elite long before the accession of George III in 1760. Before that date the constitution had established the rule of law without seriously infringing the civil liberties of the subject. The recognition that British citizens were free men living in a free state was particularly marked among the middling orders living in urban communities. A century of commercial expansion and modest population growth had created towns in which moderately prosperous men had learned to exercise increasing control over their own lives. In the larger urban communities such men had already proved their ability to form pressure groups capable of influencing the decisions taken in Parliament and they had come to dominate the institutions of local government. Within these urban centres they had set up a variety of voluntary associations: Dissenting chapels and clubs or societies serving commercial, cultural and educational purposes. These associations enabled them to meet together and to act independently of the patrician elite. Urban communities were also the location for a whole range of civic ceremonies and public rituals that were able to unite significant bodies of citizens and allow them to demonstrate their political loyalties. Towns, moreover, were the places where political information and new ideas could reach large numbers of people, even those beyond the middling orders, by means of the printed word and where large popular demonstrations on public issues were most likely to occur.[1]

Before 1760 therefore it was already apparent that the aristocratic elite could not totally ignore the political opinions of the British people as a whole, neither could they entirely control their political actions. None the less, although the British people were convinced that they were free men living in a free state and they were able at times to restrict the ruling elite's room for political manoeuvre, they did not seek to initiate government policy and did not campaign to reform the constitution. In the later eighteenth century, however, extra-parliamentary forces attempted to achieve both of these objectives and a reform movement, with considerable popular support, arrived on the political scene. To understand this new political force we need to examine its ideological assumptions and its declared aims, and to explore its composition, structure and activities. First, however, we need to look at the circumstances which persuaded relatively humble men to mount a more sustained challenge to the aristocratic domination of politics than had ever been achieved in early Hanoverian Britain.

I ORIGINS AND ISSUES

By 1760 the preconditions for the development of extra-parliamentary radicalism already existed and over the coming decades the tensions produced by economic expansion and foreign wars, and by the social dislocations which both of these brought in their train, did much to focus attention on the failings of the governing elite. None the less, it was popular reactions to serious *political* crises that did most to stimulate the quite sudden growth of a radical movement 'out-of-doors'. It was the actions of the new king, the dramatic irruption of John Wilkes onto the political stage, and the prolonged and ultimately disastrous dispute with the American colonies that generated the pressure which turned potential critics of the ruling oligarchy into political radicals ready to demand constitutional reform and willing to join extra-parliamentary pressure groups dedicated to political change. Moreover, these three

political crises had a cumulative effect in that, as one followed
the other, they deepened the sense of unease about the existing
constitution and widened the circle of those who supported the
cause of reform.[2]

While no historian now believes that George III waged a
determined campaign to increase his own prerogative powers at
the expense of the rights of Parliament or the liberties of the
subject, a considerable body of opinion in the 1760s did believe
that the king was threatening to disturb the delicate balance of
the constitution and was leading a conspiracy against liberty.
Public alarm was deliberately created by disgruntled politicians, who resented their sudden loss of power, by an unscru-
pulous John Wilkes, who was prepared to use any tactic to
advance his own political career, and by American colonists
who were seeking ideological justifications for their resistance
to British interference in their internal affairs. The consequence of all these efforts was a widespread conviction that a
constitutional crisis had been created by the political ambitions
of George III and his deeply unpopular favourite, the Earl of
Bute.[3] The king was accused of exploiting crown patronage as a
means of increasing his personal power, whereas George I and
George II had used it to create ministerial stability and to
secure a measure of consensus in Parliament. Edmund Burke
and the other Rockingham Whigs, who opposed the king's
policies, were soon convinced that 'the power of the crown,
almost dead and rotten as prerogative, has grown up anew,
with much more strength, and far less odium, under the name
of influence'.[4] By April 1780 they were supporting John
Dunning's celebrated parliamentary motion that 'the influence
of the crown has increased, is increasing, and ought to be
diminished'.[5] The Rockingham Whigs developed a conspiracy
theory about the unconstitutional aims of George III and they
eventually turned to economical reforms as a means of reducing the patronage at the disposal of the crown. Their fears were
given wide currency in the press and their critique won over
considerable extra-parliamentary support to the cause of economical reform if not to the Rockingham party.

John Wilkes was even more successful at convincing a
significant number of people 'out-of-doors' that he was a
political victim of men who were seeking to undermine the

independence of Parliament and subvert the liberties of the subject. With unrivalled skill he raised his personal disputes with the government into issues involving fundamental constitutional principles. When, in 1763, following his notorious attack on the king in number 45 of *The North Briton*, the ministry issued general warrants in order to secure incriminating evidence against him, Wilkes exploited the situation to condemn the authorities for abusing their power. He gave his personal plight a more general application by claiming that English liberties were at stake. When, in 1768, a majority of MPs were persuaded to embark on a policy of repeatedly expelling him from the House of Commons, although he consistently won the backing of a majority of the electors of Middlesex, Wilkes was able to warn the public of the serious constitutional implications of this action: 'If ministers can once usurp the power of declaring who *shall not* be your representative, the next step is very easy, and will follow speedily. It is that of telling you whom you *shall* send to Parliament, and then the boasted Constitution of England will be entirely torn up by the roots.'[6] This prediction was rapidly borne out by events. After he had won a third by-election in Middlesex, in April 1769, the House of Commons not only expelled Wilkes yet again, but decided that his defeated rival, Henry Luttrell, had been duly elected for this large and important constituency. Wilkes could now claim that the issue was no longer confined to his own political fate, but had raised the whole question of the freedom of the voters to choose their own representatives. If the decision in the Middlesex election case was not reversed, then, he argued, the rights of the electorate would be reduced to a hollow sham. The issue clearly transcended the question of whether John Wilkes should or should not represent Middlesex. It posed the question of whether Parliament was to be manipulated by a narrow aristocratic elite or was to represent the interests of the electorate as a whole. Wilkes tried to persuade a very wide public to understand the issue in these stark terms.

Even more fundamental questions were raised by the American crisis which developed over a period of twenty years or more. The ill-judged policies of successive British administrations aroused widespread resentment in the American colonies.

They eventually provoked an armed resistance which led to a prolonged war that Britain was unable to win. Within Britain the whole dispute generated intense discussion about the very nature of the British constitution.[7] Many domestic critics of government policies supported the American challenge to the doctrine of parliamentary sovereignty and they endorsed the American stand on the principle of 'no taxation without representation'. These critics began to argue that Parliament was not sovereign, but should be accountable to the people at large. To make the people and not Parliament the sovereign authority in the state, crown patronage would need to be reduced and the whole system of representation overhauled. Inspired initially by Christopher Wyvill, a nationwide campaign was launched to reform a political system which had failed the nation and which had plunged the country into a war Britain appeared incapable of winning.

II IDEOLOGICAL CONTEXT AND POLITICAL PROGRAMME

The political crises of the 1760s and 1770s did not produce a single, integrated radical ideology. Instead, those seeking reform drew upon several different political discourses and a wide array of moral principles and political ideals in order to provide themselves with a set of values capable of underpinning the practical programme which they favoured. In seeking to appeal to a wide range of opinion some of the leading reformers adopted the traditional Country ideology (itself a combination of old Whig and Tory criticism of executive power and ministerial corruption) in order to demand a return to the original principles of the balanced constitution and to secure an independent House of Commons free of crown and aristocratic influence. Other reformers were influenced by a radical Protestant discourse which stressed personal and individual virtues rather than public or civic virtue. Praising such personal qualities as industry, sobriety, frugality and enterprise, they encouraged self-improvement and they desired equal opportunities and careers open to talent. The most radical reformers went beyond demands for a meritocracy and emphasised instead the importance of universal and inalienable natural rights. Adopting and developing the ideas of John Locke, they began to proclaim the political equality of all men. Although modern scholars can detect the differences between these ideological approaches, radicals then were quite capable of appealing both to Country principles and to natural rights theories at the same time. They often managed to proclaim the glories of the ancient constitution and the traditional rights of Englishmen, while simultaneously advocating future progress on the basis of abstract, rational principles.[8]

The radicals and reformers were not only influenced by different ideological assumptions; the reform movement itself was divided on what programme to support. Unfortunately for the historian seeking to understand the connection between ideology and programme, a particular ideological approach did not automatically lead to a specific reform programme. Those seeking reform were influenced by a whole range of ideas and by their own political experience. As a result, different reformers tended to see the political crisis of the age in a different light and so they produced different solutions to the problem as they saw it. Wyvill and the more moderate supporters of the Association movement were convinced that the real danger was that the existing political system was being corrupted by the misuse of crown and aristocratic patronage. Hence their solution was to urge the adoption of a Country programme which would reduce the patronage available and weaken its ability to influence the composition of the House of Commons. The metropolitan radicals, who supported Wilkes and later the Westminster Association, believed that the political system was too aristocratic and was not sufficiently accountable to all those who had a material stake in society, particularly the commercial and professional middle classes. Their solution was to reform Parliament so that a redistribution of seats and an extension of the franchise would give at least the urban middle classes greater representation in the House of Commons. The so-called Rational Dissenters, who were more concerned with politics at a moral and philosophical level, were particularly anxious to defend the universal right to freedom of conscience. It was this religious motivation which led most of these theorists to advocate the inalienable natural rights of all men.

They were persuaded that all men had the right to take an active role in the decision-making processes of the state.

Many Wilkite radicals in the late 1760s and most adherents of Wyvill's Association movement a decade and more later were influenced by the Country ideology which had previously been advanced by Whig Commonwealthmen in the late seventeenth century and by Tory critics of the Whig ascendancy in the early Hanoverian period. These reformers in the later eighteenth century still greatly admired Britain's constitution, which mixed the three simple forms of government (monarchy, aristocracy and democracy) in the balanced institutions of King, Lords and Commons in an effort to achieve both liberty and order. Unfortunately, the delicate balance of the constitution, which had been rescued by the Glorious Revolution from the threat posed by the royal prerogative, was subsequently in constant danger of being undermined by the corrupting influence of crown and aristocratic patronage. To defeat this insidious threat the people were urged to adopt the patriot ethic of civic virtue. They were encouraged to be active citizens determined to defend their liberty and they were asked to support measures which would cut off patronage at its source or at least ensure that it could not corrupt either the electorate or their representatives. The people were encouraged to prize their liberties and the voters were urged to reject courtiers, placemen and moneyed men as their representatives and to elect honest, independent country gentlemen in their stead. It was also suggested that voters should instruct their representatives on how to act in Parliament and secure their support in particular for measures which would reduce the influence of crown and aristocratic patronage. Support was also given to proposals to exclude placemen from Parliament, to eliminate bribery and corruption in elections, to secure more frequent general elections and to redistribute some parliamentary seats from the rotten boroughs to the largest counties and more populous urban centres. Christopher Wyvill wanted to abolish at least fifty rotten boroughs and to transfer the hundred seats to the counties and large towns. He showed little interest in securing direct representation for such growing manufacturing centres as Birmingham, Manchester and Sheffield, however, and he was content to restrict the franchise to men who possessed sufficient property to be independent of crown and aristocracy.[9] The Wilkites were perhaps willing to contemplate a more drastic redistribution of seats and John Wilkes himself appeared to favour an extension of the franchise. He certainly raised the issue in a speech which he delivered to Parliament in 1776.[10] But these particular metropolitan radicals made only limited advances on the Country platform. They did not endorse a genuinely democratic programme.

The metropolitan radicals, who supported Wilkes and, later, the Westminster Association, clearly prized their independence and they undoubtedly sought a greater public role for the commercial and professional classes. Critical of both the idle rich and the idle poor they praised the virtues of the industrious middle classes. They insisted that independence could derive from all kinds of property, not simply from the possession of landed estates, but they stressed that independence could also be a matter of conviction and attitude. They were convinced that the middling ranks of urban society had the capacity to judge the merits of those who governed them and that they ought to have the right to choose more of the nation's representatives. In their opinion industry, frugality and talent had gained the middling orders sufficient wealth, status and expertise to engage actively in public affairs. Seeking to increase their own power by association, they desired to render the governing elite more accountable to men like themselves and more responsive to their economic interests. Besides seeking to achieve a stronger representation in Parliament, mainly by more frequent elections and a major redistribution of seats (rather than by a radical extension of the franchise), they also campaigned for changes in the way that the law was made, administered and executed, and for religious equality, an end to the press gang and the game laws, and for greater freedom of the press.[11]

A small minority of reformers, chiefly Rational Dissenters, were mainly interested in spreading political ideas rather than in joining political organisations. These theorists looked back to earlier notions about the ancient constitution and to the ideas of John Locke. On these foundations they developed a more progressive ideology and a more democratic platform. Major John Cartwright, for example, was one of the leading propagandists who gave a radical twist to the traditional view of England's ancient constitution and to the historic rights of Englishmen. He insisted that before the Norman Conquest the Anglo-Saxons had accepted the sovereignty of the people. He wrongly believed that the Anglo-Saxons had possessed a parliament and that they had allowed all men to vote for their representatives in annual general elections. In Cartwright's view the people had waged a prolonged campaign ever since 1066 in order to recover their lost rights.[12] Other radical theorists, such as Joseph Priestley, James Burgh and Richard Price, were led by their belief that freedom of conscience was a universal, inalienable natural right into campaigning for greater political liberty as the means of safeguarding religious freedom. Clearly influenced by John Locke and by the American colonists of their own day, they insisted that all legitimate governments must be based on consent and must seek to translate the universal, natural rights of man to life, liberty and property into civil liberties. More explicit than Locke, they claimed that a man's life, liberty and property could not be safeguarded unless he possessed the right to vote for those who sat in the nation's legislature.[13]

Whether they appealed to ancient or to natural rights, Rational Dissenters such as Cartwright, Burgh and Price began to adopt a radical programme of parliamentary reform. Undoubtedly influenced by the American concept of 'no taxation without representation', James Burgh condemned the inequitable features of the existing system of representation in Britain and urged the need for a substantial redistribution of seats and a major extension of the franchise. Since he accepted the maxim that those who contributed to the expenses of government should be represented in the legislature, Burgh was able to claim that all those householders who paid rates or other specific taxes deserved to possess the vote.[14] By 1776 John Cartwright was persuaded of the view that, since all men paid taxes, no man could be denied the franchise.[15] In 1780 John Jebb and other members of the subcommittee of the Westminster Association were convinced that political equality could be achieved only by a radical reform of Parliament. They endorsed what later became known as the famous six points of parliamentary reform: universal manhood suffrage, equal constituencies, annual elections, the secret ballot, the abolition of property qualifications for parliamentary candidates and the payment of MPs.[16]

Very few reformers endorsed such a radical programme of parliamentary reform, but clearly the discussion about constitutional changes and the political rights of the subject had made major strides since the later 1760s. None the less, even the supporters of the six points of parliamentary reform were not as democratic as such a programme might indicate. None of them advocated votes for women, for example, and most of them were confident that even if poor men did secure the vote they would defer to men of superior fortune or better education. Moreover, while these radicals wished to make the House of Commons a more democratic institution, they did not attack monarchy or aristocracy as such and they still trumpeted the virtues of mixed government and a balanced constitution.[17] Neither is there much evidence to suggest that they saw parliamentary reform as the prelude to a major restructuring of the economic and social order. Most radicals and reformers were mainly concerned about ending corruption and about increasing the political influence of the propertied middle classes, but they did not seek to redistribute property in order to allow the poor to become active in politics. Even those radical theorists who emphasised the natural rights of all men were primarily concerned with the political freedom of the individual and showed little interest in improving the social welfare or the economic condition of the labouring poor. Only Thomas Spence attacked the concept of private property and sought a more equitable distribution of wealth. The most that the poor could expect if the aims of the other radicals were achieved was some reduction in government expenditure and hence a smaller tax burden placed upon them.[18]

III LEADERS AND SUPPORTERS

In the early Hanoverian period the critics of the ruling oligarchy had no effective national leaders outside Parliament and only occasionally (as in 1733, 1739–41 and 1756) did they enlist widespread popular support for their aims. By contrast, after

1760, radicals and reformers actively sought, and were more successful in securing, national leaders outside Parliament, and greater popular support for their cause.

Although he was a rake, and a politician whose sincerity and integrity are open to serious question, John Wilkes played an indispensable role in exciting popular interest in major constitutional issues. He was neither a great orator nor an able organiser, but he was a bold and brilliant propagandist who achieved unrivalled publicity and recruited unprecedented support for his cause. By deliberately creating incidents and issues capable of arousing intense excitement he was able for several years to sustain unrelenting pressure on the governing elite. Employing his pen, his wit and his theatrical talents to brilliant effect, he was able to exploit his charismatic personality and his outrageous behaviour in order to reach and captivate a wide public. Capitalising on the misjudgements of his political opponents he was able to create dramatic incidents and to raise explosive issues that allowed him to pose as the defender of liberty against arbitrary power. His own personal objectives were raised to the level of grand constitutional principles. Abstract concepts of liberty and justice were made tangible and intelligible to ordinary people. Wilkes made himself the personification of liberty and played the role of a political martyr suffering at the hands of an unprincipled and corrupt oligarchy. Never remote, aloof or patronising, he deliberately flattered his public by praising the political sense and even the political sophistication of ordinary freeholders and tradesmen. Endeavouring to enlist their support, he told the people that he was dependent upon their goodwill and could achieve nothing without their backing.[19]

Wilkes publicised his activities in the press across the whole country, but in organising his supporters he relied heavily on a small group of metropolitan radicals including John Horne (later Horne Tooke), John Sawbridge, Richard Oliver, Thomas Brand Hollis, John Glynn and Brass Crosby. These men were prepared to involve themselves in the rough and tumble of extra-parliamentary politics and to engage in the routine tasks essential to mobilising popular support. They provided a lead for provincial activists across the country, including such men as George Grieve, Richard Gardiner and Crisp Molyneux who played leading roles in such towns as Newcastle, Norwich and King's Lynn.[20] A decade later Christopher Wyvill was the indispensable link holding together the scattered elements of the Association movement. In many ways the antithesis of Wilkes, Wyvill was sober, honest, direct and industrious. A man of courage, broad humanity and scrupulous integrity, he had a clear vision of what was needed and he displayed a remarkable tenacity and persistence in pursuit of his goals. Subtle in his management of men and skilful as a political organiser he did his best to avoid rancour and to quell unnecessary disputes. Both the inspiration and the driving force of the Association movement, he showed a respect for the opinion of others and remained an excellent judge of what was politically feasible.[21]

With its heavy reliance on the printed word the radical movement was dependent upon the skills of political theorists and publicists. James Burgh, John Cartwright, Capel Lofft, Richard Price, Joseph Priestley and a host of other writers provided the radicals with convincing moral, historical and intellectual justifications for their practical proposals. The ideas and activities of the radicals were propagated by a whole coterie of publishers and distributers in London, including John Almon, Isaac Fell, John Williams, Thomas Hollis, Thomas Brand Hollis and Thomas Day, as well as by many newspaper proprietors in the provinces.[22]

Support for radical reform covered a wide spectrum of society, but it was mainly drawn from the middle orders. A handful of the propertied elite, most notably the Duke of Richmond, took an interest in parliamentary reform. Wilkes was also occasionally able to involve some of the urban poor in his activities. Spitalfields weavers, coalheavers on the Thames and day labourers from the east end of London certainly joined in some of the Wilkite festivities and crowd demonstrations. In general, however, most popular urban disturbances at this time were concerned with economic grievances rather than with demands for political reform.[23] It seems clear that most of the support for extra-parliamentary radicalism came from the middling ranks of society, especially those who lived in urban areas. Both Wilkes in Middlesex and Wyvill in Yorkshire secured some support from rural freeholders, but most of their support came from the urban areas of these counties. They recruited sympathisers from among the moderately prosperous merchants, wholesalers, manufacturers, shopkeepers, retailers, traders, master craftsmen and professional men, as well as from more humble tradesmen and artisans.[24] Men such as these could sometimes see their economic prospects severely damaged by those ill-judged decisions of the ruling oligarchy that resulted in wars, financial crises or commercial disasters.[25] Some urban groups were particularly prominent in the reform movement precisely because their fortunes were closely tied up with the success or failure of radicalism. These groups included middle-income lawyers involved in the campaign for the reform of legal abuses, those involved in the print and book trades which provided information about radical opinions and activities, those who kept or supplied the inns, taverns and public houses frequented by the various radical groups, and those tradesmen who manufactured the pottery, ceramic and other commemorative artefacts bought by radical sympathisers.[26] A few Rational Dissenters played a distinguished part in developing a radical ideology, but there is little evidence to suggest that the majority of ordinary Dissenters were deeply involved in the reform movement.[27] None the less, Dissenters in general had more sympathy with the reform movement than did committed Anglicans or Methodists, who mainly rallied to the defence of the established order.[28]

Throughout the period radicalism flourished in and around London, in the urbanised areas of the southeast and in the small clothing towns of the West Country and the rather larger clothing towns of the West Riding of Yorkshire, in the manufacturing areas of the West Midlands and in a number of important ports or commercial centres such as Norwich, Portsmouth, Bristol, Liverpool, King's Lynn, Worcester and Newcastle. Perhaps surprisingly the rapidly expanding towns of Birmingham, Manchester and Sheffield were not as involved in radical politics as were the older urban centres with a longer tradition of partisan involvement in civic and parliamentary politics. The campaign for parliamentary reform certainly made very little headway in Scotland, Wales or in deeply rural counties such as Westmorland.

IV ORGANISATIONS

The Wilkite movement benefited from the existence of dozens of clubs, lodges and associations which had been set up in London and other large towns long before the 1760s. The majority of these voluntary associations, including the Albions, the Bucks, the Leeches, the Lumber Troop, the Free and Easy Johns and the Robin Hood debating societies, had been established for commercial, educational, convivial and civic purposes, but most of them soon rallied to the radical cause in the late 1760s. The club of Honest Whigs, which brought together many of the leading Rational Dissenters in London, also soon changed its focus from debates on general religious or philosophical questions to discussions on more explicitly political subjects.[30] The issues raised by Wilkes soon spawned new, overtly political, clubs, such as the Anti-Caledonian Club, the Retribution Club, the Liberty Beefsteak Club and, most important of all, the Society of the Supporters of the Bill of Rights (SSBR) and the Constitutional Societies.[31]

The SSBR, which was explicitly Wilkite, was only the tip of a broad base of clubs in the metropolis. It was set up on 20 February 1769 by a band of London radicals, including John Horne Tooke, John Sawbridge, James Townsend, William Beckford and Richard Oliver. It sought to provide the organisation needed to mount a nationwide petitioning campaign in support of Wilkes. By collecting funds and distributing propaganda it was able to give a lead to protesters not only in London, Westminster and Middlesex, but also in Yorkshire and parts of the West Country. Much to the chagrin of Wilkes, the leaders of the SSBR were not devoted only to advancing his personal political career or to reversing the decision in the Middlesex election case. They were also concerned to achieve shorter parliaments and a redistribution of seats and they believed such objectives could be gained only if they embarked on a long-term programme of political education. Such aims soon clashed with the more limited and immediate goals of Wilkes. The resulting dispute rapidly revealed that many of these metropolitan radicals distrusted Wilkes and were suspicious of his delight in promoting crowd demonstrations. John Horne Tooke was soon accusing Wilkes of making patriotism a trade and a fraudulent trade at that. By 1771 the breach between them was a matter of public and acrimonious debate. In order to retain influence with the SSBR Wilkes had to adopt its more radical programme, but even this did not prevent Horne Tooke, Sawbridge, Oliver and Townsend from resigning from the SSBR on 9 April 1771 and setting up a rival Constitutional Society in London. The SSBR thereafter lost momentum, but, within a short time, there were provincial Constitutional Societies in such towns as Birmingham, Norwich and Newcastle. Wherever they were established they worked hard to return candidates to Parliament who had explicitly pledged to support political reform.[32]

The whole range of clubs and societies was vital to Wilkes and the radical cause. They were experienced in raising subscriptions, staging celebrations and coordinating activities. Fund-raising was one of their most important functions once they had rallied to Wilkes's banner. Money and presents, often in units of 45, were sent to Wilkes from bands of sympathisers from many parts of the country and even from the American colonies. Appreciable sums were raised by securing small subscriptions from large numbers of individuals. The nation-wide network of clubs was also responsible for renting rooms where political meetings, discussions, lectures and dinners could be held. Their members canvassed voters in elections, secured signatures on petitions, publicised their aims and activities in the press, distributed propaganda and organised public demonstrations and celebrations. Relatively humble men in a wide range of clubs demonstrated their political convictions and proved their collective power by such means as these.[33]

After Wilkes was returned to Parliament in 1774 the SSBR foundered and the Constitutional Societies languished. It was another five years before the heavy costs of an unsuccessful conflict with the American colonies encouraged Christopher Wyvill to enter the political fray. In 1779 he set up a committee designed to act as a steering group for the Yorkshire Association which was itself dedicated to economical reform. Wyvill was soon in regular correspondence with sympathisers in Yorkshire and with more radical reformers in many parts of the country. He fully recognised the necessity for association and

he organised a conference in London in order to unite reformers in a coordinated campaign for a common programme. At
least sixteen counties and several boroughs established associations modelled on that set up in Yorkshire and, in March 1780,
some 30 to 40 reformers from these associations attended
Wyvill's conference in London. Some of these associations
proved to be short-lived and the whole movement was torn by
internal disputes and suffered from frequent defections. Some
associations, such as those in Dorset, Hertfordshire and
Gloucestershire, were only prepared to support economical
reform, whereas the committee of the Westminster Association
adopted the six points of parliamentary reform in 1780. Wyvill
performed heroics to keep the Association movement united
and in being. He was able to mount a significant nationwide
petitioning campaign in 1780, but a second convention in
March–April 1781 was attended by delegates from only eight
counties and from London and Westminster. Further efforts
were made to revive the Association movement in October
1782, and again in May 1785, but they achieved only limited
success. Wracked by continuous quarrels, the associations were
divided over what programme to adopt.[34]

Less of a national movement, but a major contributor to the
education of political reformers, was the Society for Constitutional Information (SCI). Set up in London in April 1780 by a
number of prominent Rational Dissenters, including John Cartwright, John Jebb, Thomas Brand Hollis and Capel Lofft, the
SCI sought to increase support for political reform by the
systematic production and distribution of printed propaganda.
Although anyone was free to join, the subscription rate of a
guinea each year effectively excluded the lower orders. Always
small in size its membership included several peers and about
15 MPs, but its more active members were recruited from the
professional middle classes. Four general meetings were sche-
duled each year, but the main work was done by the committee
responsible for printing and correspondence. Composed of 21
members, this committee met once a week from October to
May and once a month in summer. Supported by funds raised
from members and other sympathisers the SCI undertook the
printing of a vast range of political propaganda, including
broadsheets, original pamphlets and reprints of earlier political

works. Most of its publications supported more radical reforms than those proposed by the Wilkites or Wyvill's Yorkshire Association. Indeed, it largely endorsed the programme of parliamentary reform favoured by the committee of the Westminster Association. Many of its publications were distributed free of charge and it achieved a great deal in educating reformers across the country. None the less, it was too radical to secure widespread support and it declined like the other reform movements after the failure of Pitt's Reform Bill in 1785. After the outbreak of the French Revolution, however, the SCI renewed its efforts to distribute radical propaganda across the country and it helped to educate a new generation of reformers.[35]

V METHODS AND ACTIVITIES

The extra-parliamentary radicals in the age of Wilkes and Wyvill did their best to use the existing political processes. They sought to win elections, dominate local institutions and exploit loopholes in the judicial system. Although they recorded some successes, their achievements in these areas were not substantial. To appreciate their success therefore we also have to examine their efforts outside the usual political channels.

The electoral system was not entirely open or truly representative even of the propertied classes of society, but there were some constituencies with quite large electorates that were not dominated by the aristocratic elite. In these constituencies the radicals achieved some successes. Although John Wilkes's failure to secure one of the Middlesex seats in 1768–9 demonstrated the control which the ruling oligarchy could exercise over who sat in Parliament, the radicals did win quite a few seats in this period. William Beckford, James Townsend, John Glynn and John Sawbridge, all soon to be allied with Wilkes, won seats in 1768 or even earlier. Richard Oliver and Frederick Bull, two other metropolitan radicals, won by-elections in London in 1770 and 1773 respectively. In the general election of 1774 Wilkes and Glynn won the two Middlesex seats, radical candidates captured all four City of London seats and candidates sympathetic to reform won seats in Southwark, Bristol,

Bedford, Dover, Nottingham, Northumberland and Warwick-shire. Altogether a dozen or so reformers were returned to Parliament and significant challenges were mounted in several other constituencies, including Surrey, Cambridge, Newcastle, Seaford and Worcester.[36] Many of those elected in 1774 retained their seats in 1780, when the American crisis led to renewed efforts to return reformers to Parliament. Although only a tiny minority with little real influence on the decisions taken by Parliament, these radicals did at least propose various constitutional reforms in the 1770s and early 1780s.

The Wilkite radicals in particular also made great efforts to gain power at the municipal level. They were very active in London where they were embroiled for a decade or more with the merchant oligarchy which traditionally dominated the Court of Aldermen in the city's corporation. Wilkes and his allies soon won over the majority of the city's liverymen and from this base they were able to gain power in the wards, in Common Hall and in the Common Council. Wilkes himself was elected alderman in 1769, sheriff in 1771, lord mayor in 1774, and then city chamberlain for life in 1779. Several Wilkite radicals were also elected to the posts of alderman, sheriff, recorder and lord mayor. They were able to dominate city politics for a decade or more and this enabled them to secure popular support for a whole series of petitions critical of government policies, particularly those which led to the dis-astrous conflict with the American colonies.[37] Provincial radic-als never achieved such a strong municipal platform in any other town, but they were able to form a significant opposition to the conservative ruling group in such towns as Norwich, Nottingham, Newcastle, Cambridge, Southampton, Ports-mouth, Gloucester, Exeter, Leicester and King's Lynn.[38]

Wilkes and several of his lawyer friends, including John Glynn, Arthur Lee and John Reynolds, proved adept at exploiting loopholes in the law, generating drama in the courtroom and successfully proclaiming their political opinions from the public platform afforded by the law courts. They fought cases, some of them with spectacular success, over such issues as the use of general warrants, Parliament's efforts to restrict press reports of its debates, and the abuse of their authority by officials seeking to control crowd demonstrations.[39] In the Printers' Case of 1771 the corporate privilege of the House of Commons to restrict press reports of its debates was opposed by the jurisdictional autonomy of the City of London in order to protect those printers who published parliamentary debates. In a brilliant campaign, executed with characteristic audacity, Wilkes won a major victory.[40] John Glynn also won several victories in libel cases and he was instrumental in preserving the ancient rights of the freemen of Newcastle over the common land of the Town Moor.[41]

More important than any of these achievements, however, were the radical successes in educating a wide public on political questions and in securing popular support for their reform programme. The radicals were very active in exploiting the opportunities provided by the press, which grew significantly in the age of Wilkes and Wyvill. Many newspapers in both London and the provinces were highly critical of the ruling oligarchy in this period. The *London Evening Post*, the *Middlesex Journal*, the *Newcastle Chronicle*, the *Bath Journal*, the *Leeds Mercury*, the *Birmingham and Stafford Chronicle* and many other newspapers publicised the activities and the objectives of the radicals and condemned government policies towards the American colonists and domestic critics.[42] Individual pamphlets, highly critical of the existing political system, poured from the presses. Well over 1000 separate pamphlets on the American crisis were published in London in the twenty-year period beginning in 1763.[43] Edmund Burke's *Thoughts on the Cause of the Present Discontents* (1770), with its critique of George III and the Earl of Bute, sold about 3250 copies, a respectable total, but its central thesis reached a much larger public because it appeared in review or extract in five London newspapers, several provincial newspapers and six magazines.[44] Richard Price's more radical *Observations on the Nature of Civil Liberty* sold an impressive 60,000 copies in some 14 editions.[45] Wilkes himself exploited the press to an astonishing extent. He used newspapers, pamphlets, periodicals, handbills, posters, ballads, verse, cartoons and even joke books to publicise his activities. In the first Middlesex election of 1768 he distributed over 40,000 handbills and he was the inspiration behind *English Liberty Established*, the most famous single-sheet publication of the age.[46] The SCI, concentrating as it did on distributing political propaganda, sent out at least 88,000 copies of some 33 different publications between 1780 and 1783 alone.[47]

Wilkes more than any other radical made a determined effort to encourage the less literate and more humble sectors of society to take an interest in politics and public affairs. He did much to persuade tradesmen to commercialise radical politics by producing a whole range of artefacts with a political connotation. Pottery of all kinds, including porcelain figures, plates, teapots, shaving mugs and snuff boxes, all appeared with Wilkite decorations. So did medals, buttons, rings, brooches, badges and candles. The number '45' appeared on a vast range of products because it was easy to execute, it was recognisable even by the illiterate, and it could be attached or drawn on almost any object. It could be used to denote a unit of time, space or mass. It was even chalked on walls and doors, and embroidered on clothes. This simple device became a sign or symbol for Wilkes, liberty and the whole radical cause.[48]

As well as educating a wide public the radicals devised a variety of means to recruit popular support for their aims and to show that unity was strength. Regular club meetings were one way to achieve this and national conferences or conventions were another, but such tactics involved only the dedicated activists. The radicals needed to think of other ways of demonstrating mass sympathy for their cause. They occasionally held large public meetings, such as that attended by about 2500 liverymen in Common Hall on 24 June 1775 where the government was urged to adopt a conciliatory stance towards the American colonies.[49] The most marked and consistent feature of their public campaigning, however, was the petition. In 1769 the SSBR organised the first nationwide petitioning campaign clearly initiated and fully orchestrated by extra-parliamentary groups rather than being inspired by opposition elements within Parliament. The SSBR urged clubs, societies and individuals across the country to petition Parliament over the Middlesex election case. About eighteen counties petitioned and a further eight groups discussed doing so. A dozen boroughs also sent in petitions and several others indicated some degree of support for Wilkes. Nearly 60,000 people altogether signed these petitions; some 38,000 of them were freeholders and about 11,000 of them lived in Yorkshire.[50]

During the long dispute with the American colonies petitioning was a major response of those who took issue with government policies. As early as 1765 some 25 petitions were sent in against the Stamp Act, while at the height of the American crisis in 1774–6 a positive flood of petitions reached king or Parliament. More than a dozen counties and nearly 60 towns in England alone sent petitions; in many places rival petitions urging either conciliation or coercion were drafted. In 1775 over 44,000 signatures were attached to the petitions drafted in England, over 10,000 of them in Lancashire alone, while several thousand signatures were gathered in Scotland and Ireland. Clearly, a large number of people was both well informed and deeply concerned about the actions of the British government in the American colonies.[51]

Wyvill and the Association movement mounted petitioning campaigns more consistently than any other radical organisation. Their greatest effort was made in 1780 when about 60,000 signatures were secured in 26 counties (over 8000 in Yorkshire alone) and in a handful of boroughs. Another petitioning campaign in 1782–3 had less support from the counties (only 12 petitioned), but it aroused greater interest in the boroughs, 23 of which produced petitions. Apart from London, Westminster, York and Gloucester, however, few of these boroughs were of great significance. Several large towns, including Bristol, Liverpool, Nottingham, Newcastle, Manchester and Birmingham, did not petition on this occasion, though they had organised other petitions in recent years. The total number of people who signed the petitions in 1782–3 was only about 20,000; half of them from Yorkshire alone. In 1785 when the Prime Minister himself proposed a modest reform bill, Wyvill could only encourage two counties and 12 boroughs to petition.[52]

John Wilkes was never as active as Wyvill in organising petitioning campaigns, but he was remarkably successful in his attempts to make politics enjoyable, entertaining and exciting. He made extra-parliamentary politics a communal activity by recognising the impact of ritual, spectacle and ceremony. Public celebrations, feasts, processions and crowd demonstrations were all seen as vehicles for attaching popular support to the radical cause. Such activities coordinated behaviour, established unity and created a sense of community and equality among the participants. The authority of the established elite was explicitly challenged in such rituals as burning opponents in effigy, while support for Wilkes was demonstrated in a whole series of celebrations commemorating the various achievements of his career. Bonfires, gun salutes, fireworks, music and heavy drinking were features of many of these celebrations. In many parts of the country Wilkite festivities were marked by inspired use of the number '45'.[53] Wilkes's release from prison on 18 April 1770 was celebrated in communities across England. In Gateshead, for example, a tobacco pipemaker produced 45 pipes 45 inches long for local radicals, while his journeymen prepared a feast of 45 lbs of mutton, 45 large potatoes, 45 biscuits and 45 quarts of ale. A farmer near Berwick planned an even greater feast for 45 guests with every item on the menu in units of 45.[54]

Much of the crowd behaviour in Wilkite demonstrations was rich in anti-authority ritual, but most of them remained orderly. Workers involved in violent industrial disputes at the time occasionally used Wilkite slogans, but they were motivated more by economic grievances than by political demands. There was undoubtedly some violence and intimidation by Wilkite crowds, but violence was not usually seen as a means of applying pressure to the ruling elite. There was certainly nothing revolutionary about these disturbances. Indeed, it is not certain what positive political aims were shared by these crowds. In general it is doubtful whether they were committed to an extensive programme of parliamentary reform. The crowds were protesting about the abuse of power by those in positions of authority and they wanted to proclaim their independence from the patrician elite, but they were less articulate than those who supported the petitioning campaigns. Wilkes himself and nearly all the radicals of the period had a horror of mob violence and, apart from Wilkes, they rather disdained the labouring poor.[55]

VI

Because the radicals failed to gain a significant representation in Parliament and failed to carry through a reform of Parliament, it is easy to conclude that they had little influence on British politics. It is a mistake, however, to make such a crude assessment of their achievement. Even if we look only at the radicals' influence on the existing political institutions, it is possible to point to a number of successes. Crown patronage was slowly reduced from the early 1780s onwards and there was a significant revival of partisan politics in the larger, more open constituencies.[56] Parliamentary reform was not achieved, but the Reform Bill of 1785 did secure the support of 174 MPs. The condemnation of general warrants and the relaxation of restrictions on press reports of parliamentary debates were also significant achievements.

The really important successes of the radicals, however, were achieved at the local level where they experimented in how to rally support among the middling orders of society. The radicals began to challenge local elites in many of the large towns and they exploited the press more effectively than ever before. Clubs and pressure groups had existed before 1760, but they had not been directed so explicitly towards overtly political objectives. Petitioning and instruction campaigns had also been waged earlier in the eighteenth century, but rarely had they been so widespread and so independent of the parliamentary elite. Crowd demonstrations were also an endemic feature of eighteenth-century Britain, but they had rarely been enlisted in the cause of extra-parliamentary forces challenging the political power of the patrician elite. Never before had politics seemed so exciting, instructive and relevant to so many people outside the ruling classes as they did in the age of Wilkes.

The extent to which extra-parliamentary politics had been transformed by the radicals can be seen most clearly by examining their impact on other groups who sought to influence the decisions of the governing elite. If we look at other extra-parliamentary movements in the era of Wilkes and Wyvill we can see how much they had learned from studying the strategy and tactics of the radicals. The Protestant Association, for example, had a charismatic leader in Lord George Gordon, established societies across the country, distributed a great deal of propaganda, organised public meetings and crowd demonstrations, and its London branch presented a truly massive petition to Parliament. The largescale violence which occurred during the Gordon Riots of June 1780 was not planned, however, and it took most of the Association's leaders by surprise.[57] A whole series of economic and moral pressure groups in the late 1780s also demonstrated how much they had learned from the radicals. The ironmasters of the West Midlands, the potters of Staffordshire, the cottonmasters of Manchester, the Dissenters seeking the repeal of the Test and Corporation Acts and, most of all, those who wished to abolish the slave trade all adopted most of the methods used by the radicals in their efforts to influence Parliament.[58] Perhaps even more significant was the extent to which those extra-parliamentary groups seeking to defend the existing political system adopted similar tactics to those who were seeking to challenge it. The loyalists who wished to protect the constitution from the attacks of colonial rebels or domestic radicals used the press and organised petitions as effectively as their opponents.[59] Extra-parliamentary politics were not restricted to the dissatisfied elements seeking constitutional reform, but involved those who approved of existing policies and practices, such as those who rallied to George III and the Younger Pitt in 1783–4.[60] Politics 'out-of-doors' became a vital part of the whole political culture of Britain in the age of Wilkes and Wyvill. While it is true that interest in parliamentary reform slumped in the mid 1780s, when the political crises created by George III, John Wilkes and the American Revolution were things of the past, the outbreak of the French Revolution in 1789 soon generated even greater interest in extra-parliamentary radicalism. These later radicals demonstrated that they had learned many of the lessons of those who had been active at the time of Wilkes and Wyvill.

6
Foreign Policy and the British State 1742–1793

JEREMY BLACK

I

A KEY subject in any examination of the operation of the British state is foreign policy. It was generally seen as of crucial importance, was frequently controversial and involved in its formulation, execution and debate all the leading political institutions and forces in the country. For the scholar and student of the period these arguably were the most important features of foreign policy. The details of diplomacy, though important in their own right, appear less consequential in hindsight. In order to provide a chronological background they will be sketched briefly, before attention is directed to the political context of policy.

Between 1742 and 1793 Britain fought four wars. The War of Jenkins' Ear with Spain, essentially a struggle over trade in the West Indies, had already begun in 1739 and Britain remained at war with Spain until 1748. However, the ministry that replaced Walpole in 1742, whose most influential figure in the field of foreign policy was Lord Carteret, was more concerned about French progress against Austria in the War of the Austrian Succession (1740–8). In 1742 British troops were sent to the Austrian Netherlands (modern Belgium), in 1743 they first fought French troops and in 1744 war was formally declared. The war did not go well, although Louisbourg, the French base on Cape Breton Island guarding the approach to Canada, was captured in 1745 and French forces overran the Austrian Netherlands, invading Britain's ally the United Provinces (modern Netherlands) in 1747. The inability of the Dutch to

147

continue the struggle lent urgency to pressure for peace from within the ministry and by the Treaty of Aix-la-Chapelle (1748) peace was restored on the basis, as far as Britain and France were concerned, of the status quo before the war.

The war was followed by a sustained government debate over policy. The Duke of Newcastle, a Secretary of State since 1724 who, after the fall of Carteret in 1744, was the leading ministerial figure in foreign policy, pressed for an active interventionalist policy in concert with Austria and the United Provinces, the concept of the 'Old Alliance' that looked back to the wars of William III and Marlborough. This system was designed to prevent France and her ally Prussia from increasing their influence. In 1748 Newcastle wrote to his brother Henry Pelham, the more cautious First Lord of the Treasury: 'Do but concur in the necessity of supporting the Old System and Alliance, and all will do well, this you know was, and always must be my point.' His view was supported by George II's influential younger son, the Duke of Cumberland, who wrote that year, 'whatever slips our allies make, they may be over-looked, provided there is hopes of pursuing the old system, and maintaining the old alliance', and by the British pleni-potentiaries at Aix-la-Chapelle who wrote of 'the alliance so necessary at all times, and upon all occasions between the House of Austria and the Maritime Powers'. The following spring George II told the Sardinian envoy that the only way to restrain France's excessive power was for the allies to expand their alliance system.[1]

This system triumphed, although alternatives were put forward in 1748. Criticism of Austria and a sense that Britain should ally with the rising power of Prussia led to an overture to Frederick II that year, the mission of Henry Legge, but this was quashed by Newcastle's insistence that such an alliance could be negotiated only as part of the 'Old System'. Another possibility was opened up by French overtures for better relations, but these were not probed, Newcastle writing that October: 'I can see the follies and the vanity of the court of Vienna, but I see the danger and ruin of being dependent upon France. I was once caught in the year 1725 . . . no considera-tion shall ever catch me again.'[2] The third alternative was a more cautious approach to continental entanglements, designed to avoid expenditure on the subsidy treaties supported by Newcastle, and looking back to the policies of Walpole. It was supported by Pelham and in late 1748 Newcastle complained, 'I see a great inclination to lie by, and engage as little as possible'.[3]

Pelham's inclination was to be vindicated by events, for Newcastle's interventionist diplomacy was a failure both in the short and the long term. The Imperial Election scheme, a plan actively sponsored by Newcastle for the election of the heir to the Austrian dominions, the future Joseph II, as successor to the Emperor in order to stabilise the situation in the Empire (roughly modern Germany) failed, despite considerable British financial inducements. More serious was the failure of Britain's allies to adopt an appropriate position when Anglo-French hostilities broke out in 1754 in the disputed borderlands of North America, spreading the following year to a state of undeclared war: formal hostilities began in 1756 when the French successfully attacked the British Mediterranean base of Minorca. Concern about a possible French or Prussian attack on the Low Countries and Hanover did not meet with the envisaged Austrian response, and the British ministry negotiated agreements with Russia (1755) and, thanks to Frederick's fear of Russia, Prussia (1756). However, far from stabilising the Continent while Britain waged a maritime and colonial war, these new alliances did not turn out as intended. Austrian and Russian plans to attack Frederick led him to launch a preemptive war in 1756, while the Russians argued that their British alliance had been voided by the subsequent Anglo-Prussian Convention of Westminster.

Britain thus found herself aligned with the weaker side in the Seven Years War (1756–63), though the only one of Prussia's enemies she was actually at war with was France. Initially the war did not go well for Britain. There was an invasion panic, anger at the humiliation of the loss of Minorca was only partly propitiated by the execution of Admiral Byng, and in 1757 Cumberland failed to defend Hanover successfully against a French invasion. However, the commitment of British troops and money, ostensibly to assist Frederick, helped to shore up the defences of Hanover, while most of the French colonial bases fell to British amphibious attacks including Louisbourg

and Goree (1758), Guadeloupe and Quebec (1759) and Martinique (1762). The French tried to reverse the war by an
invasion attempt in 1759, but their fleet was defeated at Lagos
and Quibéron Bay.[4] Had they succeeded then judgements of
the wisdom of Britain's war and of the dispersal of British
strength overseas by Pitt might have differed radically. The
French plan was unrealistic in so far as it anticipated significant
Jacobite support, and it is unlikely that the regular forces
intended to invade Essex from Ostend and the Clyde from
Brest could have conquered Britain. But the plan involved the
landing of a regular force, several times greater than the
Jacobite army which had invaded England from Scotland in
1745 and had then helped to divert British forces from the war
in the Austrian Netherlands; this would have posed serious
problems for the British ministry, and would possibly have led
them to accept a peace based on terms more favourable to
France than she could otherwise have expected.

British success against France had owed something to Spanish neutrality, which was important in the vital matter of the
arithmetic of comparative naval strength. However, Charles
III, who acceded to the Spanish throne in 1759, signed an
alliance with France – the Third Family Compact – in August
1761 and the following January war began with Britain. The
British capture of Manila and Havanna in 1762 indicated that
success had not left the ministry with Pitt, who had resigned in
October 1761 over his call for a pre-emptive strike against
Spain.

Far from wishing to continue or expand the conflict, George
III, who had acceded in 1760, and his favourite, the third Earl
of Bute, who was first minister in 1762–3, both sought peace
and were disenchanted with Frederick II. In April 1762 Bute
wrote to Andrew Mitchell, envoy in Berlin:

There were not in the late reign wanting many worthy men,
who tho' unable to stop the torrent; saw with great anxiety
the vitals of this country daily exhausting; without the least
prospect of putting an end to a war that however proper
under certain limitation became frightful when carried to the
annual expence of 20 millions, and that part of it alone
regarding Germany, above 8, a sum almost incredible when

compared to the utmost laid out in any one year of Queen Anne or King William's wars; The King on mounting the throne beheld with the utmost horror the situation he was to act in.[5]

The ministry was accused of abandoning Prussia, but these claims are difficult to justify.[6] The Commons majority of 319–65 on 9 December 1762 on the Preliminaries indicated the general eagerness for peace shown by a country that was fiscally exhausted, and widespread satisfaction with the preliminary peace terms. Certainly, Guadeloupe, Martinique, St Lucia and Goree were returned to France and concessions were made over Newfoundland fishing rights by the Peace of Paris (1763), but the recognition of Britain's gains in the West Indies (Grenada, Tobago, Dominica, St Vincent) and India and of Canada and Senegal and the restoration of Minorca all from France, and the gain of Florida from Spain, amounted to an impressive triumph. These were the most important colonial acquisitions by a European power in any eighteenth-century peace treaty.

To a certain extent the accession of George III led to a move away from European diplomacy.[7] As most European wars of this period ended as a result of negotiations offered unilaterally by members of alliances they were frequently followed by the collapse of wartime alignments. This had been true for Britain after the War of the Spanish Succession (1702–13); both that and the War of the Austrian Succession had been followed by periods of active interventionalist diplomacy. Once the prospect of peace drew near, George III and his ministers revived the search for allies, directing their attention to Austria and Russia, the same powers that Newcastle had wooed in 1748–55, but there was a difference in both commitment and willingness to make concessions. The personal, indeed emotional, attachments to Hanover of George II and to continental interventionalism of Newcastle were not matched by their successors in the 1760s, while the stress on the financial and diplomatic consequences of the concessions demanded by possible allies accorded with a post-war period of retrenchment. In negotiations with Russia in 1763, the ministry revealed an unwillingness to become embroiled with a demanding ally. Russia wanted the defensive alliance to include the eventuality of a Turkish attack on Russia, a far from distant prospect given their competing views in Poland, to support intervention in which the Russians also demanded financial assistance. In September 1763 the Cabinet rejected the Russian proposals, the British envoy being instructed to tell the Russians, 'how improper it would be to enter into the disputes about the succession to the crown of Poland, and thereby incur the danger of involving these kingdoms in a new war, for purposes in which they are no ways concerned'.[8]

This was not to be the end of negotiations between the two powers, but in essence the political differences that were to prevent alliance had already been clearly stated. Britain was unwilling to intervene effectively in eastern Europe. In a similar fashion Britain had been uninvolved in negotiations involving Holstein and Poland in 1732–3, and was unwilling to support her own hostility to Russian steps in eastern Europe with action in 1720–1 and, later, in 1772 and 1791. In the 1760s, as in 1733 over Poland and 1749–51 against Sweden, Britain refused to support Russian expansionism. Britain's attitude to Russian gains was not to alter significantly until the Prussian and Austrian failure to defeat France in 1792 ushered in a new international situation with France apparently able to dominate western Europe. At that time Britain sought to call in the 'New World' – Russia – to right the balance in the Old, rather as in 1748 she had encouraged the march of Russian troops towards the Rhine in order to counteract French triumphs. However, before the 1790s successive British ministries viewed Russia as an ally who could serve to assist in keeping Europe politically stable, rather than as a dynamic power whose expansive schemes should be supported. Arguably this view can be defended. In the long term, France was to be less of a threat to the European political system than Russia. In the short term, British disinclination to accept Russian demands in the 1760s was not a misjudgement, as Michael Roberts has suggested it was.[9] Aside from the crucial importance of following a policy that was viable in domestic political and financial terms, no 'necessary' diplomatic objectives were to be served by supporting Russia. The history of Anglo-Russian relations over the previous half century had revealed that Russian rulers and ministers would only accept British diplomatic initiatives on their own terms. In continental European terms Britain, the only major power without a large army, sought stability after 1763. Alliance with an aggressive power was not the obvious way to achieve this.

If British policy in Europe can be described as pacific and cautious – there was no serious response to the French annexation of Corsica in 1768 or the First Partition of Poland in 1772, although neither were welcomed by the ministry – outside Europe a more assertive attitude was maintained. Gunboat diplomacy was employed to obtain a satisfactory settlement of disputes with France over Turks Island and the Gambia (1764–5) and with Spain over logwood cutting on the coast of Honduras (1764) and the Falkland Islands (1770). In the last and most serious crisis France nearly came to the support of her ally when Britain threatened Spain with war for expelling a British settlement. However, the anti-British French foreign minister Choiseul was dismissed. His replacement D'Aiguillon (1771–4) sought a reconciliation with Britain, rather as Puysieulx (1747–51) had done, especially as he was concerned about the need to resist what he saw as the threat of Russian power to the European system. However, George III and the few ministers who were aware of French approaches were hesitant about responding, as they were concerned about the domestic and Russian response, the stability of the French ministry and Hanoverian vulnerability to Prussia, one of the partitioning powers. In 1763 a French envoy in London had reported that he was certain George III wanted peace, 'but I will not promise that it will last. Every day one sees the Kings of England forced to follow the wishes of the English nation, always unsettled, always jealous and always an enemy to France.'[10] Such attitudes had not prevented the Anglo-French alliance of 1716–31, but it could be suggested that hostility to France was more clearly part of British political culture by the second half of the century. Furthermore, George III did not benefit as to a certain extent his two predecessors had done from the sense that the Jacobite threat was an additional encouragement to most ministers to support royal views on foreign policy.

In the twelve years that followed the first Partition of Poland continental diplomacy was far from stagnant and a number of events, including the War of the Bavarian Succession (1778–9), the move of Russia from a Prussian to an Austrian alliance (1781) and the Russian annexation of the Crimea (1783) provided opportunities for diplomatic manoeuvre, for establishing whether the Sardinian envoy had been correct when he wrote in 1772 that everyone would agree that the sole discernible principle of the British government in foreign affairs was to avoid all foreign commitments.[11] However, Britain was instead committed to the American War in which France (1778) and Spain (1779) intervened on the rebel side. This intervention helped to destroy the best chance for the British, defeating the rebels sufficiently to encourage them to accept a compromise peace. Bourbon, especially French, naval power helped to alter the maritime balance, to crucial effect in 1781 when General Cornwallis, blockaded by the Americans and the French, was forced to surrender.

The war was not as disastrous as it could have been. The American attempt to conquer Canada, the Bourbon attempt to invade England in 1779 and the siege of Gibraltar all failed, and at the Battle of the Saints (1782) Admiral Rodney saved Jamaica and the reputation of British naval power. Nevertheless the loss of America was a serious blow, though in the long term commercial sense far less so than was feared, and if the Treaty of Versailles (1783) left Britain in control of Canada and British India, it was still the after-effect of defeat. France acquired Senegal and Tobago, Spain Florida and Minorca.

A decade later France and Britain were to be at war again, but it was not the conflict that had been anticipated in 1784–7. In Britain in those years suspicion of French intentions had been strong and it was widely believed that France would seek to undermine the British position in Canada, Ireland and India. The British were most sensitive about the French threat to India and feared that this threat would be taken closer to realisation should the French gain control of the Dutch navy and the Dutch empire, with its important bases in the East Indies and Ceylon and at Cape Town. Opposition to France was viewed as a necessary policy by the Foreign Secretary, the Marquis of Carmarthen, much of the ministry, many diplomats and most of the Opposition. Pitt the Younger, in contrast, preferred to hope that commercial negotiations with France, which led to the Eden Treaty of 1786, could have a diplomatic benefit. In the summer of 1787 his attitude altered, in accord with a hardening of the government's general stance towards France and an almost obsessive concentration on the struggle between British and French protégés in the United Provinces to the detriment of other aspects of Anglo-French relations. The situation was resolved in September by a Prussian military intervention, instigated by British diplomatic action and supported by a British naval armament. French attempts to forestall this intervention by means of military preparations failed. Carmarthen and Sir James Harris, the British envoy in The Hague, were determined to use Prussian power to serve British ends, and the Prussian invasion was made without any British commitments to Prussian interests in eastern Europe.[12] The overcommitment of subsequent years that began arguably with the Anglo-Prussian alliance of August 1788 and culminated in the Ochakov crisis of 1791 cannot be ascribed to the negotiations of 1787, but rather to those of subsequent years, especially to the confusion and inattention that afflicted British policy during the Regency Crisis of 1788–9. The Ochakov crisis, a confrontation with Russia in which Britain appeared to be willing to fight in order to ensure the territorial integrity of the Turkish empire, was mishandled diplomatically in the face of Catherine (the Great) II's refusal to oblige and amid domestic concern about the prospect of war with Russia.[13] The ministry backed down, leading to Carmarthen's resignation, a Russo-Turkish peace was negotiated without Britain, the Anglo-Prussian alliance collapsed and by the summer of 1791 Britain was without a powerful ally.

Developments in eastern Europe dominated government concern in the first years of the French Revolution, which was welcomed for its apparent nullification of French strength and stability, though fears were expressed that the crisis might lead to a growth in French power through reforms. Worries of greater French influence in the rebellious Austrian Netherlands in 1789–90 proved misplaced and in 1790 France was unable to help Spain in the Nootka Sound crisis when the seizure by Spanish warships of British vessels trading on Vancouver Island rapidly escalated towards war. The Family Compact allowed

Spain to call for French assistance, providing France with an opportunity to escape from diplomatic nullity, and in May 1790 Louis XVI announced orders to fit out a fleet. However, political divisions reduced the credibility of French promises and the Spaniards felt obliged to yield to British pressure. If the Dutch crisis of 1787 marked the diplomatic bankruptcy of *ancien régime* France, that of Nootka Sound suggested that the subsequent changes had brought no improvement. Despite French fears that the British sought gains from their colonies, the Pitt ministry was essentially satisfied if France was reduced to the situation she was in in early 1791, a nullity that was diplomatically isolated. The radicalisation of French politics was not generally seen as a threat. In 1788–90 the prospect of a revived France entailed a monarchy that was stronger because of constitutional and administrative reform and national unity, a powerful challenge to Britain and an attractive proposition as an ally for other monarchs. From 1791, however, it was increasingly likely that, short of a successful counter-revolution, which would probably bring chaos, a stronger France would be a politically radical France that would threaten, intentionally or not, the domestic position of other monarchs. As a result, in the event of war Britain would not be without allies. This in fact was to be the case. When France declared war on Britain on 1 February 1793, as the result of a deterioration of relations that essentially reflected different views over the Low Countries, Austria and Prussia were already fighting her.[14] The great problem of fighting any war on the Continent, the existence of powerful allies, had been solved not by skilful diplomacy but by the alignment of comparable interests. Unfortunately this alignment was to prove difficult to maintain while, as in the Seven Years War, the outnumbered power was to be surprisingly successful.

II

The role of the crown was an important element in the formulation and execution of foreign policy, which was essentially within the constitutional domain of the monarch who appointed diplomats and had the right of making war and peace. Of the two monarchs of this period George II (1727–60) was a more controversial figure as far as foreign policy was concerned than his grandson, George III (1760–1820). This was partly because George III, though interested in foreign policy and concerned to advance his own views, was more prominently associated with controversial views on constitutional matters, ministerial politics and American affairs, while George II appeared most interested in the advancement of Hanover. In the past diplomatic historians had arguably paid insufficient attention to the role of the crown, largely because they based their studies substantially on British diplomatic instructions and reports, sources that do not reveal this role as they are concerned with the execution of policy, not its formulation. However, the more recent attention devoted to the archives of other states has thrown considerable light on the influence of the monarchs, often seen by foreign diplomats as the crucial source of initiatives. This shift accords with one in British political history, which for many years devoted little attention to the eighteenth-century monarchy. The Closet had been stormed, Britain was a 'Venetian Oligarchy', political stability required and stemmed from a rejection of Stuart traditions of monarchical activity; Queen Anne was putty in the hands of favourites and ministers; George I an elderly buffoon whose limited control of English, gratitude at obtaining the British throne and concern over the alleged Jacobitism of the Tories delivered him into the hands of his Whig ministers; George II a 'King of Toils' unable to maintain favoured ministers in office, Walpole in 1742, Carteret in 1744 and 1746, or to prevent the rise of Pitt; and George III controversial precisely because he sought to create a new form of monarchical authority. Management of the Commons was seen as the crucial element of political skill, the court and the Lords, as spheres of policy formulation and political management, being generally ignored.

In recent years, however, there has been an obvious increase in interest in the eighteenth-century monarchy. Baxter, Clark and Owen have all produced work stressing the political independence and importance of George II. It is clear from Roberts' examination of the Swedish crisis of 1772 and Blanning's study of the *Fürstenbund* (League of Princes) of 1785 that George III was capable of taking initiatives with scant consultation of his ministers. Mackesy has recently underlined royal influence in his study of the fall of the younger Pitt's administration.[15] There was clearly a certain amount of contemporary confusion about the situation in Britain. In 1753 Joseph Yorke, the envoy in The Hague, wrote to his brother: 'I am convinced that the constitution of no country is so little known, as that of England, half the world imagine that all government is confusion with us; and the other half that our kings are as arbitrary as any other, and that all they do in a view to satisfy the nation is pure grimace.' The same year Frederick II wrote to his envoy in London: 'when you say that such a thing could make an impression on the nation I regard the word nation as inappropriate, as I know that at present the king gives whatever impression he pleases to the nation which he governs absolutely.'[16]

A stress on the role of the monarch links foreign policy and political history in a two-way relationship. It alters our understanding of the former and, by making clear the continued power of the monarch in a crucial sphere, underlines the significance of foreign policy for the political history of the period. Though George I considered the idea of an eventual division of Britain and Hanover, he essentially created a new polity. In common with the general European trend, this did not lead to novel constitutional, political or administrative arrangements, but was instead a personal union, a territorial agglomeration. However, though not fused, it was given common purpose at the international level by the dynastic interests of the monarch. This was recognised by contemporary diplomats, impatient with British attempts to differentiate between the two dominions. It was also recognised by Hanoverian ministers, faced in 1741, 1753, 1757 and 1772 with threatened attacks designed to influence British conduct. The monarchs appreciated the consequences of the personal union, but the bulk of the British political nation did not, and this provided the basis for political dissension. What was criticised in British political debate as the pursuit of Hanoverian interests was in practice the consequences of royal intervention arising from the interests of the personal union. Not only did the charge of Hanoverian counsels fail to do justice to the divisions within the government of the Electorate, that were at times quite marked, but it also neglected the extent to which dynastic interests were often different from those of the Electorate, as understood by its ministers. Ministerial attempts, such as that of Carteret in 1743, to argue that Anglo-Hanoverian interests were 'inseparable and would be inseparable, even though the same person were not sovereign of both dominions,'[17] were unconvincing.

George II in his later years was still interested in the aggrandisement of Hanover, but his British ministers were not always willing to support him. In 1748 Newcastle wrote to the Earl of Sandwich, a plenipotentiary at the peace congress of Aix-la-Chapelle, about British opposition to the guarantee to Prussia of East Friesland, to which George as Elector had claims: 'What I have mentioned about the Guaranty of Oost Frise, I was ordered to do; But I am sure your prudence will prevent your taking any notice of it, till the time comes, and then in a way not to give any offence to the King of Prussia.' This letter revealed Newcastle's awareness of a conflict of interests between Britain and George's wishes as King-Elector, as did his instructions to Sandwich concerning the claims of the house of Hanover to Osnabrück.[18] This awareness of conflict had dulled after the deterioration of British relations with Prussia in 1726–32, but it revived again in importance as Anglo-Prussian relations became more significant from 1740. British ministers were willing to accept the need to protect Hanover from attack, as in the negotiations with Russia in the early 1750s, but they were less keen to support particular Hanoverian pretensions. This distinction was not always apparent to contemporaries, and it is not surprising that Frederick II, faced by hostile Austro-Hanoverian moves, wrote to his envoy in London in 1745, 'dois-je regarder le roi d'Angleterre comme une ou comme deux personnes?' Five years later Newcastle informed the envoy in The Hague, the Earl of Holdenesse, that Dutch demands that George II should pay one-third of the joint subsidy to the Elector of Cologne as King and one-third as Elector was unacceptable, because, 'contrary to all practice, for His Majesty, in the same act, to enter into any engagements in two different capacities.'[19]

Relatively little is known about Hanoverian policy or George III as Elector for the period 1760–84 due to archival destruction and insufficient scholarly attention. British diplomats felt that Hanoverian measures affected the attitudes of other powers[20] and an absence of consultation led to British complaints. The highpoint of tension occurred in the 1780s, as a result of George's negotiation as Elector of an anti-Austrian league of German princes at a time when his British ministers sought better relations with the Emperor. In 1786 Carmarthen wrote to Pitt that the League's consequences 'must be provided against'. The following year, another senior minister, the Duke of Richmond, suggested to Pitt that:

If some idea could be conveyed to the Emperor that the effects of the German league would probably be much weakened and in time done away by an alliance between him and England, I should think it would have a very good effect. And . . . it would be saying no more than the truth for without the assistance of England Hanover would make but a poor figure in a continental war, and I do not believe that His Majesty's German purse could possibly support his army in the field above one campaign. But if England was on the other side it is next to impossible he could act at all.[21]

Though George III was clearly interested in Hanoverian affairs, and unwilling to abandon the chance of following an Electoral policy for the sake of whatever his British ministers believed might be national interests, there is no doubt that in 1760–93 the consequences of the *Personalunion* were less serious for British policy than they had been in 1714–60. This owed much to Hanoverian neutrality in the wars of both American Independence and Bavarian Succession, to the comparative non-interventionist nature of British foreign policy in the period 1763–86 and to the generally peaceful nature of imperial politics in 1763–92, with the important exception of the War of the Bavarian Succession, a period when there was some divergence between British and Hanoverian policy. George III was concerned about Hanover, but not its territorial aggrandisement. As Elector his stance was essentially defensive, and the decision to join the League of Princes, as well as the general hostility to the Emperor Joseph II, can be explained as responses to the aggressive attitude and bold plans of

Joseph. Essentially pacific and defensive, George's policy as Elector complemented the continental views of his British ministers, and the differences between them were largely over tactics, not strategy. Probably as a result, Hanover and royal wishes and actions played a far smaller role in the British public debate over foreign policy than in 1714–60. There was criticism of what were regarded as Germanic habits, but though the effects of Hanover on British policy were condemned, the condemnation was less sustained and severe than, for example, that of the early 1740s.

III

It is possible to present the influence of Parliament in foreign policy in a number of ways. The potentially negative political role that it could play can be stressed by directing attention to the inability of Carteret to sustain his position. It could also appear to have an active or potential restraining role. The opposition *Westminster Journal* argued that Parliament should play a greater role, its issue of 3 December 1748 noting: 'In several papers hath endeavoured to show, that the right of making peace, war, and alliances, was in ancient times thought to be cognisable in Parliament, and that the best and greatest of our kings were most frequent in their consultations with the great assemblies upon those important subjects; and that the conduct of ministers was not fully justified till it had received the sanction of a parliamentary approbation.' British ministers stressed the problems posed by parliamentary management, Holdernesse responding thus in 1749 to Dutch pressure for a subsidy to the Elector of Cologne: 'I laid great stress upon the difficulty I supposed His Majesty would be under, from the nature of our constitution, in granting subsidies to foreign princes in time of peace.'[22]

And yet both constitutionally and politically the government had far more leeway. The Tory Earl of Lichfield was correct in complaining in 1743 that 'this House has not of late years been let into any secrets relating to our foreign transactions.'[23] The constitutional possibilities of Parliament's role could not be pushed because of the political fact of ministerial power. In

1751 Joseph Yorke wrote from Paris: 'The Parisians say their Parliament is less corrupt than yours, for that their remonstrances are different from your polite addresses.'[24]

However, this power could not be simply assumed, and both parliamentary management and discussions about policy were important for this reason. In 1747 the ministry called a general election a year earlier than necessary, because they feared the electoral and thus parliamentary consequences of a bad peace, Newcastle writing to Cumberland:

any final conclusion of the war, by almost any peace that can be obtained, would undoubtedly give strength to opposition, raise some flame in the nation, and render the choice of a Parliament more difficult. . . . The present New Opposition is yet unsupported, unconnected, and not in high reputation; what the course of a year may produce nobody can tell; unfortunate public events, or private disappointments, and personal views, may render that opposition formidable, what at present is far from being so.[25]

There was at times therefore a sense of precariousness, and concern about the domestic perception and impact of foreign policy had a definite focus in the shape of Parliament. The absence of well-disciplined political parties helped to ensure that politicians were conscious of the importance both of foreign policy and of specific international conjunctures, and this naturally produced clashes between ministers. At the end of 1749 Newcastle told the Sardinian envoy that he was completely discouraged by the obstacles he encountered, not in Parliament, where the government had a massive majority, but within the majority itself, 'because most of them only think of making themselves popular, and to that end only seek the means to cut taxes,'[26] an attitude that hindered Newcastle's efforts to grant foreign subsidies. Two years earlier Horatio Walpole complained to Pelham of the priority of parliamentary over policy considerations:

our ministers in England have no plan for peace or war, but we shall depend upon a great majority in Parliament; for God's sake what will that do, why vote what you please; will votes without means and men extricate us from these endless difficulties.[27]

And yet it is important not to present a crude contrast of parliamentary pressure and foreign policy, or to exaggerate the difficulties of parliamentary management, or ignore the advantages that Parliament offered. The decision in 1748 to return the popular gain of Cape Breton to France in the peace settlement, despite vociferous demands that it be retained, suggests that domestic opposition was far from being a determinant of policy, as does the success of pushing through peacetime subsidies to allies in the early 1750s, despite claims that Parliament would never accept it. Government success at general elections and the resources available for parliamentary management did not prevent serious criticism of British foreign policy, but it lessened their impact. It is salutary to contrast the criticism of peacetime subsidies with their minor role in the general election of 1754.

The parliamentary system could be a source of considerable strength in foreign policy and was recognised as such by some contemporaries. By regarding Parliament as partly a sphere in which the disputes of politicians in and out of favour could be contested, it can be seen as a stage for, rather than a source of, political difficulties. These difficulties were not unique to Britain; they were an essential feature of court-based political systems that lacked the organisation and attitudes of disciplined parties. Conversely, Parliament offered a solution to the most serious domestic problem of the states of eighteenth-century Europe: public finance. It provided a means for linking government to the politically powerful throughout the country, a means whose constitutional and institutional expression was the voting of substantial sums for approved policies. The contrast between Britain and her continental counterparts was not solely a matter of sums raised and the speed with which they were voted and produced. It was also a matter of lower rates of interest, flexible financial methods, sources of revenue that could be anticipated without difficulty and relatively low collection costs, both in administrative and political terms. Politically this led to the voting and collection of large sums without significant levels of public disorder. Parliamentary financial arrangements and taxation were accepted as legal even if they could produce criticism. While many continental states found it difficult to devise politically acceptable methods to raise taxation, largely because the politically and socially powerful were unwilling to increase their commitments, Britain used parliamentary taxation and a parliamentary-funded national debt to raise large sums.

The content of parliamentary debates has received insufficient attention, though caution is necessary, owing to the problems associated with establishing what was actually said. For whatever reason there are no significant private papers for several senior politicians, including Carteret and Harrington, while others have left only patchy remnants of their correspondence. After the death of Frederick Prince of Wales in 1751 his papers were burned, while those of William Pulteney, Earl of Bath, were destroyed after his death in 1764 by his brother.

Aside from possibly leading to an overemphasis of papers that survive, especially the readily accessible Newcastle correspondence, such destruction leaves unclear the significance of parliamentary discussions of foreign policy to the senior participants and what specific issues their speeches were intended to address. There is also the problem of bias in the sources that survive. It is likely that many commentators, especially newspapers, simplified the arguments in order to represent two clear-cut positions, and deliberately stressed rhetorical attitudes at the expense of cautious discussion and the use of evidence.

Despite these problems, it is clear that one of the most impressive features of debates was the knowledge of international relations displayed by some parliamentarians. Expert opinion could be presented in Parliament, which contained both diplomats and former diplomats, some of whom contributed their knowledge. The quality of debates has been criticised,[28] and it is certainly true that much parliamentary language, for example in the debates over the Peace of Paris, was aggressive. Rhetoric, however, was not necessarily incompatible with an intelligent assessment of the situation and in judging opposition speakers, it is necessary to consider the particular problems of lack of information that they faced. In addition, criticism of the role of the monarch had to be indirect, helping to ensure that, for example, the issue for Hanoverian subsidies during the War of the Austrian Succession was treated both as a very significant matter, being used to discuss fundamental questions of constitutional propriety and dynastic legitimacy and in a very general fashion. The Opposition was also appealing to a wider public, most obviously in the printed Protests of their peers. In appealing to such an audience it was possibly felt best, either by the speakers or by the reporters whose accounts we are substantially dependent upon, to adopt a broad and rhetorical approach. Furthermore, it is possible that the euphoria of public speaking, the conceit of conviction and the sense that once in opposition there was no harm in embarrassing the government as much as possible, all combined to encourage a strident style and aggressive approach.

IV

One particular sphere in which an aggressive policy was frequently advocated was that of colonial and commercial policy. This became more important from mid-century both in ministerial thinking and in public debate. The War of the Austrian Succession focused disenchantments with continental interventionalism and raised interest in North America. Whereas during the previous period of confrontation with France (1689–1713), attention had been concentrated on the continent, in that of 1742–63 there was a stronger and increasing sense of opportunity and anxiety relating to maritime and colonial matters. In July 1749 Admiral Vernon, an opposition MP, wrote to a colleague:

I look on the fate of this country to be drawing to a speedy period whenever France should attain to a superior maritime power to Britain, which by the present of Cape Breton, we have given them an extensive foundation for ... I may say without the spirit of prophesy, that whenever they think themselves so, the first blow they will strike, will be to strip us, of every one of our sugar colonies, which I know to be easily attainable by them, whenever they have a superior force by sea; and that the natural consequence of that will be, that you will by the same blow, lose all your American colonies as to their dependence on Britain. And then what must become of a nation . . . with eighty millions of debt, and deprived of those branches of commerce that principally produced the revenues, to pay the interest of those debts, is a melancholy consideration.[29]

To Vernon and other opposition figures the Pelham ministry displayed a scandalous neglect for Britain's colonial position, and indeed Newcastle's Imperial Election Scheme had little purchase in public support. Nevertheless, it would be mistaken to imagine that trade was neglected. In 1748, for example, the consul at the crucial Mediterranean port of Leghorn (Livorno) was ordered to preserve British commercial privileges from any innovations whatever, and his efforts were supplemented by the envoy in Florence. The following year the Duke of Bedford, Secretary of State for the Southern Department, ordered Benjamin Keene, envoy in Madrid, to 'insist that the trade between the two nations should be on the same footing, as it was before the war', while in 1752 Newcastle moved to protect the export of paper hangings to Russia and the following year he wrote to the envoy in Vienna concerning the situation in the Austrian Netherlands, 'our manufacturers in Yorkshire are already full of complaints upon this head; and if they were, by such a Convention, to be precluded from all hopes of redress, there would be no standing their importunities.'[30]

Ministers were exposed to and often heeded commercial pressure. In early 1749 Bedford was pressed by a general meeting of London merchants engaged in the West Indies sugar trade over the position of certain Caribbean islands, and received information from Lord Chancellor Hardwicke, 'I herewith transmit to your Grace the third volume of the *British Merchant*, in which are contained the tracts concerning the Spanish duties'. Two years later Newcastle instructed the envoy in The Hague to follow the directions of the East India Company in helping them in their quarrel with the Dutch company.[31]

There is no doubt that trade was an important slogan in debate over foreign policy and that diplomats were instructed to protect merchants and their interests, but it could be suggested that it is misleading to press too far the view that British policy was motivated primarily by commercial consideration. This view accords with the notion that Britain after the Glorious Revolution was somehow a bourgeois state or motivated by bourgeois considerations. Trade is an explanatory device that is clear, comprehensive, and attractive, is not specific to the period, and demands little specialised knowledge. If Britain is seen as an 'open' political system in which the parliamentary machinery, however corrupt, was open to pressure groups and the amorphous, and therefore very convenient, concept of public opinion is regarded as of great importance, trade appears as crucial to foreign policy. Public opinion and commercial lobbyists are seen as influencing policy through Parliament and the administration. This is less clear if the stress in the period is on royal power, aristocratic dominance, social conservatism, religious ideologcial presuppositions, and a fundamentally non-secular society. Then arguably the position of trade becomes problematic and marginal in terms of the central political interests of society. Ministries were usually willing to seek and eager to receive advice, though they did not consider themselves obliged to follow it. Concerned to maximise national wealth, ministries obtained contradictory advice from conflicting interests. Diplomats instructed to support merchants were nevertheless not expected to act in any way liable to endanger diplomatic relations.

Many ministries were accused of being opposed to trade, easy polemic for successive oppositions that was nevertheless expected to stick. The contemptuous references by many diplomats to merchants and the failure of ministries to jeopardise diplomatic for commercial ends, lent some substance to these charges. Despite having trumpeted the 1786 commercial treaty with France, the Pitt ministry was willing to compromise it by confronting the French in the United Provinces the following year. Catherine the Great's agenda for Anglo-Russian political relations was not accepted despite the importance of the Russia trade. In 1783 W. Morton Pitt forwarded to the Foreign Secretary, the Earl of Grantham, a memorial from some of his constituents, the mayor and merchants of Poole, opposing the idea of concessions in Newfoundland to France, Pitt asked for an answer to quiet their fears but added that he was not 'so unreasonable as to expect any confidential information, nor so presumptious as to suppose you want any information from Poole touching the importance of Newfoundland to this country'. Grantham's overt reply stating a readiness to receive information, was accompanied by a private note: 'You are fully sensible how impossible it is for me to say more or less to them. I wish they could be at all convinced of the impropriety of their interference.'[32] This was very much the standard ministerial attitude. Advice would be accepted only if judged suitable. Any reassessment of the role of commerce will clearly require more work. It is not enough simply to note the existence of a lobby, discuss its purposes and activities, and assume that it was responsible if its policies were adopted. Instead, it is necessary to explain why this happened in the context of a system in which mercantile demands were not automatically heeded.

And yet it is as unsatisfactory to deny the importance of colonial and commercial considerations as it would be to exaggerate them. Arguably the most important international developments affecting Britain in this period were her acquisition of substantial trans-oceanic territories so that by 1763 she was the most powerful European power in North America and India. Between 1763 and 1793, whether at peace or war, she struggled to retain and strengthen this position, and ministerial correspondence was filled with such matters as the respective naval strength of Britain and the Bourbon powers, or speculation concerning Bourbon intentions. This concern did not reflect the pressure of colonial interests, but rather the strong post-Newcastle government sense that power was a function and cause of wealth, colonial possessions and trade, and maritime strength. However, ministers were determined to retain the right to define what policies should be followed in order to pursue these goals and they refused to yield to jingoistic pressure for war whether, for example, against Spain in the Falkland Islands crisis of 1770 or against Spain in the Nootka Sound crisis of 1790. The British stance might appear aggressive, especially to continental commentators who queried the existence of a maritime balance of power and criticised wartime Britain's policy towards neutral traders, but no British ministry sought unprovoked war for the sake of seizing new territories. In 1754–5 there was hesitation in the ministry over the escalating confrontation with France over the contested North American frontier, and the government saw itself as responding to French aggression. In 1761 the Duke of Bedford, a former Secretary of State who was shortly to play a major role in negotiating the Peace of Paris, suggested to Bute that: 'we have too much already, more than we know what to do with, and I very much fear, that if we retain the greatest part of our conquests out of Europe we shall be in danger of over colonizing and undoing ourselves by them, as the Spaniards have done.'[33] In the years of 'gunboat diplomacy' immediately after the Seven Years War, the Grenville ministry saw itself as responding to Bourbon provocation, and the same was true of the Falklands and Nootka Sound crises.

It is possible to present British activity in a different light. The construction of a base on the Falklands, alongside exploratory voyages in the Pacific, the foundation of the colony of Botany Bay in Australia, and the activities along the northwestern coast of North America that led to the Nootka Sound crisis can all be seen as part of a forward policy in the Pacific. It is certainly true that some prominent individuals and groups sponsored such activity, but it is equally clear that the preservation and defence of existing territories in India, the West Indies and, until their loss, North America were the central concern of government. There was no master-plan to use naval power to drive the other European powers from their empires. Naïvely over-optimistic views might be expressed, for example, about the vulnerability of the Spanish American empire in the War of Jenkins' Ear (1739–48), but ministries were more prudent, aware of the limitations of naval power and of the primary need to prevent a Bourbon invasion of Britain.[34] There was an acute awareness of the difficulties posed by Britain's lack of a substantial army.

V

The general, almost universal cry is, that the great acquisitions we have made, the flourishing condition of our trade, the spirit and experience of our troops by sea and land, and

the distresses of our enemies entitle us to the most advantageous terms of peace; of which an exclusive right to the
Fisheries, as the great source of trade and maritime power, is
almost universally esteemed the most essential, and indeed
the sine qua non. Whatever falls short of this will most
certainly occasion clamour, and there is but too much reason
to fear that a general clamour without doors will have an
influence within, considering how many mercenary wretches
will be wavering, till they can see which side of the question
is most likely to carry it'.

Despite these claims from John Paterson, a London commenta-
tor, in 1762,[35] in the Peace of Paris France retained a right to
fish off Newfoundland, and the terms were approved by
Parliament. It is difficult to assess the role of public opinion and
all too easy when confronted with a reversal of government
policy, as for example towards Russia in 1791, to attribute this
to public opinion, a convenient explanatory device when nothing else seems to fit. There is still much work that needs to be
done in assessing the difficult subjects of public attitudes and
the means by which they were expressed. The study of public
opinion can be approached through a consideration of the
various means of articulating and expressing opinion, but the
representativeness of these was often queried in the eighteenth
century. It is too easy to extrapolate from newspapers which
were often little more than an expression of what was largely a
certain strain of essentially metropolitan opinion. What contemporaries understood by public opinion is unclear. Xenopho-
bic idioms can be studied, but it is difficult to assess their
significance. Contemporaries commented on the interest of the
public in political news, including those whom the nature of the
franchise kept from any formal role in the parliamentary
process. A mid-century broadside declared:

Here, every man is a politician, from the King to the cobbler;
and go into the meanest hedge-alehouse you will hardly fail
finding a grimy-fingur'd mechanic that cannot regulate the
state, describe and foretel the event of a battle, had they
done so, and so, better than the whole Parliament of
England or the ablest general of the age.[36]

This concern did not have to relate to politics, let alone foreign policy. On the eve of a contentious wartime parliamentary session, the Earl of Stair noted in 1743 that London 'seems to be entirely employed about whist'.[37] The role of public opinion made some commentators pessimistic. In 1747 Horatio Walpole warned Pelham that the position of Furnes, rather than Dunkirk, was crucial, adding, 'but popularity, overbearing popularity must presage if you are drove to this dilemma, and Dunkirk must be demolished and Furnes yielded'. Two years later a French official argued that, 'in a state like England one should anticipate frequent revolutions. The nation is restless, the monarch so hated that it is impossible that sooner or later there will not arrive events which will overthrow their authority.' In 1753 the French foreign minister urged Frederick II to be accommodating in his commercial disputes with Britain on the grounds that the British ministers were under pressure to have 'reasons which can retain the impatience of the nation over this affair'. Carteret's political weakness was attributed to his failure to act in the necessary popular fashion.[38]

However, such dictates could be defied, one MP declaring in 1746 that he had always voted for Hanoverian troops and 'was not afraid to see my name in yellow letters', a reference to printed lists of how MPs had voted that were designed to stir up their constituents. Two years later the French foreign minister, referring to criticism of the British government in London that he feared might affect British policy, nevertheless added, 'we do not think that they are weak enough to let themselves be intimidated by popular insinuations.'[39]

Rather than presenting a simple balance of public opinion and policy, it is more appropriate to draw attention to the varied nature of the former. Alongside essentially urban criticisms of the return of Cape Breton in 1748 one can note rural concern for peace. Pelham wrote after a visit to his Surrey constituency, 'we had a full meeting of Gentlemen, and almost all in good humour, our peace is popular with all parties'. The following year he noted after another country visit, 'I must own they call loudly for a lessening of the Land Tax. I have promised nothing, though I feel the weight of four shillings in the pound to country gentlemen as much as anybody.' It is not surprising that Pelham declared in 1748, 'Peace you know is my

mistress; and war a rival I fear, as well as watch'. Legge wrote
to him from Berlin: 'a Minister with your intentions and
possessed of the means, as you are; who will take every
opportunity of retrenching expences, reducing interest, adding
to the Sinking Fund and paying our debts as fast as is at all
consistent with public safety, will in a few years deserve better
of Great Britain and make a much greater future himself than
all the heroes whose ashes repose in Westminster Abbey have
ever done.'[40]

Legge therefore offered a different standard of judgement to
that of warleader and strategist and conqueror of empire that
was to be adopted by Pitt. Pitt's pretensions and achievements
fascinated many Victorian historians, who commonly searched
with approval for the eighteenth-century antecedents of imperial greatness. It has been more recently argued that Pitt's
contribution to British success has been exaggerated, that the
margin between success and failure in the Seven Years War was
very tight, and that the problems posed by political expediency,
alliance politics, and overseas warfare helped to limit the
bounds of effective government action. Historians emphasising
the role of Pitt in the conduct of the war have often overlooked
the structure of eighteenth-century government. Administration was departmental: each minister managed a specific
branch of the executive for the king, leading George II to tell
Newcastle, 'There is no such thing as a First Minister in
England'. Pitt's plans were often imprecise and in practice he
followed the policies and commitments of his predecessors.
However, in contrast to the situation during the War of the
Austrian Succession, the weakness of France and neutrality of
Spain for most of the war provided the ministers with a unique
opportunity for advancing Britain's maritime and colonial
position. Nevertheless, only rarely did Pitt look ahead to
increase the resources of the nation in the matter of ship-
building, manning the fleet, recruiting the army, or producing
munitions. His abilities were primarily parliamentary, not
administrative. He failed both to comprehend the nature of the
nation's fiscal problems and to anticipate the war's
requirements.[41]

Possibly the debunking of Pitt's reputation can be taken too
far. Any reader of foreign diplomatic correspondence in the

years after his resignation in 1761 is struck by the space devoted to Pitt's position and the possibility of his return to power. The attention devoted to Pitt itself helped to make his actions and opinions appear more significant, but it also reflected an appreciation of his importance. The disasters at the beginning of the Seven Years War, particularly the fall of Minorca and the convention of Klosterseven, helped to discredit a whole generation of politicians and generals, and this facilitated Pitt's rise in prestige. By 1757 George II, born in 1683, was an old man, Cumberland discredited, Prince George and his circle an unknown quantity, and Newcastle fearful of the consequences of a conflict that he had not wanted anyway. Pitt's solutions were neither novel nor invariably successful but a political culture that personalised power required a British hero to rank alongside the 'Protestant Hero' Frederick the Great. Pitt himself was not a figure free from controversy, and Pittite publications had to deny frequent charges of opportunism, hypocrisy and egotism brought against the minister. However, he served a valuable purpose, both providing the crown with an essential House of Commons leader, after a period (1754–7) when the lack of an acceptable and successful one was both cause and consequence of ministerial instability, and helping, however unrealistically, to keep up enthusiasm for the conflict. Badly frightened and humiliated by the early stages of the war, Britain sought heroes and wished to hear the bells of victory.

And yet Pitt's popularity was not universal and other views on foreign policy were advanced. Glorying in victory in 1759, there was a widespread desire for peace two years later, the Earl of Chesterfield writing to Bute: 'The report of an approaching peace is now universal, and I hope in God, not entirely groundless, for I am sure that this, his Majesty's *native country* (I am never weary of repeating these words) stands in need of one.' Newcastle hoped 'that there may be no occasion to enter into any transaction, for raising those immense sums which would be necessary for carrying on the war another year'.[42] There were of course victims of peace. Crime rates rose, for example in north Devon in 1749, as disbanded soldiers and sailors were cast adrift with few resources.[43] However, peace was in general beneficial, both at the national and the personal scale. Merchant sailors needed no longer to fear the somewhat primitive and only partially effective method of naval recruitment by the press gang, and could sail without fear of privateers. In 1763 Hardwicke warned Newcastle:

As at present advised, I feel the project of counter addresses of application of thanks to members for the opposition to the peace would not succeed or have the effects proposed; because I am convinced that the objections to the peace, such as it is, take place much more in the town than in the counties. People in the country are in general glad to be relieved from a state of war and I believe would with great difficulty be induced to enter into any public protestations against it.

Peace reduced the pressure of national taxation in a fiscal system where military expenditure and the servicing of wartime debt were the principal commitments,[44] not social welfare and economic support. This was generally beneficial, not least because it reduced the drain of specie by the government from the rest of the economy, with its consequent effect on interest rates and the availability of money.

By stressing the value of peace, it is possible to appreciate better Legge's praise of Pelham and to offer a different judgement of leading ministers, one that rates more highly those who were faced with the difficult task of negotiating or preserving peace, as Bute was in 1762–3 and North in 1770. It is also possible to suggest that the four greatest leading ministers of the century, Walpole, Pelham, North and Pitt the Younger, were so precisely because they were great finance ministers who appreciated the financial context and consequences of government policy, including crucially foreign policy.

It is arguably this dimension of cost that is absent in much discussion of post-1763 foreign policy, where there has been criticism on the grounds that a failure to heed the requirements of other powers, especially Russia, led to isolation and thus to British vulnerability at the time of the War of the American Independence. Dubious on military[45] and diplomatic grounds, this argument suffers from the problem that Britain was not Prussia, not a state permanently prepared for major conflict with the consequent financial, governmental and social implications. The British political nation expected to have its peacetime security on the cheap and there was a significant shift between the interventionalism of the George I, Stanhope and Townshend years and the quarter-century from 1762. This was not a shift that public opinion or the political nation, however defined, had forced on government, but one that reflected new views including those of George III and the new generation of politicians that rose to prominence and power in the 1760s,[46] as well as changes in international relations. Arguably this shift was in part in response to the nature of Britain's strength and potential. Her ability to intervene effectively on the Continent, either militarily or diplomatically, was limited. Her maritime and colonial successes against the Bourbons in the Seven Years War had been won at considerable cost and the continued existence of the Bourbon Family Compact was a significant military challenge. It might appear inappropriate to stress weakness at a moment of victory, but the war had been a costly and, up to 1759, close-run affair, and it is easier to appreciate British foreign policy if the difficulties it faced and its domestic context are both considered.

7

The Eighteenth-Century Empire

P. J. MARSHALL

I

In the 1740s it would still be premature to describe Britain as the dominant power outside Europe, but a British presence in some form or other was already widely scattered across the globe. In the new world British settlements were relatively dense along the eastern seaboard of North America and in the Caribbean islands, while British subjects traded extensively with the Indian peoples of the north and the Spanish and Portuguese colonies of Central and South America. There was a large volume of British trade along the West African coast, conducted from forts and trading posts and from many other points of contact with African rulers and merchants. In Asia flourishing commercial enclaves on the Indian coast were under British management together with smaller settlements in the Persian Gulf and Sumatra and a barely tolerated presence in the Chinese port of Canton. British ships had begun to make regular incursions into the Pacific.

This far-flung British presence took varying forms in different parts of the world. British North America and the British West Indies were divided into a series of distinct 'colonies'. Although the origins of these colonies were very diverse, by the middle of the eighteenth century they had come to share certain characteristics. In Johnson's *Dictionary* colonies were defined as 'a body of people drawn from the mother country to inhabit some distant place'. Even though in the Caribbean up to 90 per cent of the colonial population were drawn from Africa, not from Britain, and there were very considerable

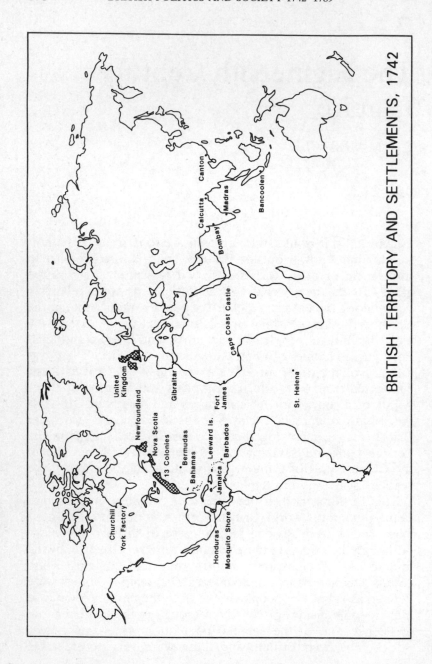

BRITISH TERRITORY AND SETTLEMENTS, 1742

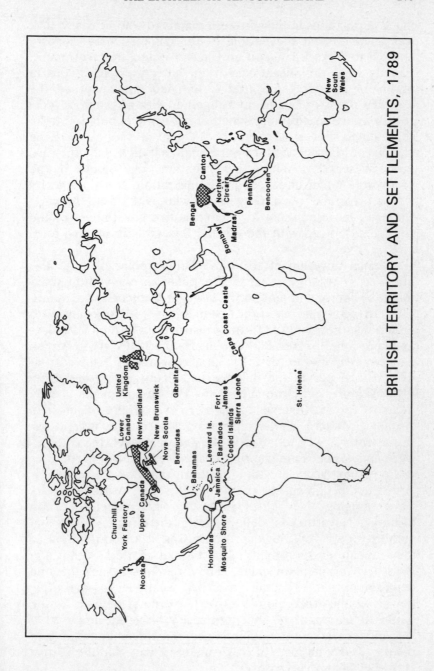

BRITISH TERRITORY AND SETTLEMENTS, 1789

black populations in the southern mainland colonies as well, it was assumed that the people of the colonies were English, entitled to English law and an English system of government. Exactly what this meant was often bitterly disputed, but in outline it was accepted that it entailed enjoyment of the essential rights of Englishmen together with a system of local representative institutions, whether the white population to be represented was as large as the 180,000 in Virginia and the 150,000 of Massachusetts or very small, as was usually the case in the West Indies. With a few exceptions, the colonies by the 1740s were under direct royal administration. Royal authority was represented by a Governor, who with his nominated Council was responsible for the executive government of the colony and joined with the elected Assembly in making local laws.

Colonial government from the British point of view was intended to ensure that colonial populations enjoyed the maximum of liberty and autonomy, thought to be essential stimulants to economic exertion, compatible with obedience to imperial authority in the form of instructions to the Governors and occasional Acts of Parliament. By the 1740s, those British agencies responsible for colonial administration believed that over a long period the balance had been tipping decisively towards more and more autonomy. By the end of the decade 'fears of colonial independence were everywhere manifest in Britain'.[1] Modern scholarship does not necessarily accept that this alarm was well founded. On a practical level, the colonies were perhaps becoming more manageable, as the opportunities arising from increasing trade with Britain and the need for British protection against the threats posed by worldwide wars were bringing their elites into a greater dependence on London.[2] Nevertheless, deficiencies in the structure of formal authority were very obvious. There was little coordination of departmental responsibility for colonial matters within the British government machine. The Board of Trade, the one department that had some expertise, usually lacked executive power. Within the colonies most Governors fought a losing battle to maintain the independence of the executive from Assemblies who controlled finance and involved themselves in the day-to-day business of government in ways that the British House of Commons rarely did.

Few historians are inclined to see the colonial elites who dominated these Assemblies as being inspired by any concept of 'national' identity against what they might regard as 'foreign' rule. The tendency is in fact to stress their increasing 'anglicisation', that is their closer identification with British social and cultural values.[3] But the elites were very committed to protecting and enhancing what they saw as local rights and privileges and to asserting the 'rights of Englishmen' in general, in terms which evoked seventeenth-century Whig traditions reinforced by the writings of later 'patriot' and 'country' oppositions to 'oligarchy'.[4] In the mainland colonies at least, the elites, drawn from landowning, merchant and professional families in the north or from planters in the south, represented considerable political communities. The franchise was very widely diffused among a mass of small property owners. The extent of actual popular participation in colonial politics is widely debated. But even if the elites were consolidating their authority by the middle of the century, the values which they claimed to uphold in the Assembly were the values of politically conscious and articulate communities, to whom in a real sense they were accountable.[5] Few would argue that the continental colonies were moving inexorably towards rebellion by the 1740s, but they were in a volatile state and attempts to reform what most British opinion regarded as an unsatisfactory imperial connection could have explosive results.

In areas where the British had been able to establish links with an effectively functioning indigenous economy, colonies of rule and immigration had not developed. The British presence was limited to what contemporaries called 'factories' or 'settlements', that is to coastal trading posts, some of which had in fact grown into very considerable commercial enclaves. Only in eastern India had the British commercial network extended inland to any degree. The simplest trading posts were those where a few agents bought furs from Indians along the shores of Hudson's Bay; the largest enclaves were the cities of Calcutta and Madras, where over 100,000 local inhabitants lived under effective British rule. For all their diversity, settlements had certain features in common. They existed as commercial bases from which British exports were sold to indigenous merchants and to which these merchants brought commodities which the British wished to export: furs, African slaves, Indian textiles or Chinese tea. They originated in concessions granted to groups of British merchants by local rulers. Within the settlements authority was exercised by Governors appointed by merchant companies, not by the British state. Indeed it was a nice question as to whether the territory of most of the settlements belonged to Britain at all. The Hudson's Bay Company, the Company of Merchants Trading to Africa or the East India Company, the bodies that managed the overseas settlements, were relics of seventeenth-century monopoly grants. In the case of the East India Company the monopoly of trade to Asia was jealously guarded by a highly successful trading organisation, which, if in no sense an agent of the British state, worked in close cooperation with the national government.[6] Most British commercial settlements had established relatively stable relations with the African or Asian polities where they had gained a lodgement, but in parts of India the dominant position which the British had won for themselves in local trade was creating friction that was to have important consequences.

By the 1740s there was also a wide spread of British trade beyond the colonies or the settlements of the trading companies. Ships either from Britain or owned by merchant communities operating from British North American, Caribbean or Indian ports did business in the harbours of many independent African or Asian states and frequently called at ports within the colonial domains of other European powers, the Spanish, the Portuguese and the Dutch. Such trading contacts were usually breaches of the colonial codes of the powers concerned. They were particularly resented by the Spanish, whose efforts to suppress them had led to conflict in the Caribbean.

Viewed from Britain itself, the British presence that was taking so many different forms in so many parts of the world was seen as an essentially commercial one, judged to be capable of making an invaluable contribution to Britain's national well-being. Since the mid seventeenth century the state had been taking action to try to regulate and increase the contribution of trade outside Europe by the creation of a system usually referred to as the Laws of Trade or Navigation Acts. In the first place, these Acts were intended to encourage

British shipping and therefore the potential pool of seamen for the Royal Navy, by confining all trade with British colonies to British or colonial ships. Beyond that, all shipments of certain named tropical commodities from British sources were to be exported to Britain in the first instance, to ensure that British needs were met and to enable Britain to become the distribution point for such commodities by re-exporting them to Europe. Finally, colonial markets were to be developed as an outlet for British manufactured goods, foreign imports and local manufacturing being discouraged.

The contribution being made by trade outside Europe by the 1740s seemed to be a significant one.[7] For two of the tropical commodities most in demand, tobacco and Indian textiles, Britain had succeeded in becoming the major European distributor. The tobacco came from the colonies on the Chesapeake, Virginia and Maryland. The textiles were shipped in by the East India Company, who were the largest importers into Europe of Indian cotton cloth.[8] The British West Indies were no longer the world's major supplier of sugar, but their increasing output generally kept up with the growing British domestic demand. By the 1740s re-exports, mostly of tropical commodities, could amount to up to a half the total of domestic British exports. An increasing proportion of those domestic exports were going to the colonies in America. Growing population and rising living standards were making North America a particularly important market for British manufactured goods. The colonial population was rising towards a total of 1,200,000 (doubling again by the 1770s), whose per capita consumption of imports is calculated to have increased by 50 per cent between 1720 and 1770.[9] The British West Indies consumed less, but they were the main staging post for the flow of illegal exports into Spanish America. The boom in America contrasted with slow growth of exports to Europe. As a result, the share of American exports in the British total rose spectacularly: from 10 per cent in 1700–1 to 37 per cent in 1772–3.[10]

The expansion of trade outside Europe and the advantages it appeared to offer Britain made a deep impression on contemporaries. It seemed to them to be the dynamic sector in an economy whose overall growth in the first half of the eighteenth century appeared to be slow. Not only was it creating new sources of private wealth, but it was contributing powerfully to the national finances, through the very high level of customs collected on colonial imports and re-exports, and to the national balance of trade by reducing the level of foreign imports and putting Europe into Britain's debt for re-exports. It was becoming commonplace to regard worldwide trade as the vital increment of wealth which enabled Britain to sustain military and naval forces appropriate to a power with a much greater endowment of territory and population. A treatise on trade, for instance, urged that the American plantations should now 'demand of *us* the *first* and *highest* regard, preferably to any other commercial consideration whatever', because of

> the vast increase of their people, and of the commodities by them raised for our own use, for our manufactures and re-exportations and more especially by the perpetually increasing demands from thence for all kinds of our manufactures, productions, etc. in immense quantities: (whereby probably about or near one million of our people are employed at home, many stout ships, and many thousands of mariners constantly employed; much wealth and considerable quantities of bullion of both gold and silver continually brought home to us).[11]

There was, however, a price to be paid for the advantages of worldwide trade. It must be protected and fought for, if necessary. Heavy extra commitments were thus added to the navy, often fully stretched to protect Britain from invasion and to maintain British interests in European waters. Worldwide naval supremacy was a vastly expensive ambition, probably only attained in the later stages of the Seven Years War. Even when it was attained, it could not be taken for granted. Britain must be constantly vigilant lest other powers erode her commercial gains and match her naval spending. Pre-emptive war on competitors could even be a legitimate tactic. Throughout the eighteenth century there was no doubt that France was Britain's major competitor. By the 1730s, if not earlier, the success of French trade throughout the world was becoming all too apparent. Anglo-French commercial rivalry was by no means the only cause of the antagonism between the two countries which so often led to war. It was, however, a major cause and it turned European wars into worldwide wars, forcing British strategists to make choices, which were rarely as simple as exponents of a 'blue-water' policy of concentrating on war outside Europe often assumed.

In the first half of the eighteenth century, the exponents of such a policy were likely to have overt economic or political motives for doing so. Trade expansion backed by a war at sea was of course the cause of merchants who traded outside Europe, but it was also the cause of parliamentary oppositions, who used the appeal of supposedly cheap and truly 'national' naval war against what were said to be costly continental campaigns waged on behalf of foreign powers by the ministers of Hanoverian kings. Yet for all the political opportunism of such campaigns, a recent study of one mounted in the early 1740s to commemorate limited successes in the Caribbean suggests that they could evoke widespread public response.[12] The naval war against Spain begun in 1739 merged into full-scale involvement in the continental War of the Austrian Succession. By 1746, however, attempts were again being made to concentrate British resources on war in America. With the coming of peace in 1748 this trend was not reversed. In 1750 the Duke of Newcastle wrote of the dangers to the 'Northern Colonies, which are inestimable to us. . . . For if we lose our American possessions; or the influence and weight of them, in time of peace; France will, with great ease, make war with us, whenever they please hereafter.'[13] The link between Britain's trade and her standing as a major power was on the way to becoming an orthodoxy accepted by almost all shades of opinion.

Increasing enthusiasm for global trade and the deployment of seapower led to many effusions about Britain having created an empire over the seas of the world, but a careful study has found little evidence of the use of concepts of empire in the sense of lands and peoples subject to British rule.[14] Johnson chose a maxim of Sir William Temple's to illustrate the definition of 'empire' for his *Dictionary*: 'A nation extended over vast tracts of land and numbers of people arrives in time at the ancient name of kingdom or modern of *empire*.' The assortment of colonies or plantations, enclaves and trading posts in all parts of the world hardly measured up to this standard and seems not yet to have been dignified with the title of the British Empire. No doubt in contemporary eyes it had very little in common with what were recognised to be empires, those of Rome or of Spain. The British presence overseas in the 1740s was still very much a series of uncoordinated private enterprises in which the initiative lay with individual merchants, the representatives of trading companies or the leaders of the colonial communities. It was, however, a presence with a high potential both for conflict and for growth.

II

The conflicts that erupted in the second half of the eighteenth century had their roots very much earlier. Spanish counter-measures against illegal British trade were the pretext for war in 1739. France was inevitably drawn in. This was the first of a series of wars against the French to be fought in North America, in the West Indies, off the coast of Africa and in India. Britain and France were officially at war from 1756 to 1763, from 1778 to 1783 and from 1793, and undeclared war was waged outside Europe in other years. At times Spain and the Netherlands were added to Britain's enemies. In India Anglo-French rivalry exacerbated existing tensions between the East India Company and Indian rulers who wished to contain foreign commercial expansion. Fighting broke out in Bengal in 1756, setting off events which were to turn the Company into a major Indian territorial power. As such, it was repeatedly to be involved in war with neighbouring Indian states. The tensions between local autonomy and imperial regulation in America came to the surface in the 1760s, as successive British governments tried in a piecemeal and incoherent way to impose a limited imperial control, only to encounter determined resistance from colonial communities who saw a threat to what they conceived to be their established liberties. In 1775 British regular troops were being deployed and were encountering armed resistance. In 1776 thirteen colonies declared their independence, which was recognised by Britain after six years of war.

The loss of most of the North American colonies took some 2.5 million people out of the political orbit of the British, if not necessarily out of their commercial one. Contraction was, however, highly untypical of what was happening to Britain's commitments outside Europe in this period. By nearly all criteria they grew very rapidly. Territory was conquered from the empires of other European powers and Indian states were annexed. Vast additions were made to the population living under British rule by conquest and there was a considerable flow of migration from the British Isles and from Africa.[15] The volume of British trade with America, Asia and Africa continued to grow. Migration of British capital was still on a small scale but much of the commercial development of the western hemisphere depended on credit being extended by British merchants.[16]

Expansion took place in all quarters of the globe. Even in North America, the loss of the Thirteen Colonies was preceded by huge acquisitions at the expense of France and Spain in 1763. France surrendered its Canadian settlements together with its claims to western lands from the Great Lakes to the Gulf of Mexico. Spain surrendered Florida. Ex-French Canada and Nova Scotia, both much reinforced with American loyalists who chose to remain under British rule, alone survived the debacle of the Revolution. But of much greater significance, at least in the short run, was the recovery of British exports to the new United States, which by the 1790s were running at a higher rate than at the end of the colonial period.

Older theories that the British West Indies entered into a decline in the later eighteenth century now seem to be untenable.[17] Much new Caribbean territory was acquired. New islands were annexed in 1763. During the war with Revolutionary France losses sustained in the War of the American Revolution were recovered, while British forces occupied Spanish Trinidad and the Dutch territories on the mainland of South America, which are the origin of modern Guyana. The new acquisitions together with increased output from old colonies, especially Jamaica, boosted British sugar production and turned the West Indies into a major source of raw cotton. With the destruction by slave revolt and war of exports from the French Caribbean, Britain's most formidable rival, British sugar was able to capture European markets in the 1790s. The weakening of the Spanish colonial system at the end of the century stimulated an increased flow of British exports to Spanish America through the British colonies.

Growth in the Caribbean economy was inevitably reflected in growing trade with Africa; increased production of sugar and cotton meant increased imports of slaves. Already the world's largest dealers in slaves by the middle of the century, the British maintained their lead until they abolished the trade in 1807. Estimates of how many slaves the British carried between 1750 and 1807 vary widely, but about 2 million seems likely.[18] Commercial expansion in Africa was not accompanied by any marked extension of territorial control. The largest part of the slave trade was conducted in independent African ports. A new settlement was, however, established at Sierra Leone.

The British position in Asia underwent a revolution in the second half of the eighteenth century. The commercial enclave of Calcutta expanded to conquer the provinces of Bengal and Bihar, which were inhabited by perhaps 20 to 30 million people. The roots of the conquest of Bengal probably lie in the commercial inroads which the British had been making into the province since early in the eighteenth century and in the increasing resentment which its rulers felt at the assertive foreign presence in their midst. Events came to a head when the ruler of Bengal attacked and took Calcutta in 1756, only to lose it again the following year and to be deposed after his army had been defeated at the battle of Plassey by East India Company troops sent up from Madras. For the next eight years the Company tried to manage Bengal through a succession of client rulers before turning rulers themselves by accepting the office of *Diwan* or deputy to the Mughal Emperor in 1765. As rulers of Bengal the Company disposed of a revenue, derived largely from taxation of land, of some £3 million. With such a revenue it was able to support an army of 80,000 British and Indian soldiers. This army became a potent instrument for extending British influence far beyond the frontiers of Bengal and eventually for further conquests. The enclave at Madras expanded less spectacularly. There the British had fought the French throughout the 1740s and 1750s, becoming involved with Indian allies, whom they dominated but preserved. Largescale territorial conquests did not begin from Madras until the 1790s.[19]

The acquisition by a British trading company of a huge new empire, generating a revenue about one-third of that of Britain itself, naturally aroused high expectations that Britain would be greatly enriched. Although very large fortunes were made by certain individuals, the yield to the nation as a whole was generally judged to be disappointing. Most of the Indian revenues were absorbed by the costs of defence and government, including handsome salaries for British officials. It was hoped that much of what remained could be syphoned back to Britain through an increased flow of Indian goods. Imports of textiles from India and of Chinese tea, in large part financed from India, increased significantly after the conquest of Bengal. In 1794–6 British imports from Asia were valued at £7.3 million compared with £8.6 million imported from the West Indies. But India remained a limited outlet for British exports until well into the nineteenth century. In 1794–6 Asian exports were worth £3.5 million; those to the West Indies and the United States were £4.5 million and £6.5 million respectively.[20]

In spite of increasing foreign intrusion, the Pacific Ocean in the middle of the eighteenth century was still effectively a Spanish preserve. In the second half of the century the Spanish were reduced to trying to defend the western coast of America, leaving the Pacific Ocean open to others. The largest number of ships entering the ocean were British: British exploration had done most to map it. British naval power had forced the Spanish to make formal concessions after the Nootka Sound crisis of 1790 and a permanent British presence was being maintained at Sydney Cove on the western rim of the Pacific. The tangible rewards for Britain of all of this activity were still slight. A brief fur trade had developed along the northwest coast of America. Whaling and sealing were taking place in the southern oceans. The New South Wales settlement was relieving Britain of convicts. Whether other advantages were envisaged from it is a matter of intense controversy among historians. There can be no doubt of the acuteness of the convict problem or that other outlets for transportation had been thoroughly explored. It is, however, tempting to see the decision to send convicts such an immense distance at enormous expense as part of a British strategy to force open the Pacific. Much has been written in support of such a supposition, but decisive evidence to sustain it has yet to be found.[21]

III

Half a century of great accretions of territory, people and trade, together with the virtual elimination of French overseas interests in the 1790s, had undoubtedly left Britain supreme outside Europe. That Britain's strength throughout the world was an essential prop to her national greatness had long since ceased to be the slogan of interested pressure groups or dissident politicians and become the orthodoxy of all but a handful. In 1754, as in 1739, Britain was again driven towards a European war by hostilities in America. This time, however, the government seems to have been in no doubt that it must respond to what it took to be French threats to the frontiers of the North American colonies by the deployment of troops and, as the commitment escalated, to make total victory in North America the main objective of the Seven Years War, almost regardless of the huge price in men and money. 'Should our trade and plantations be exposed to the ravages of the French, a national bankruptcy would probably in a very few years ensue', a minister told the House of Lords.[22]

The gains of the Seven Years War were for contemporaries a startling demonstration of Britain's power, but they also believed that her eminence left her vulnerable to her enemies, who were scheming to attack her at any point of weakness throughout the world. Garrisons and naval squadrons must therefore be kept at the ready in North America, the West Indies and India. The American colonies must on no account be allowed to undermine metropolitan control to the point where a significant proportion of the trade that was so vital to Britain passed to her rivals. Faced with this prospect, British ministers were ultimately prepared to risk civil war and the almost certain prospect of renewed world war in order to restore control. Between 1778 and 1783 Britain fought a desperate war on many fronts to limit the damage to her worldwide interests. From 1783 she was again vigilant in the defence of her global position, increasing her commitment of forces to India and threatening to fight for access to the Pacific. For British ministers the war against Revolutionary France soon became yet another stage in the long struggle to maintain Britain's position outside Europe. The major part of the British army was sent to the West Indies in 1795. In 1799 Henry Dundas, who directed the war effort, could still write that:

> Great Britain can at no time propose to maintain an exten-sive and complicated war but by destroying the colonial resources of our enemies and adding proportionately to our commercial resources, which are, and must ever be, the sole basis of our maritime strength. By our commerce and our fleet, we have been enabled to perform those prodigies of exertion which have placed us in the proud state of pre-eminence we now hold.[23]

The consensus among historians would probably be that, while contemporary opinion generally over-exaggerated the role of Britain's worldwide interests in her economic develop-ment, very significant advantages had accrued to her, at a high price in public expenditure. Close links between worldwide expansion and the onset of industrialisation are difficult to establish. Assertions, for instance, that wealth accumulated in trading and plundering outside Europe 'financed' the Industrial Revolution are hard to reconcile with studies of how industrial enterprises met their capital needs. Savings in the domestic economy were in any case at such a level that inputs from overseas were most unlikely to have had any decisive effect. Historians seem to be cautious about the role of exports in stimulating industrial development, at least until the very end of the eighteenth century. At that point exports to markets outside Europe, especially of cotton goods to America, acceler-ated very sharply.[24] But in terms of growth, not necessarily directly related to industrialisation, the value of increasing worldwide trade seems to be beyond dispute. By the 1790s Britain had to a very large extent achieved her long-standing objective of becoming the principal emporium for American and Asian goods for Europe as a whole.

For British opinion in the early eighteenth century Britain's involvement throughout the world had a significance that transcended expectations of material gain. Overseas trade supported by naval power was activity worthy of a free people. Successful war at sea against Catholic absolutist enemies both vindicated British freedom abroad and asserted it at home against the dangers to the constitution thought to be implicit in the heavy taxation and standing armies needed to wage war on the Continent. In the second half of the eighteenth century, however, Britain's role overseas was beginning to be invested with political associations of a different kind. The language of empire was being used to imply not merely dominion over the seas but rule over territory and peoples throughout the world.

Gains made after the Seven Years War seem to have given the decisive impetus to theories about territorial empire. Commentators in the years after 1763 were beginning to write that Britain should be:

> no more considered as the kingdom of this isle only with many appendages and provinces, colonies, settlements, and other extraneous parts, but as a grand marine dominion consisting of our possessions in the Atlantic and in America united into one empire in a one center where the seat of government is.[25]

By the 1770s 'survey' books which included the 'British Empire' in their titles became commonplace.[26] African and Asian settlements were usually included with American colonies in one whole, at whose grandeur readers were invited to wonder. The British empire, one of these books claimed, 'may now be esteemed the greatest sovereignty upon earth either considered as to its extent or its power'.[27] The very varied nature of the British possessions meant that precise definitions of empire were elusive. The status of Ireland was an obvious difficulty: was it an imperial partner or a subordinate part? There was still a tendency to see the empire as peopled by free-born Englishmen and thus to consign the conquered Indian provinces to a separate 'empire in India'. But there was increasing acceptance that some kind of unity transcended the diversity of British overseas possessions. For Edmund Burke, for instance, the Indian provinces had become 'the most considerable part of the British empire', an empire that certainly included Ireland.[28]

Recent studies have identified new strands in British nationalism in the later eighteenth century, arguing that it was taking conservative or authoritarian forms in which state institutions, like the army or the monarchy, were becoming increasingly acceptable as national symbols.[29] Empire of the seas had for long been a very powerful focus for a narrowly English nationalism. The tradition of Britannia ruling the waves certainly retained an unabated popularity with all sections of society, as the apotheosis of Nelson was to show. There are also indications, which need further investigation, that newer concepts of territorial empire were winning acceptance as an element of British national self-identification. It has been suggested that 'the existence of Britain' and 'the existence of a British empire beyond the seas were inseparable notions' in the late eighteenth century.[30] How widely held such notions were and how far down society they had penetrated remains obscure. Interesting evidence of the potential popularity of territorial empire is, however, provided by the reception of Lord Cornwallis, when he returned from India in 1794. He was hailed as victor over Tipu Sultan of Mysore with an enthusiasm in the past accorded to successful admirals rather than to rulers of British India, who were liable to be called to account by Parliament. Cornwallis was granted the freedom of the City of London, 'the populace taking his horses from his carriage and drawing him through the streets'.[31]

If those who ruled Britain in the second half of the eighteenth century were conscious that they were also the rulers of a worldwide territorial empire, to what extent and in what ways did they try to shape its growth? Such questions have long been debated. On the one hand, there are scholars who see the emergence of more or less purposeful imperial policies, which British ministers were applying from the 1760s onwards. Historians who try to delineate strands of colonial policy usually also look for turning points between 'old' and 'new' or 'first' and 'second' British empires, the turning points being marked by the adoption of new policies. The end of the Seven Years War in 1763 or the recognition of the independence of the Thirteen Colonies in 1783 are conventionally selected as turning points.

For instance, a very influential interpretation was launched by C. M. Andrews in 1924, when he argued that the gains of the Seven Years War marked a shift from an empire based on 'mercantilist' policies of trade regulation to one based on new policies of 'imperialism', that is on concern for 'extent of territory and the exercise of authority' as ends in themselves. These new policies of imperialism drove the Thirteen Colonies to rebellion.[32] For Vincent Harlow, whose two volumes on *The Founding of the Second British Empire 1763–93*[33] offer an extremely elaborate interpretation of colonial policy, 1763 has a very different significance. He saw it as marking a turning away from territorial empire in the old sense of colonies of settlement in the Americas to policies of promoting worldwide commercial expansion through tapping new markets in Asia and the Pacific from a chain of trading bases.

The prevailing view among historians at present seems to be one of scepticism about changes in policy and indeed scepticism as to whether such a thing as colonial policy in any real sense even existed. The emphasis is on the weakness of British authority. British ministers are said to have had very little capacity to impose any shape on the processes of expansion overseas and few ideas of what to do with such power as they did possess, beyond the repetition of trusted maxims going back to the seventeenth century. Most recent accounts stress that the measures that British ministers sought to enforce in the North American colonies after 1763 were in no sense new. There was a 'profound continuity in the purposes and aspirations of colonial rule'.[34] Other scholars depict a continuity that extended far beyond the American crisis and the secession of the Thirteen Colonies, which are not seen as having forced profound changes on imperial thought or practice. A study of the years 1783 to 1801 sees only the survival of a set of old-fashioned 'assumptions and priorities'; ministers could not 'conceptualise' alternatives.[35]

The case for continuity and lack of coherent policy-making seems to be a powerful one. No uniformity of structure was imposed either at home or overseas on what was increasingly being called the British empire. At the end of the eighteenth century the empire was still a mixture of old-style colonies and trading settlements, to which newer models, Indian provinces or conquered territories predominantly inhabited by foreign Europeans, had been added. Patterns of local government varied from the traditional Governor, Council and elected Assembly to an authoritarian system in New South Wales. Indian provinces were ruled by a Governor or Governor General and Council at the head of a hierarchy of officials, British and Indian. Authority in Britain was still uncoordinated and overlapping. After an experiment between 1768 and 1782 with a Third or Colonial Secretary, the main executive responsibility was passed to a Secretary of State primarily concerned with home affairs and then with waging war. The old Board of Trade was abolished, but a similar body was later created in its place. The new Indian territories were managed from Britain by an entirely separate bureaucracy. In the first instance they were still the concern of the clerks, secretaries and directors of the East India Company at Leadenhall Street. After 1784 indirect supervision was also exercised by a government department called the Board of Control. The Cabinet or a group of senior ministers might at times, according to some historians, exert themselves to take an overall view of Britain's interests around the world, but there was no government body charged with formulating policy for the empire as a whole.

It is therefore scarcely surprising that such policy as there was remained extremely conservative. The only guidelines that more or less applied to the whole British empire were the seventeenth-century Navigation Acts, reinforced in 1764 and again from 1783 to 1786 to exclude the independent United States. Quite significant modifications were made in the system from time to time, but the theoretical debate on free trade, most obviously associated with Adam Smith, did very little to weaken commitment to old ideals of maintaining the colonial trades for British shipping, reserving colonial markets for British manufactures and directing colonial products to Britain.

Debates about the desirability of empire in one part of the world or in another or about such concepts as trading access being preferable to actual rule also seem to have had very little effect on what actually happened. There was in fact a great increase in the volume of trade going to areas outside Europe, such as Spanish America or the United States, over which Britain did not exercise political control; but the area under

British rule increased as well. Here old priorities survived virtually unchanged. The West Indies retained their central place in British concerns throughout the century. Neither the unreal debate about whether to choose Canada over Guadeloupe at the end of the Seven Years War nor later hostility to the slave trade signified any weakening of commitment to the West Indies. Commitment to colonies on the North American mainland grew rapidly with awareness of the demographic and economic transformation taking place there by mid-century. They were deemed worth wars to defend them from the French and to retain authority against rebellion. Many anticipated that after their loss Britain would sink down the scale of European powers. The great change from commercial settlements to territorial empire in India was at first regarded with misgivings and repeated efforts were made to curb further expansion. Within a few years, however, phrases like the 'brightest jewel' in the king's crown began to be coined and it was being argued that the loss of the Indian provinces to another European power would fatally weaken Britain.[36] Empire in India had been incorporated into the list of national assets, but not as a substitute for what had been lost or for what remained in the West. This seems to have been characteristic of eighteenth-century policy making: gains could be absorbed but a reassessment of priorities was not undertaken.

Arguments that the British policies around which American resistance crystallised in the 1760s were impeccably traditional seem to be irrefutable. The decisions to keep sizeable British garrisons in America in 1763, that they should be in part paid for by a stamp duty, that the enforcement of the Navigation Acts should be tightened up, as in the Sugar Act of 1764, that the colonial customs should be reformed, that salaries for colonial judges and other officials should, as Townshend proposed in 1767, be provided from sources that did not depend on the Assemblies, and even that unsatisfactory colonial charters should be revised, as was attempted for Massachusetts in 1774, could all be traced back to proposals made by the Board of Trade or by other officials in the first half of the eighteenth century. In their own eyes British governments were not threatening the colonies with fundamental changes. They were merely seeking to ensure that trade flowed in the prescribed directions, that adequate provisions were made for defence and that what were seen as usurpations of the power of the Governors by the Assemblies should be reversed. Most opinion in Britain seems to have accepted this view. There was very little controversy at the time in Britain about the measures proposed by George Grenville or Charles Townshend.

It seems equally undeniable that no systematic attempt was made to reconstruct the British empire after the loss of the Thirteen Colonies. The Navigation Acts were reimposed. Old patterns of government survived in those colonies, mostly in the Caribbean, that had not rebelled. Ex-French Canada had been successfully defended against the Americans and had attracted a considerable immigration of loyalists after 1783. In 1791 a limited new departure in colonial constitutions was launched with provisions to strengthen the Governors of the Canadian colonies against their Assemblies.

The weight of evidence seems clearly to favour those historians who argue for lack of overall planning and for continuity of attitudes against those who discern the development of new imperial policies in the second half of the eighteenth century. Such a conclusion may, however, give a misleading impression of the extent to which the rulers of Britain did in fact engage with the problems of empire. This engagement took place not, as was to be characteristic of the later empire, through the creation of administrative structures or by policy-making within the machinery of government, but, as was characteristic of the eighteenth century, through Parliament.

The measures affecting the colonies that were introduced in the 1760s may not have been new in themselves, but frequent resort to Parliament to implement them was new. In the first half of the eighteenth century parliamentary intervention in colonial matters was virtually limited to trade regulation. As a consequence colonial opinion began to formulate doctrines that Parliament had no jurisdiction in other areas, which were the exclusive preserve of the colonial Assemblies.[37] Such doctrines were entirely unacceptable in Britain. In the 1760s, 'Parliament insisted on its character as a government, making laws and directing policy and extending increasingly into every corner of the colonies'.[38] Parliamentary sovereignty in all aspects was unequivocally stated in the Declaratory Act of 1766. A recent study has suggested that, once the British government had decided in 1769 to retain a duty on tea and thus to give a practical application to Parliament's claims to sovereignty, a violent outcome was very difficult to avoid.[39]

In an effort to bring peace to America, Parliament renounced its power to impose taxes on colonies in 1778, but by then it had effectively extended its authority to other parts of the empire. In 1774 the new colony of Quebec was given a constitution by an Act of Parliament that has proved as contentious for historians as it was for contemporaries. The Quebec Act appeared to mark at least a temporary departure from the principle that colonial constitutions should be based on the essential liberties of Englishmen by affording some protection to French law and the rights of the Catholic Church. The Act's critics regarded these provisions as a gross betrayal; its defenders argued that it showed Parliament's willingness impartially to uphold the interests of all the peoples of the empire, French as well as English.

Parliament even purported to consider the interests of Hindus and Muslims. For all the ambiguities about British sovereignty in India, Parliament asserted its right not only to interfere in the affairs of the chartered East India Company at home, but to try to regulate its government of its Indian provinces. In the King's Speech in December 1782 the Commons was told that: 'The regulation of a vast territory in Asia opens a large field for your wisdom, prudence and foresight.'[40] By then Indian affairs had already been referred to committees of the House and one major statute, Lord North's Regulating Act of 1773, had been passed in an attempt to define relations between the state and the East India Company and to check what were thought to be abuses in the government of India. Another major statute for the same purposes, Pitt's India Act, was to be passed in 1784. From 1786 to 1795 the House of Commons and the House of Lords devoted a great deal of time to the prosecution of Warren Hastings, former Governor General. Burke, who promoted the prosecution, called it an act of 'imperial justice which you owe to the people that call to you from all parts of a great disjointed empire'.[41]

In its record of the events of 1791 the *Annual Register* for that year reported that: 'The attention of the British Parliament which guards with unceasing solicitude the interests of our widely extended dominions (dominions from which according to the old boast of the Spanish monarchy, the light of the sun may be said never to be withdrawn) was next attracted from our eastern to our western dominions.'[42] The article then went on to describe the third year of parliamentary investigations into the slave trade in response to a powerfully organised campaign spearheaded by William Wilberforce. There was of course nothing new about Parliament's concerning itself with trade, but large, if not yet decisive, votes for abolishing a very major commercial enterprise were breaking new ground. Wider implications were also being raised. If the institution of slavery were to be reformed, let alone abolished, the imperial Parliament would have to assert its authority over the West Indian Assemblies which had devised the slave codes. In a most unreal way Parliament was also presuming to exercise some authority over Africa itself. Petitions were inviting 'the legislature' to 'extend its protection to the Africans, the most injured and defenceless of our fellow creatures' by opening a 'friendly commercial intercourse' with Africa 'to introduce into it the comforts of social life and the advantages of true religion'.[43]

Parliament's frequent involvement with colonial affairs was certainly a reflection of the almost universally held belief that worldwide trade sustained Britain as a great power. But much that was said in the debates suggests that contemporaries believed that more than commercial success was at stake in the management of what they were coming to recognise as the British empire. Successful rebellion in the American colonies would shake the stability of the British Isles. The influx of ill-gotten Indian wealth could corrupt British society. The apparent injustices of the slave trade or of misrule in India would discredit Britain's good name, and, to the lively apprehensions of Evangelical Christians, would bring divine retribution. Conversely, a worldwide empire was a stage on which the British people could display those qualities, such as enterprise and vigour, benevolence or love of justice, with which the writer or speaker deemed it appropriate to endow them. Empire was a part of Britain's national identity, distinguishing it, for instance, from competitors like the Netherlands, whose concerns were thought to have remained narrowly commercial.[44]

For all the evidence for continuity throughout the eighteenth century, some things evidently did change and probably did so round about the time of the Seven Years War. New policies were certainly not devised, but there was a new determination to enforce old policies. More resources must be allocated to worldwide war and colonial prevarication could no longer be tolerated. Underlying this new determination seems to have been a new and much wider awareness of a world outside Europe, in the first place as a source of wealth and power through its trade, but secondly as including an empire which, however ill-defined it might be itself, gave definition to Britain. To see 'an imperialistic system of administration' coming into existence in the 1760s[45] is probably going further than the evidence warrants, but a new sense of empire seems clearly perceptible.

8

Religion in British Society 1740–1790

DAVID HEMPTON

IT HAS been unusually difficult for historians to offer satisfactory organising principles for the study of religion in eighteenth-century British society. One reason for that is that many of the dominant historiographical traditions of the eighteenth-century Church had their origins in the period of constitutional revolution between 1828 and 1835 when the terms under which the established churches in Britain operated were forever altered. The ideologues of the early Oxford Movement and enthusiastic evangelicals had much in common in decrying both the theory and practice of Whig erastianism which in their view had spiritually impoverished the Church by subjecting it to political manipulation through lay-controlled patronage. Similarly, both Nonconformists and anticlerical radicals had a vested interest in exposing establishment defects, especially those occasioned by excessive wealth and pastoral neglect. Even those as ideologically far apart as Irish Catholics and utilitarian radicals regarded the episcopal established churches of the eighteenth century as bulwarks of unmerited privileges enjoyed by the few against the legitimate interests of the many. Hence many treatments of religion in this period are dominated by either attacks or defences of established churches in which moral judgements often take the place of realistic assessments of how churches could be expected to operate in an eighteenth-century setting.

An equally important historiographical problem to be aware of is that assessments of the Church of England in particular often depend on whether a date of *c.* 1740 is chosen as the start or the end of a period of study. In the latter case it is appropriate to emphasise the ecclesiastical continuities with the Caroline past, the comparative weakness of religious Dissent in England, Scotland and Wales, and the relative decline of religion as a disruptive force in British politics. Conversely, although it is accepted that the establishment principle remained central to the *weltanschauung* of ruling elites until well into the nineteenth century, social historians of religion have detected forces operating from around the middle of the eighteenth century which were inexorably eroding established churches throughout the British Isles. These include rapid demographic growth, the commercialisation of agriculture, an increase in the pace of industrial and urban expansion, the rise of popular evangelicalism, the growing unacceptability, especially in Scotland, of the secular exercise of ecclesiastical patronage and the renewed vitality of older forms of both Protestant and Catholic Dissent. All these, it is held, undermined the social deference and dependency upon which established churches relied.[1] On a statistical level at least the impact of such changes is striking. Whereas in 1750 the established churches in Britain accounted for over 90 per cent of all churchgoers, the proportions had altered dramatically by the time of the census on public worship in 1851. By then Nonconformity was in the ascendancy in every census registration district in Wales; in Scotland the Established Church accounted for only one-third of all churchgoers – a decline unduly magnified by the disruption of 1843 – and in England Nonconformist churchgoers of all sorts made up approximately half the total.[2]

While accepting that statistics of churchgoing are not a very reliable guide to the social influence of established churches, it is clear that British society was considerably more pluralistic in 1850 than it had been a century before. It is equally clear, however, that the pace of religious change in the half century after 1790 was much more rapid than in the preceding fifty years and historians need to exercise care lest in explaining the remarkable growth in alternatives to established churches they exaggerate both the speed and the extent of their decline. The most dramatic change in the pattern of denominational adherence, for example, occurred in Wales, yet it seems probable that Welsh Nonconformity in its home county of Monmouthshire actually lost ground from 1700 to 1800. The real leap forward in Welsh Nonconformity took place in the first half of the nineteenth century.[3] A third historiographical problem confronting students of eighteenth-century religion is that until quite recently wide generalisations have been made about the state of the Church of England, for example, on the basis of a restricted range of local studies of dubious typicality.[4] As it is now clear that there were often enormous variations of belief and practice between neighbouring parishes within the same diocese and equally wide regional variations within the country as a whole, national projections from local studies need to be based on much wider samples than have customarily been the case. The recent upsurge of interest in eighteenth-century religion, manifested both in published works and in thesis literature, has made that task easier. The aim of this essay is to seek to offer some organising principles within which to view British religion in the second half of the eighteenth century and to highlight some of the period's most important continuities and changes.

One important aspect of recent work has been the renewed emphasis on the religious foundations of much political and social ideology in the eighteenth century. Both attacks and defences of established churches were based more on theological and historical frameworks of understanding than on principles of utility or natural rights. Moreover, it is becoming clear that the most intellectually influential ideas on the relationship between Church and State were not so much based on Locke and Warburton as on Hooker and Filmer. Far from being regarded as a protected subsidiary of the State, the Church of England was an integral and indispensable part of the theory and practice of governing. It was therefore 'the identity of sentiment between Church and State that most impressed contemporaries about the social and political attitudes of the Church in the last two decades of the eighteenth century'. The Church as a genuinely nationwide institution 'upheld the "natural" hierarchy of mutual obligations which were thought to provide social cohesion', and the state protected the legal establishment as the appropriate agent of benevolence and public morality.[5] Church and State were thus regarded as interdependent; if the one suffered damage so too did the other. In Burke's words the English regarded their church establishment 'as the foundation of their whole constitution with which, and with every part of which, it holds an indissoluble union'.[6] It must be stressed that such views were not the preserve of a coterie of High Churchmen, the intellectual vitality of whom should not be underestimated, but were the commonly accepted maxims of both governors and the governed in the late eighteenth century. Of course the foundations of such beliefs were repeatedly challenged, both theologically and politically, from the Deism of the early Hanoverian period and the radicalism of the 1760s to the more serious threats posed by the French Revolution in the 1790s, but they emerged, if anything, stronger than they were before. Some of the more radical figures within the Church either turned unitarian or were seen to be peripheral to the main body of Anglican opinion. Although their views have disproportionately interested historians, their achievements, at least in the short term, were negligible.

Part of the badge of loyalty to Church and State in the eighteenth century was devotion to monarchy and acceptance of the State's right to have a say in ecclesiastical appointments and preferments. Whereas the former, according to J. C. D. Clark, survived the dynastic vicissitudes of the early Hanoverian period to underpin the fundamental concept of a patriarchal society until well into the nineteenth century, the latter has been at the sharp edge of much of the criticism of the eighteenth-century Church. It is commonly alleged that the Whig exercise of patronage immeasurably weakened the spiritual vitality of the Church by subjecting it to political control and nepotism. In this area much heat is often generated by a view of patronage quite inappropriate to eighteenth-century circumstances. A recent study of ministerial patronage during the Newcastle years from 1742 to 1762, for example, has shown that patronage was not so much a tool of party as an instrument of government.[7] As the Church was recognised to have a vital role to play in the maintenance of social stability and state security, Newcastle's priority, in so far as power was delegated to him by the king, was to select men of pastoral and administrative ability who could be relied upon to support the Hanoverian regime and steer clear of political controversy. Moreover, it was well understood that no successful system of patronage could be based upon the long-term separation of reward from ability, since both patrons and protégés benefited from each other's success. Uppermost in Newcastle's mind then, when making ecclesiastical appointments, were neither theological nor parliamentary considerations, but rather the need to combine the reward of talent with the good governance of the nation. Here was a policy scarcely designed to enliven the Church's holy mission, but neither was it employed to create an army of political toadies responsive to the will of those in power.

A far more serious problem for the established churches in Britain than the exercise of ministerial patronage and political control was the way in which appointments to livings were made throughout the country. In England about half of all advowsons were in the hands of private patrons and pluralism rose in direct proportion to the number of livings owned by a layman. According to the most recent estimates 36 per cent of the Anglican clergy were pluralists in 1780 and only 38 per cent of parishes had resident incumbents.[8] Although there are wide regional variations there seems little doubt that pluralism was more extensive at the end of the eighteenth century than at the beginning. This was not a problem caused solely by lay impropriation and clerical poverty, because when there was a transfer of livings from the laity to the clergy in Norfolk in the period 1780–1830 pluralism did not decline. Moreover the richer English clergy were as non-resident and pluralistic as their poorer Welsh counterparts. Of course not all parishes without a resident incumbent were pastorally neglected and not all clerical pluralists were indulging in rich pickings, but it would be foolish to underestimate the deep-seated structural and administrative problems of the eighteenth-century Church. The reason they lasted so long is not entirely attributable to the difficulties of reforming such a cumbersome institution; the fact of the matter is that neither wealthy laymen nor bishops had any great desire to alter a system from which they benefited. Perhaps the ultimate proof of the centrality of the Church in the eighteenth-century state is the reluctance of those in authority to tamper with it. In Scotland in the same period the exercise of patronage was both more contentious and more divisive. In the period 1750–80 there was a steady stream of secessions from the Church of Scotland – mainly in Lowland rural parishes – over patronage disputes. The failure to resolve this problem, combined with the resurgence of evangelicalism, led to even greater problems in the nineteenth century.

The criticism that the eighteenth-century Church suffered from the iron grip of Whig patronage has often gone hand in hand with the view that the Church's wealth and resources were inappropriately directed to the tasks confronting it. There is, of course, no shortage of material to support such claims whether one looks at income distribution within the Church, the utilisation of clerical manpower or the growing disparities occasioned by rapid demographic change within a relatively static parish system. Not only did the Church inherit many of its most intractable problems from the past, but by the end of the eighteenth century it had to accommodate social and economic changes of unprecedented magnitude. The Church was therefore not an easy institution for its bishops to manage. Recent studies of the early Georgian episcopate have largely exonerated the bishops from allegations of fabulous wealth and ruthless exploitation of their ecclesiastical estates.[9] Some sees were of course exceptionally wealthy, but the majority sustained a comfortable rather than exotic lifestyle. In the period after 1760 rising land values did bring about a remarkable increase in the landed income of the Church and there were more bishops with aristocratic connections. The real weakness of the Hanoverian episcopate, however, has less to do with unacceptable wealth and erastian dependency as on more prosaic structural and administrative problems. Most prelates were appointed late in life, had limited administrative experience, were required to spend much of their time in London, presided over dioceses of irregular size and poor communications, and held their jobs until death regardless of incapacitating infirmities. Without a powerful reforming stimulus from outside such conditions were unlikely to give rise to dynamic leadership.

Below episcopal level the social structure of the Church, as with the wider society, resembled a pyramid with a broad base. At the beginning of the eighteenth century around half of Anglican livings were worth less than £50 a year and the salaries of stipendiary curates were notoriously inadequate. Detailed studies of the diocese of London and elsewhere have shown that there was a decline of unacceptably poor livings in the first half of the century due largely to the effects of Queen Anne's Bounty which in modern parlance was a successful marriage of public and private capital.[10] But the results were regionally uneven with Wales and the East of England benefiting less than the Midlands and the North, and most of the gains were made before 1750 and after 1800. Money alone, however, is not an adequate measure of the life and conditions of humble Hanoverian curates. As Peter Virgin has shown, out of every hundred men ordained in late Georgian England a fifth never held a benefice, a quarter died young, emigrated or went into teaching, and over a third took more than six years to find a living. Only a well-connected minority, a fifth of the total, found a benefice within five years of ordination.[11] Moreover, as is the case with all major employers in all periods, the eighteenth-century Church found it difficult to achieve a perfect balance of supply and demand. There was probably an undersupply of clergy in the middle decades of the century and an oversupply in the early nineteenth century. The former inevitably fuelled pluralism and the latter further exposed weaknesses in the Church's career structure. Most of the stresses and strains associated with such problems had to be absorbed by those at the bottom of the pile, the stipendiary and assistant curates. Stipends in the late eighteenth century were less generous than Sykes supposed, especially in the poorer dioceses of the North and Wales and were not substantially improved until after the Stipendiary Curates Act of 1813. For the most part these worker bees of the eighteenth-century Church lived a life of peripatetic poverty with few incentives, little supervision, an absence of like-minded company and an element of rural boredom. The vast majority dutifully performed the tasks required of them, which were mainly the conduct of services and other Anglican formularies, but only an enthusiastic minority devoted themselves to a more wide-ranging pastoral ministry. As with their much wealthier bishops, therefore, such deficiencies as there were among stipendiary curates were not so much caused by excessive moral and theological inadequacy as by deep-seated structural and economic deficiencies at the heart of the Established Church. In the eighteenth century the forces, including self-interest and complacency, operating against effective reform were stronger than those on the other side, and those who grappled with ecclesiastical reform in the early nineteenth century soon appreciated the very considerable obstacles in the way.

It would be misleading, however, to give the impression that the Church of England in the second half of the eighteenth century was suffering from undue economic hardship for there is much evidence to the contrary. Many clerics, especially in central and eastern counties, benefited from the widespread tithe commutation for land associated with enclosure between 1750 and 1830. Many incumbents in areas of new enclosure became substantial farmers as their average glebe size more than doubled and a new phase of parsonage building got under way. Thus, according to W. R. Ward, 'at the very time when churches within reach of revolutionary France were losing property wholesale, the Church of England was gaining it on a considerable scale throughout the midlands and the east'.[12] Similarly, a pilot study of the occupations of younger sons in the peerage, baronetage and landed gentry carried out by F. M. L. Thompson has shown that the Church was the most common identifiable career choice in the second half of the eighteenth century.[13] It seems likely that for a variety of reasons the Church of England was a more desirable occupation for younger sons after 1740 than it had been in Walpole's England. The rise in the social status of clergy benefiting from structural changes in the English countryside was reflected also in the remarkable increase in the proportion of clerical magistrates during the reign of George III. The most recent estimate is that clerical membership of the rural magistracy trebled in the three-quarters of a century after 1761 and there is a rough correlation between counties in which tithe commutation for land was most prevalent and those with the highest proportion of clerical magistrates.[14] There were many even within the Church itself who recognised that the pastoral and judicial responsibilities of the clergy were not entirely compatible.

Before assessing the implications of such developments on the position of the Church in the English countryside it is appropriate to introduce a few cautionary remarks. In the first place there are considerable regional and chronological variations which need to be taken into account. In Derbyshire, for example, it seems that the benefits of tithe commutation for land were passed on to tenants in the form of twenty-one year leases at fixed rents. In other counties of ancient enclosure and small glebes such as Cheshire the growing weakness of the Church of England towards the end of the eighteenth century is not primarily attributable to the rising social status of the clergy, who were in any case a far from homogeneous social group in any county at any period in the eighteenth century.[15] Only a minority of Anglican clergy were wealthy and well connected, only a minority were pluralists or magistrates and only a minority were vigorous and insensitive tithe litigants. Moreover, several local studies have shown that wise use of patronage and clerical zeal could substantially improve the fortunes of the Church in areas where the social and economic structure have been traditionally regarded as antithetical to Anglican success.[16] But even with all the necessary qualifications there seems little doubt that the rising social status of many incumbents, especially in areas of new enclosure, did nothing for the pastoral efficiency of the Church in a period when social and religious deference was by no means unconditional. It has been suggested, for example, that the combination of enclosures, tithe collection and clerical magistrates led to more overt anti-clericalism in rural England in this period than at any time since the Interregnum.[17] Similarly, Ward has stated that the real tragedy for the Church in this period was not so much that 'industrialisation concentrated people where her endowments, manpower and accommodation were thinly spread, but that things went so badly where her resources were concentrated'.[18] All was not well, therefore, in the rural heartlands of the established Church long before manufacturing and urban growth posed new problems of control for a parish system which the Georgian Church admired far too uncritically. As has been pointed out, the real problem with parishes by the late eighteenth century is that they did not easily accommodate social change on a large scale without major restructuring. As a result the failure of the Established Church to expand from its old parish centres cost it dear in parts of the country beginning to experience economic and demographic change.[19] In such circumstances Anglican neglect probably counted for more than social protest in the expansion of Nonconformity.

Turning aside from the structural problems of the Hanoverian Church to the performance of its duties, much of the recent historical writing has been kinder to the Church of England than once was the case. F. C. Mather, for example, has shown that north and west of a line from Portland Bill to the Tees the performance of two services on a Sunday was the rule, not the exception, especially in upland areas.[20] The same is true of market towns and well-populated parishes, whereas 'single duty' was more common in the lowlands of southern and eastern England where pluralism and non-residence militated against the frequency of services. A similar pattern exists for the holding of weekday services and the celebration of Communion. Although weekly Communion was rare outside some of the great city churches, and although quarterly Communion was probably close to the average in the country as a whole, many of the more populous parishes in town and country celebrated Communion more regularly than four times a year. Attendances at Communion services were nevertheless low partly due to apathy and puritan anti-sacramentalism, but also due to the timing of services and a genuine fear of incurring personal judgement by profaning the ordinance. In a study of Restoration Wiltshire, for example, Donald Spaeth has shown that some preferred to wait until old age to lessen the risk of spoiling their devotion with subsequent sin.[21] The poor were also less likely to receive Communion than the more wealthy, and it would be interesting to know if these patterns are capable of a wider geographical and chronological application. In the meantime the three most important points to be made about the public worship of the Church of England in the eighteenth century are that paradoxically the Church was at its most diligent in those areas, including the North and Wales, where its large parishes and dispersed settlements made it pastorally vulnerable to evangelical Nonconformity. Secondly, what emerges from the welter of statistics on all aspects of public worship in this period is the sheer diversity of church life in eighteenth-century England. Finally, it is clearly inappropriate to measure the religious and social influence of the established Church in terms of frequency of services, churchgoing, figures and numbers of communicants, though there is patchy evidence to suggest that all three were in decline during the course of the eighteenth century before signs of improvement can be detected in some dioceses by around 1800.

While statistics alone may not be a very useful guide to the popular religious beliefs and practices of the eighteenth-century laity, finding alternative organising principles that do justice to the complexity of the subject is not easy. There is moreover a thinner vein of historiography to draw upon than there is for both the seventeenth and nineteenth centuries, while the ideological differences among historians are just as sharp. Edward Thompson, for example, is of the opinion that the Church was both instigator and victim of the increasing gap between patrician and plebeian cultures in the eighteenth century and consequently lost control of the ritualistic and leisure activities of the poor.[22] The sheer erastianism of the Church prevented it from exercising an effective paternalist influence over the mass of the people and left the door open for groups such as the Methodists to offer a more compelling alternative. Conversely, Jonathan Clark has suggested that the ideological centrality of Anglicanism in the Hanoverian state penetrated more deeply into the population as a whole than many suppose. Not only was the divine right of kings embedded in popular consciousness by religious celebrations of royal anniversaries and the persistence of belief in the healing powers of monarchs, but the Church was intimately involved in the life of the community through its uncontested monopoly over the rites of passage, its provision of welfare and education, its widespread distribution of popular forms of religious literature and its thorough identification with the political, legal and social institutions of the state both at the centre and in the localities.[23] Thus, the Church was not simply the religious arm of the state, but rather offered a framework of loyalty and allegiance within which other activities had their meaning. This debate is probably not resolvable in the terms within which it has been presented and it therefore seems more profitable to concentrate on those areas amplified by recent work. It is clear, for example, that the eighteenth-century Church enjoyed a high level of conformity, a low level of attendance, an even lower participation in Communion and yet was widely, almost universally, used for baptism, confirmation, marriage and burials. It is equally clear that religion, however that is to be defined, played an important part in the celebratory rhythms of the state and of the local customs associated with the agricultural calendar. In the Rogation week perambulations of the parish, for example, Bob Bushaway suggests that the Church helped underpin for the labouring poor 'the geographical basis of the community as a ceremonial unit' and 'reaffirmed an older economic and social structure'.[24] Moreover, to say that much popular celebration was impious and bawdlerised is not to deny the symbolic importance of the Church or the central role occupied by many clergymen in village festivities. Similarly, to conclude that Christian ceremonies were relatively less important as religious occasions than as social events is to introduce an unhelpful distinction into the function of religion in eighteenth-century communities. There is no denying the fact, however, that the religious content in rituals and ceremonies declined towards the end of the eighteenth century, particularly in the towns. Another method historians have used to uncover the religious beliefs and practices of the lower orders has been to investigate the various forms of cheap literature in common circulation. The results of such enquiries are predictably ambiguous. There is no doubt that the Church, through the distribution of catechisms, tracts and manuals, and devotional and prayer aids made a more serious attempt to communicate with the poor than was once supposed. Moreover, as one would expect, there is a continuation of religious chapbook literature with a strong emphasis on prophecies, judgements, signs and wonders. But much chapbook literature was concerned more with popular entertainment than with piety. There is therefore a romantic, irreverent and disrespectful tone to much of this genre which Hannah More's Cheap Repository Tracts set out to counteract. Ironically her best selling tracts were also the most sensational. What the various surveys of popular literature in the early modern period have shown is that, not surprisingly, there was a wide range of material to suit a wide range of tastes.[25] The reading materials of the poor, no less than their rituals and festivals, show a breadth of meaning and experience which crude divisions into two broad categories, whether based on social class or level of religious commitment, can never hope to encapsulate. Most communities in the eighteenth century, as with the seventeenth, contained a minority of the truly pious, some completely indifferent, and a great many more who professed what has been called an 'unspectacular orthodoxy', which was flexible enough to accommodate life-cycle changes and eclectic enough to serve a variety of religious and social functions. Such popular devotion as there was to Anglicanism in the eighteenth century was, therefore, a delicate mixture of social utility, rural entertainment and moral consensus in which the parish church and all its associated values was closely enmeshed, albeit within certain defined limits set by the community. It is possible also to demonstrate the influence of Anglicanism on popular music-making, health and healing, law and public morality and even on the common usage of language itself. None of this is to deny the importance of what historians have inadequately described as 'pagan' and 'superstitious' elements in popular religion or to minimise the profound gap which often existed between clerical expectations and popular practices, but no treatment of religion in eighteenth-century communities can afford to underestimate the centrality of church and religion in the social life of the parish.

So far the emphasis has been chiefly on established religion and on the continuities with the past evident from the importance of Anglican ideology, its persistent structural problems and the nature of popular religion. But arguably one of the great discontinuities of eighteenth-century religion is the evangelical revival which began to make some headway in all parts of the British Isles from the 1730s. While many have demonstrated that evangelicalism in general and Methodism in particular had roots in the old High Church tradition, in puritanism and in the Anglican religious societies that were common in London and provincial market towns at the beginning of the eighteenth century, and while others have interpreted the growth of evangelical religion as a reaction against erastianism, latitudinarianism, deism and economic disorder, much of the recent work has taken a rather different approach. Most striking has been the renewed emphasis on the international dimensions of pietism and revivalism which has shown that the British experience was neither unique nor isolated from wider currents in European and American Protestantism. Not only has it been shown that many of the distinctive organisational characteristics of Methodism, including itinerant preaching, class meetings and love feasts, were common among the persecuted and displaced Protestant minorities of Habsburg-dominated Central Europe, but it is now clear that there were more personal contacts between popular evangelicals across national frontiers than was once supposed.[26] This research has not solved the mystery of how it was that so many evangelicals in different parts of England and Wales in the 1730s and 1740s began to preach the same kind of message independently of one another, but it does confirm that popular evangelicalism was not the mere product of a particular set of social and economic circumstances, and that religious cultures, once established, have an internal dynamic of their own. The cruder forms of economic reductionism in explaining the origins and growth of evangelicalism now seem redundant.

Placing the rise of evangelicalism in the early Hanoverian period within a wider international setting should not detract from some of its more novel characteristics in terms of the British religious tradition. Methodist societies, for example, can be distinguished from the early eighteenth-century Anglican societies by their organisation into a connectional system as distinct from a group of independent cells, their use of itinerant and lay preachers, their openness to men and women of all denominations and their sheer pragmatism in devising new forms of religious expression suitable to the plebeian members they recruited. Here was an associational and voluntaryist form of religion which was a direct challenge to the confessional and territorial model of a state church.[27] Wesley did not of course view this challenge in political or social terms, neither was he prepared to allow his societies to drift into the Dissenting camp, but his desire to shelter under the umbrella of the Church of England while developing a religious community with its own style and structure became one of the most vexed ecclesiastical and legal problems of the half century after 1740.[28] The fact that English law, despite its long experience in dealing with religious deviance, was unable both in theory and in practice to establish coherent guidelines for application to the manifold disputes occasioned by Methodist expansion is itself proof of the novelty of the Methodist system. A different kind of novelty has been explored recently by D. W. Bebbington in his attempt to explain why the origins of the evangelical revival in the English-speaking world can be dated so precisely to the 1730s. For him the essential novel ingredient was the change in the high cultural environment produced by the Enlightenment emphasis on empiricism. In particular, it was 'Wesley's application of an empiricist philosophy to religious experience' – his emphasis on a person's ability to *know* and *experience* salvation – that led to an evangelical doctrine of assurance essentially different from what came before.[29] Bebbington's excellent work now stands in a vibrant new tradition of scholarship on the evangelical revival which has sought to demonstrate that evangelicalism was more of a product of the Enlightenment than an enthusiastic reaction against it. One welcome by-product of this work has been to rescue Methodist and evangelical theology from the bland dismissals conferred upon it by Norman Sykes and others writing within the broad Anglican tradition, but there is a danger of going too far in the opposite direction. The Methodism that is brought to life in the correspondence of Bishop Lavington from Cornwall in the 1740s or in the legal records of quarter sessions and church courts in different parts of the country throughout the period is an altogether more earthy, rumbustious and colourful phenomenon than is discoverable from erudite theological discussion.[30] Thus, it is by no means clear that the religious motivation of those 'mean illiterate tinners' complained of by Cornish magistrates in the 1740s or the 'prophetic sons and daughters' brought to life by Deborah Valenze at the end of the century is explicable any more within an Enlightenment framework than it is within economic categories.[31]

Turning from the origins of evangelicalism to its progress and development during the eighteenth century, one of the difficulties in assessing its strength is the fact that it flowed through many denominational tributaries apart from Methodism itself. The Church of England had an influential coterie of evangelicals who employed Methodist forms but repudiated what they considered to be Wesley's separatist tendencies. English orthodox Dissent, which had grown slowly but steadily from its nadir

in the 1730s, was influenced by Whitefield's calvinistic Methodism and Doddridge's patient mediation, but it was not until the
last two decades of the century, with the employment of
itinerant preachers and the formation of county associations,
that evangelicalism made substantial headway.[32] Thereafter the
speed of evangelical nonconformist growth in England and
Wales in the early nineteenth century is one of the most
remarkable features of British social history. In Scotland, as in
the Presbyterian settlements of Ulster, Methodism did not
make much of an impact, despite some early gains in the 1740s
and 1750s. There was, however, a strong evangelical presence
in the Established Church of Scotland which led to conflict
between the so-called Moderate and Popular parties and resulted in a stream of secessions in the late eighteenth century.
According to one recent survey the growth of evangelicalism in
Scotland was 'simultaneous in timing to the rise of evangelicalism and Methodism in England and bore strong similarities in
social appeal and religious temper'.[33] Thus, most of the support
for evangelicalism seems to have come from the new entre-
preneurial classes and from the lower orders who were experiencing profound social changes as a result of structural
changes in the Scottish economy. By the end of the eighteenth
century, therefore, a predominantly evangelical Presbyterian
Dissent had established a firm foothold in many Scottish towns
and cities.

In England the geographical distribution and social constituency of popular evangelicalism have been subjected to rigor-
ous scrutiny. By the end of the eighteenth century Methodism
had been particularly successful in the small-scale manufacturing districts of the North-East, the north Midlands, the West
Riding and the Potteries. It was strong too in mining areas,
especially Cornwall, in seaports and fishing villages, and in
those rural areas where gentry and clerical control was at its
weakest or was most resented. In terms of social status a
number of occupational surveys of Methodism from different
parts of the country have drawn attention to the preponderance
of skilled artisans – admittedly a broad category of jobs and
wage levels – semi-skilled workers and servants.[34] Conversely,
both the gentry and the labouring poor were under-represented
by comparison with the population as a whole. More strikingly,

almost all statistical surveys have shown a high ratio of women to men, a substantial proportion of whom were unmarried or widowed. One important point rarely made in the occupational surveys of Methodism, however, is that although certain social groups such as skilled artisans are over-represented in relation to figures for the country as a whole, the occupational profile of evangelical Nonconformity often closely parallels that of the communities in which it took root. Hence the work that has been done on the textile districts of the West Riding has shown a high preponderance of spinners and weavers in Methodist societies and similar conclusions have been reached in communities with a different kind of occupational structure. The point is that popular evangelicalism was not so much a religion of a particular social group as the beneficiary of the pastoral inadequacy of the Established Church in those geographical areas where demographic and manufacturing growth exposed serious weaknesses in the Church's parochial structure. In some parts of the country such as Lincolnshire, for example, the rise of popular evangelicalism was associated with an element of protest against a whole system of social values represented by Anglicanism, while in other areas the desire to create a more lively and pastorally efficient form of religion was the more important motive. Perhaps the time has arrived, therefore, for historians to spend more time on the motives of those itinerants and class members who were ultimately responsible for the growth of popular evangelicalism than in delineating the social and economic framework within which such growth took place. The one is not complete without the other.

Popular evangelicalism, especially of the Methodist variety, was not the only religious challenge to the stability and dominance of established churches in the second half of the eighteenth century. By 1790 it seems probable that there were slightly more Roman Catholics in Britain than members of Methodist societies, though comparisons are invidious because of widely different tests of membership and levels of commitment. Estimates of the total Catholic population in Hanoverian Britain are notoriously hard to make, but according to John Bossy numbers began to rise from about 1720 after a century of equilibrium and began to accelerate even faster from about

1770.[35] The areas with the highest density of Catholics were Monmouthshire, Lancashire, Durham and a narrow band across the Highlands and islands of northern Scotland, but there were also appreciable numbers in many English counties as far apart as Northumberland and Hampshire. The most important change in the internal structure of the Catholic community in the modern period was caused by the impact of mass immigration from Ireland, but this did not gather pace until the end of the century. Before that there is evidence from several local studies to suggest that the English Catholic community was already changing quite rapidly because of its disproportionate concentration in those parts of the country most affected by economic and social changes. Thus, by the end of the century probably a higher proportion of Catholics were engaged in non-agricultural occupations than the population as a whole and the consequent weakening of landlord control within Catholicism enabled the clergy to extend their influence. Certainly Bossy's estimate of a threefold increase in Catholic numbers in the four Lancashire towns of Manchester, Liverpool, Preston and Wigan in the period 1783–1800 is quite striking. A chronic shortage of funds and sometimes of manpower prevented the Catholic Church from fully realising the potential of its growing urban congregations.

With Catholic numbers still relatively small and with penal statutes either unenforced or gradually repealed the eighteenth century has been traditionally regarded as an oasis of tranquillity between the vigorous anti-Catholicism of the seventeenth century and its recrudescence in the early Victorian period. The Gordon Riots of 1780 are an acknowledged exception, but by concentrating on the metropolitan epicentre of the riots and by discovering elements of class hostility in them it was possible to suggest that they were not attributable to a bedrock of anti-Catholicism anything like as powerful as that which existed in the previous century. More recent work on the popular world view of eighteenth-century Englishmen, from a wide range of different sources and perspectives, has drawn attention to a strong continuity of anti-Catholicism from the seventeenth century. Not only were there more widespread no popery disturbances in English provinces in 1745 and 1780 than was previously thought, but anti-Catholicism remained a strong element in the traditional beliefs and moral economy of the English lower orders throughout the period.[36] It is remarkable, for example, how often early Methodism was attacked for its alleged popish beliefs and practices. Thus, fear of religious novelty, chauvinistic notions of liberty, anti-French feeling and vivid ritualistic celebrations of England's Protestant past all contributed to a profound distrust of Roman Catholicism. This mental framework was rarely channelled into active hostility against Roman Catholic neighbours unless fuelled by wider dynastic or political crises. What is different about the anti-Catholicism of the later eighteenth century, however, is that among social elites, including those responsible for government, it was increasingly recognised that the English Catholic community was a relatively harmless minority worthy of a greater degree of religious toleration. This difference in perception between social superiors and the bulk of the English population, as much as anything, accounts for the events leading up to the Gordon Riots. A similar pattern continued into the nineteenth century when the Catholic Emancipation Act was passed, against the wishes of the great majority of the English people.

The growth in the number of Methodists and Roman Catholics in the second half of the eighteenth century is paralleled by the growth of Old Dissent from its base level in the 1730s. It has been estimated, for example, that the number of Independents and Particular Baptists more than doubled in the period 1750–1800 and this growth was sustained well into the nineteenth century. Although much of this growth has been explained by the influence of evangelicalism, particularly calvinistic Methodism, Old Dissent had its own traditions of itinerancy and evangelism upon which to draw, and the evangelical revival by no means obliterated denominational distinctions in the late eighteenth century. Evangelicalism influenced, but did not entirely transform, the theology, religious practices and politics of the old Dissenting tradition. Much of the historical interest in that tradition in the second half of the century has been focused on its political characteristics. The idea that religious Dissent in this period was important in the evolution of British radicalism is not new, but it was restated with characteristic boldness by Jonathan Clark in his book

English Society 1688–1832. He states that the intellectual structure of the arguments against the established social and political order – anachronistically called radicalism by historians – was ultimately based on theological, not social and economic, principles. Thus, whether one looks at Wilkes or Paine, or Price and Priestley, or even those Anglicans who drifted into Unitarianism after the failure in 1772 of the Feather's Tavern petition against subscription to the Thirty-Nine Articles, the common denominator is that religious heterodoxy was the intellectual foundation of their critique of Church and State.[37] Although his work is a timely corrective to some trends in the historiography of late eighteenth-century radicalism, Clark's analysis, of necessity, does not penetrate very far into the Dissenting community itself. Here the picture is rather more complex and still far from complete. Many Dissenters were of course not much interested in politics and if they were the chances are that their energies were more concentrated on local struggles for power in the boroughs than in campaigns for parliamentary reform or repeal of the Test and Corporation Acts.[38] Moreover, those so-called rational Dissenters who formed cohesive chapel elites in the major commercial centres of the country were neither representative of Dissent as a whole nor rigidly excluded from the political structures of the towns they helped to build.[39] It was possible for them, as with many Methodists, to be upset on occasions by the niggardly limits of religious toleration under the Toleration Act without necessarily capitulating to an all-out attack on Church and State. Many no doubt became more emboldened in the late 1780s when it seemed that political events in England and France were going their way, but a combination of Pitt's policies and Church and King mobs soon dampened their ardour. Rational Dissenters suffered the same kind of fate in the 1790s as did the low church liberals within the Established Church, as the forces of reaction made ground in all the major British religious traditions.[40] Only in the Celtic fringes, and especially in Ireland, was religious deviance a serious threat to the stability of the Hanoverian state. To take this view is not to deny the importance of civic rivalry in the provincial towns of eighteenth-century England, where there was a surge of both Anglican and Dissenting church building in the second half of the century which helped attract a more ambitious and talented clergy. In a number of such towns religious divisions inevitably shaded off into political and administrative divisions, making it virtually impossible for the parish to function as a 'credible single focus for communal religious solidarity'.[41] This, of course, had long-term implications for the future development of social and political structures in English towns and cities.

Any search for organising principles in the religious history of this period must begin with the importance of established churches throughout the British Isles. It is possible to take a high view of their social, ideological and political significance without being blind to their structural and pastoral limitations. By 1790 the established churches, with the notable exception of Ireland, were the only religious institutions which could claim a genuinely national coverage. Dissenting denominations, though making ground, were generally located within fairly limited geographical areas. It is also possible to suggest that the social and religious influence of established churches penetrated right down the social scale, without minimising the gap between clerical expectations and popular behaviour evident, for example, in the high illegitimacy rates throughout the period. The established churches in the eighteenth century nevertheless enjoyed less coercive power than in the seventeenth century as the boundaries of religious toleration were inexorably widened at the same time as church courts began to decline, albeit at a slower rate in Scotland than in England. It is also possible to emphasise major continuities with the past in the complex mosaic of popular belief and practice, the survival of anti-Catholicism, and in the theology and devotions of the broad Anglican, Presbyterian and Catholic traditions without denying the importance of demographic and economic changes on the one hand and the rise of evangelicalism on the other in helping to undermine the old denominational order. Finally, in explaining the processes of religious change it is possible to contend for the importance of theology and religious motivation without denigrating the importance of structural changes of a social and economic kind. In the same way that many ecclesiastical myths were created in the heat of religious controversy in the 1820s and 30s, the inability to hold apparently contradictory ideas in a creative tension has limited the value of otherwise excellent work in more recent times.

List of Abbreviations

Add.	Additional Manuscripts
AE CP Ang.	Paris, Archives du Ministère des Affaires Etrangères, Correspondance Politique, Angleterre
AST LM Ing.	Turin, Archivio di Stato, Lettere Ministri, Inghilterra
BL	London, British Library
Bod.	Oxford, Bodleian Library, Department of Western Manuscripts
Cobbett	W. Cobbett, *Parliamentary History of England* (36 vols, London, 1806–20)
CRO	County Record Office
Farmington, Weston	Farmington, Connecticut, Lewis Walpole Library, Weston papers
HL	San Marino, California, Huntington Library
MO	Montagu papers
NeC	Nottingham, University Library, Clumber papers
PRO	London, Public Record Office
RA CP	Windsor, Royal Archives, Cumberland papers
SP	State Papers
STG	Stowe manuscripts
WW	Sheffield, City Library, Wentworth Woodhouse Mss

Bibliography

The place of publication is London unless otherwise stated.

INTRODUCTION

FOR reasons of space I have not referred to works mentioned in the bibliographies of other essays or the notes to this or other essays. Possibly the best approach to the period is by a careful reading of sources. There are several collections including D. B. Horn and M. Ransome (eds), *English Historical Documents, 1714–1783* (1957), A. Aspinall and E. A. Smith (eds), *English Historical Documents, 1783–1832* (1959) and E. N. Williams, *The Eighteenth-Century Constitution* (Cambridge, 1960). Parliamentary debates can be found in W. Cobbett, *A Parliamentary History of England* (1806–20). Printed correspondence tends to concentrate on political matters, especially the relevant volumes of the Historical Manuscript Commission reports and such collections as W. S. Taylor and J. H. Pringle (eds), *The Correspondence of William Pitt* (1838–40), Lord John Russell (ed.), *The Correspondence of John, Fourth Duke of Bedford* (1842–6), W. J. Smith (ed.), *The Grenville Papers* (1852–3) and Lord Edmond Fitzmaurice (ed.), *The Life of William, Earl of Shelburne* (1875–6). Unlike George II, who also still lacks a scholarly biography, there is a mass of George III's correspondence surviving: Sir John Fortescue (ed.), *The Correspondence of King George the Third 1760–1783* (1927) which, however, contains numerous errors; R. Sedgwick (ed.), *Letters from George III to Lord Bute, 1756–1766* (1939); and A. Aspinall (ed.), *The Later Correspondence of George III, I, 1783–93* (Cambridge, 1962). Recent editions include W. S. Lewis (ed.), *The Yale Edition of Horace Walpole's Correspondence* (New Haven, 1937–83); T. J. McCann (ed.), *The Correspondence of The Dukes of Richmond and Newcastle 1724–1750* (Lewes, 1984); J. Brooke (ed.), *Horace Walpole. Memoirs of King George II* (New Haven, 1985); and J. C. D. Clark (ed.), *The Memoirs and Speeches of James, 2nd Earl Waldegrave 1742–1763* (Cambridge, 1988). There is a mass of writing on ecclesiastical and religious matters, including J. Wesley, *Journal* (1904).

Less luminous individuals also left accounts, such as *The Diary of Abigail Gawthern of Nottingham 1751–1810* (Nottingham, 1980); D. Vaisey (ed.), *The Diary of Thomas Turner of East Hoathley, 1754–65* (Oxford, 1985); and J. Beresford (ed.), James Woodforde, *The Diary of a Country Parson 1758–1802* (Oxford, 1924–31). J. D. Marshall (ed.), *The Autobiography of William Stout of Lancaster 1669–1752* (Manchester, 1967) contains much of economic interest. An account closely based on the surviving accounts of a shopkeeper a little higher up the ladder of enterprise than Thomas Turner is T. S. Willan, *An Eighteenth-Century Shopkeeper. Abraham Dent of Kirkby Stephen* (Manchester, 1970).

The accounts of foreign travellers to Britain are of considerable interest. They include Casanova, *Memoirs* (1940); P. Kalm, *Account of a Visit to England* (New York, 1892); and F. de la Rochefoucauld, *A Frenchman in England, 1784*, translated by S. C. Roberts (Cambridge, 1933), and by N. Scarfe in *A Frenchman's Year in Suffolk, 1784* (Woodbridge, 1989). Different views are presented in the series, *The English Satirical Print 1600–1832*, ed. M. Duffy (Cambridge, 1986). Newspapers of the period are available in the reference departments of many central libraries, including those of Bristol, Carlisle, Gloucester, Leeds, Newcastle, Norwich, Reading and Sheffield. Modern editions include J. P. Hardy (ed.), *Political Writings of Dr. Johnson* (1968); J. Cannon (ed.), *The Letters of Junius* (Oxford, 1978); W. B. Coley (ed.), *Henry Fielding. The True Patriot and Related Writings* (Oxford, 1987); and B. A. Goldgar (ed.), *Henry Fielding. The Covent Garden Journal* (Oxford, 1988). Contemporary literature is of great value: pamphlets, magazines, plays, poetry and novels, the works of Fielding, Foote, Johnson, Richardson, Sheridan, Smollett and Sterne. Most of the major works are available in modern paperback editions and there are also scholarly editions, for example the Wesleyan edition of the works of Fielding. Collected editions, such as D. Greene (ed.), *Samuel Johnson* (Oxford, 1984), are also useful.

S. Pargellis and D. J. Medley, *Bibliography of British History. The Eighteenth Century, 1714–1789* (Oxford, 1951) covers little published after 1939. It should be supplemented by the series *Writings on British History*, by the *Annual Bulletin of Historical Literature* published by the Historical Association, by the *Annual Bibliography of British and Irish History* published under the auspices of the Royal Historical Society, by R. A. Smith, *Late Georgian and Regency England 1760–1837* (Cambridge, 1984) and W. H. Chaloner and R. C. Richardson, *A Bibliography of British Economic and Social History* (2nd edn, Manchester, 1984).

Lists of earlier works can be found in the bibliographies of P. Langford, *A Polite and Commercial Society. England 1727–83* (Oxford, 1989) and R. Porter, *English Society in the Eighteenth Century* (2nd edn, 1990). J. C. D. Clark, 'English History's Forgotten Context: Scotland, Ireland, Wales', *Historical Journal* (1989) is an important discussion of the British dimension, while S. Taylor, 'Church and Society after the Glorious Revolution', *Historical Journal* (1988) is a useful recent review article. British developments are set in a European context in J. Black, *Europe in the Eighteenth Century, 1700–89* (1990).

1. ENGLISH SOCIETY IN THE EIGHTEENTH CENTURY REVISITED

Good up-to-date broad surveys of Georgian society include J. A. Sharpe, *Early Modern England. A Social History 1550–1760* (1987), and Trevor May, *An Economic and Social History of Britain, 1760–1970* (1987). See also the second, revised edition of Roy Porter, *English Society in the Eighteenth Century* (1990), which attempts a general introduction to questions of social structure, order and change.

The definitive discussion of population change is E. A. Wrigley and R. S. Schofield, *The Population History of England, 1541–1871* (1981). Easily the freshest reassessment of the economic developments of the century is Maxine Berg, *The Age of Manufactures, 1700–1820* (1985).

Certain social ranks have been well served by historians. See John Cannon, *Aristocratic Century: The Peerage of Eighteenth Century England* (Cambridge, 1984); J. V. Beckett, *The Aristocracy in England, 1660–1914* (Oxford, 1986); Peter Earle, *The Making of the English Middle Class: Business, Society and Family Life in London, 1660–1730* (1989). There is no really satisfactory modern book on the lower orders as a whole, though see Keith Snell, *Annals of the Labouring Poor:*

Social Change in Agrarian England, 1660–1900 (Cambridge, 1985); J. Rule, *The Experience of Labour in Eighteenth Century Industry* (1981); and R. Glen, *Urban Workers in the Early Industrial Revolution* (1984). A lively account of the cultural interaction of different classes is offered in J. M. Golby and A. W. Purdue, *The Civilization of the Crowd: Popular Culture in England, 1750–1900* (1984).

As this essay has argued, it is vital that social history is not cordoned off from political history. Distinctive visions of the interplay of the social and the political are offered in J. C. D. Clark, *English Society, 1688–1832: Ideology, Social Structure and Political Practice During the Ancien Régime* (Cambridge, 1985), and his *Revolution and Rebellion. State and Society in England in the Seventeenth and Eighteenth Centuries* (Cambridge, 1986); in John Brewer, *The Sinews of Power* (1989); and in P. Corrigan and D. Sayer, *The Great Arch: English State Formation as Cultural Revolution* (Oxford, 1985).

Much of the most exciting research over the last decade has sought to integrate demographic, economic and family history within a wider social history. Admirable instances of this are Peter Mathias, *The Transformation of England* (New York, 1979); N. McKendrick, John Brewer and J. H. Plumb, *The Birth of a Consumer Society: The Commercialization of Eighteenth-Century England* (1982); E. A. Wrigley, *Continuity, Chance and Change. The Character of the Industrial Revolution in England* (Cambridge, 1988); and, above all, David Levine, *Family Formation in an Age of Nascent Capitalism* (New York, 1977), and his later *Reproducing Families: The Political Economy of English Population History* (Cambridge, 1984), which explore the interplay of family development and economic change. In a series of works, Alan Macfarlane has stressed the indissoluble links of the cultural, the social, the economic and the political, arguing for a distinctively English conformation. See *Marriage and Love in England: Modes of Reproduction, 1300–1840* (Oxford, 1986); *The Origins of English Individualism: The Family, Property and Social Transition* (Oxford, 1978); and *The Culture of Capitalism* (Oxford, 1987).

Likewise the 'politics of culture', the development of the media, and the uses of literacy have been illuminatingly examined. See Jeremy Black, *The English Press in the Eighteenth Century* (1986), and the splendid collection of cartoons which have been reprinted with illuminating introductions in Michael Duffy (ed.), *The English Satirical Print, 1600–1832*, 7 vols (Cambridge, 1986). Gerald Newman, *The Rise of English Nationalism: A Cultural History, 1740–1830* (New York, 1987) shows the social roots of political ideologies.

Family history continues to develop, though the most provocative broad introduction remains Lawrence Stone, *The Family, Sex and Marriage in England, 1500–1800* (1977). Family history is well integrated into broader social history, from a feminist viewpoint, in Leonore Davidoff and Catherine Hall, *Family Fortunes: Men and Women of the English Middle Class, 1780–1850* (1987). The best account of the changing ideas of women in respect to the family is now L. Jordanova, *Sexual Visions. Images of Gender in Science and Medicine Between the 18th and the 20th Centuries* (Madison, 1989).

2.   THE BRITISH ECONOMY IN TRANSITION, 1742–1789

A recent and extensive bibliography which includes the economic aspects of this era can be found in Immanuel Wallerstein, *The Modern World-System III: The Second Era of Great Expansion of the Capitalist World-Economy, 1730–1840s* (London and San Diego, 1989). Most of the citations in Michael Jubb's bibliographic essay in Jeremy Black (ed.), *Britain in the Age of Walpole* (1984) p. 218, are relevant for this time period as well. The best comprehensive 'new' economic history of the era remains Roderick Floud and Donald McCloskey (eds), *The Economic History of Britain, vol. 1: 1700–1860* (Cambridge, 1981). A new edition of the volume is in preparation. A recent book which challenges the primacy of industrialisation in Britain's transformation to modern growth is C. H. Lee, *The British Economy since 1700: A Macroeconomic Perspective* (Cambridge, 1986). An interesting interpretation of the relationship between industrialisation and imperial expansion can be found in P. J. Cain and A. G. Hopkins, 'Gentlemanly Capitalism and British Expansion Overseas, I. The Old Colonial System, 1688–1850', *Economic History Review*, 2nd series, xxxix (November 1986) 501–25. Two recent works by Julian Hoppitt discuss some of the economic difficulties of the eighteenth century: *Risk and Failure in English Business, 1700–1800* (Cambridge, 1987) and 'Financial Crises in Eighteenth-Century England', *Economic History Review*, 2nd series, xxxix (February 1986) 39–58. Also discussing financial developments is Larry Neal, 'The Integration and Efficiency of the London and Amsterdam Stock Markets in the Eighteenth Century', *Journal of Economic History* xlvii (March 1987) 97–115. A very interesting work which explores the evolution of social structure and income distribution in Britain is Peter H. Lindert and Jeffrey G. Williamson, 'Revising England's Social Tables 1688–1812', *Explorations in Economic History*, 19 (October 1982) 385–408. The most ambitious attempt since Gilboy to argue that demand was the moving force behind the industrial revolution is Neil McKendrick, John Brewer and J. H. Plumb, *The Birth of a Consumer Society: The Commercialization of Eighteenth-Century England* (Bloomington, Indiana, 1982). Two recent local studies of relevance are Pat Hudson, *The Genesis of Industrial Capital: A Study of the West Riding Wool Textile Industry c. 1750–1850* (Cambridge, 1986) and Gail Malmgreen, *Silk Town: Industry and Culture in Macclesfield, 1750–1835* (Hull, 1985).

3.   SCOTLAND AND IRELAND 1742–1789

Ireland: Professional history in modern Ireland is marked by high scholarly standards and speed of change in both emphasis and interpretation. Unfortunately the ambitious volumes of *A New History of Ireland* have taken extraordinary lengths of time in gestation, and of none is this more true than *vol. IV: Eighteenth Century Ireland (1691–1800)*, ed. Theodore W. Moody *et al.* (Oxford, 1985). It remains a massive summary of recognised achievement, with some fresh chapters by younger scholars. It has a notably good bibliography. Edith Mary Johnston's volume in the Gill History of Ireland, *Vol. 8: Ireland in the Eighteenth Century* (Dublin, 1974, 2nd imp. 1980) is a lively overview of manageable size.

The following titles provide a scholarly introduction to some major themes: Francis G. James, *Ireland in the Empire 1688–1770* (Cambridge, Mass., 1973); Robert B. McDowell, *Ireland in the Age of Imperialism and Revolution 1760–1801* (Oxford, 1979); James C. Beckett, *Confrontations: Studies in Irish History* (Totowa, NJ, 1972).

Scotland: The two standard introductions to the political and social history of this era are both now quite old. T. Christopher Smout's important *A History of the Scottish People 1560–1830* (1969), is ripe for a second edition. The relevant volume of the *Edinburgh History of Scotland* is William Ferguson, *vol. IV: Scotland 1689 to the Present* (Edinburgh, 1969). Bruce P. Lenman's much shorter survey in *The New History of Scotland, Vol. 6: Integration, Enlightenment and Industrialization, Scotland 1746–1832* (1981), is an extended essay on political and cultural conservatism.

The following titles provide introductions to more specialised topics: Alexander

J. Murdoch, *The People Above* (Edinburgh, 1980); Ronald N. Sunter, *Patronage and Politics in Scotland 1707–1832* (Edinburgh, 1986); David Davies, Peter Jones and Jean Jones, *A Hotbed of Genius: The Scottish Enlightenment 1730–1790* (Edinburgh, 1986); Thomas M. Devine and Rosalind M. Mitchison (eds), *People and Society in Scotland, Vol. I, 1760–1830* (Edinburgh, 1988).

Comparative Scots–Irish History: Two works, the fruits of a promising spirit of cooperation between Scottish and Irish economic and social historians, merit mention: Louis M. Cullen and T. Christopher Smout (eds), *Comparative Aspects of Scottish and Irish Economic and Social History 1600–1900* (Edinburgh, 1977); Rosalind M. Mitchison and Peter Roebuck (eds), *Economy and Society in Scotland and Ireland 1500–1939* (Edinburgh, 1988).

4.   THE CHANGING NATURE OF PARLIAMENTARY POLITICS, 1742–1789

Romney Sedgwick, *The History of Parliament. The House of Commons, 1715–1754*, 2 vols (1970), and Sir Lewis Namier and John Brooke, *The History of Parliament. The House of Commons, 1754–1790*, 3 vols (1964) provide an indispensable and far from fully exploited foundation for the study of this subject in this period but leave untouched many of its more dynamic aspects. On these there is a growing output of monographs which provide valuable insights while putting some unresolved issues in dispute. B. W. Hill, *British Parliamentary Parties, 1742–1832* (1985), and Frank O'Gorman, *The Emergence of the British Two-Party System, 1760–1832* (1982), are good general surveys, as is also within its compass A. S. Foord, *His Majesty's Opposition, 1714–1830* (Oxford, 1964). Various aspects of party politics in the later years of George II are explored in J. B. Owen, *The Rise of the Pelhams* (1957); Linda Colley, *In Defiance of Oligarchy. The Tory Party, 1714–1760* (Cambridge, 1982); Eveline Cruickshanks, *Political Untouchables. The Tories and the '45* (1979); J. C. D. Clark, *The Dynamics of Change. The Crisis of the 1750s and English Party Systems* (Cambridge, 1982); and Marie Peters, *Pitt and Popularity. The Patriot Minister and London Opinion during the Seven Years War* (Oxford, 1980). Sir Lewis Namier, *The Structure of Politics at the accession of George III* (2nd edn, 1957) and *England in the Age of the American Revolution* (2nd edn, 1961) remain pivotal for the opening years of George III's reign. For opposition politics from 1760 to 1789 two studies are indispensable: Frank O'Gorman, *The Rise of Party in England. The Rockingham Whigs, 1760–1782* (1975), and L. G. Mitchell, *Charles James Fox and the Disintegration of the Whig Party, 1782–1794* (1971). There is no comparable sustained survey for the government side, which can be followed in a series of studies and biographies: Philip Lawson, *George Grenville. A Political Life* (Oxford, 1984); Paul Langford, *The First Rockingham Administration, 1765–1766* (1973); John Brooke, *The Chatham Administration, 1766–1768* (1956); P. D. G. Thomas, *Lord North* (1976); Sir Herbert Butterfield, *George III, Lord North and the People, 1779–1780* (1949); Ian R. Christie, *The End of North's Ministry, 1780–1782* (1958); John Norris, *Shelburne and Reform* (1963); J. A. Cannon, *The Fox–North Coalition: Crisis of the Constitution, 1782–1784* (Cambridge, 1969); and John Ehrman, *The Younger Pitt: The Years of Acclaim* (1969). The wider background of ideological aspects is explored in H. T. Dickinson, *Liberty and Property. Political Ideology in Eighteenth-century Britain* (1977), J. A. W. Gunn, *Beyond Liberty and Property. The Process of Self-Recognition in Eighteenth-century Political Thought* (Kingston and Montreal, 1983), and J. C. D. Clark, *English Society, 1688–1832. Ideology, social structure and political practice during the Ancien Régime* (Cambridge, 1985).

5.   RADICALS AND REFORMERS IN THE AGE OF WILKES AND WYVILL

For the precursors of radicalism, see H. T. Dickinson, 'Popular Politics in the Age of Walpole', in Jeremy Black (ed.), *Britain in the Age of Walpole* (1984) pp. 45–68 and H. T. Dickinson, 'The Precursors of Political Radicalism in Augustan Britain', in Clyve Jones (ed.), *Britain in the First Age of Party 1680–1750* (1987) pp. 63–84. For the ideological context, see H. T. Dickinson, *Liberty and Property: Political Ideology in Eighteenth-Century Britain* (1977) ch. 6; J. G. A. Pocock, 'Radical Criticism of the Whig Order between Revolutions', in Margaret Jacob and James Jacob (eds), *The Origins of Anglo-American Radicalism* (1984) pp. 35–57; Isaac Kramnick, 'Republican Revisionism Revisited', *Amer. Hist Rev.*, 87 (1982) 629–64; and Colin C. Bonwick, *English Radicals and the American Revolution* (Chapel Hill, 1977). For the connections between the British radicals and the American cause see James E. Bradley, *Popular Politics and the American Revolution in England* (Macon, 1986) and John Sainsbury, *Disaffected Patriots: London Supporters of Revolutionary America* (Gloucester, 1987). There are numerous popular biographies of John Wilkes, but none is very satisfactory. The best remains Horace Breackley, *The Life of John Wilkes* (1917). There are, however, several useful studies of aspects of Wilkes's career and the Wilkite movement. Among the best are: George Rudé, *Wilkes and Liberty* (Oxford, 1962) and 'Wilkes and Liberty, 1768–9', *Guildhall Miscellany*, I (1952) 3–24; Peter D. G. Thomas, 'John Wilkes and the Freedom of the Press (1771)', *Bull. Inst. Hist. Res.*, xxxiii (1960) 86–98; and John Brewer, 'The Wilkites and the Law, 1763–74', in John Brewer and John Styles (eds), *An Ungovernable People* (1980) pp. 128–71 and 'The Number 45: A Wilkite Political Symbol', in Stephen Baxter (ed.), *England's Rise to Greatness* (Los Angeles, 1983) pp. 349–80. There is no biography of Christopher Wyvill, but useful studies of radical theorists include John W. Osborne, *John Cartwright* (Cambridge, 1972); D. O. Thomas, *The Honest Mind: The Thought and Work of Richard Price* (Oxford, 1977); and Carla H. Hay, *James Burgh, Spokesman for Reform in Hanoverian England* (Washington, DC, 1979). There are a number of useful studies of the radical and reform movements of this period, including George S. Veitch, *The Genesis of Parliamentary Reform* (1913; rep. 1965); S. Maccoby, *English Radicalism 1762–85* (1955); Ian R. Christie, *Wilkes, Wyvill and Reform* (1962); Eugene C. Black, *The Association: British Extraparliamentary Political Organization 1769–1793* (Cambridge, Mass., 1963); John Cannon, *Parliamentary Reform in Hanoverian England* (Washington, DC, 1979). There are a number of *Politics at the Accession of George III* (Cambridge, 1976); and John Brewer, 'English Radicalism in the Age of George III', in J. G. A. Pocock (ed.), *Three British Revolutions: 1641, 1688, 1776* (Princeton, 1980). On the social and economic context, see Walter J. Shelton, *English Hunger and Industrial Disorders* (1973) and John Brewer, 'Commercialization and Politics', in Neil McKendrick, John Brewer and J. H Plumb, *The Birth of a Consumer Society* (1982) pp. 197–262.

6.   FOREIGN POLICY AND THE BRITISH STATE 1742–1793

The best introductions to eighteenth-century British foreign policy are P. Langford, *The Eighteenth Century* (1976) and J. R. Jones, *Britain and the World 1649–1815* (1980). D. B. Horn, *Great Britain and Europe in the Eighteenth Century* (Oxford, 1967) is difficult to use; his *British Diplomatic Service 1689–1789* (Oxford, 1961) is excellent. J. Black, *Natural and Necessary Enemies. Anglo-French Relations in the Eighteenth Century* (1986) provides an important overview, while recent research can be approached through J. Black (ed.), *Knights Errant and True Englishmen. British Foreign Policy 1660–1800* (Edinburgh, 1989); J. Black, 'British Foreign Policy in the Eighteenth Century: A Survey', *Journal of British Studies* (1987);

J. Black, 'The Tory View of Eighteenth-century British Foreign Policy', *Historical Journal* (1988); and J. Black, 'Britain's Foreign Alliances in the Eighteenth Century', *Albion* (1988). On the European situation D. McKay and H. Scott, *The Rise of The Great Powers* (1983), J. Black (ed.), *The Origins of War in Early Modern Europe* (Edinburgh, 1987) and J. Black, *The Rise of the European Powers 1679–1793* (1990). On naval power, J. Black and P. Woodfine (eds), *The British Navy and the Use of Naval Power in the Eighteenth Century* (Leicester, 1988) and N. Tracy, *Navies, Deterrence, and American Independence* (Vancouver, 1988). P. Kennedy, *The Rise and Fall of British Naval Mastery* (1983) is a useful general survey. On the press and foreign policy, J. Black, *The English Press in the Eighteenth Century* (1987) chap. 7. J. Black, *British Foreign Policy in the Age of Walpole* (Edinburgh, 1985) provides a thematic account useful to an understanding of the 1740s and 1750s. On the 1740s, R. Lodge, *Studies in Eighteenth Century Diplomacy 1740–1748* (1930) is somewhat dense and there is no satisfactory biography of Carteret though Newcastle is well served by R. Browning, *The Duke of Newcastle* (New Haven, 1975). Recent perspectives can be found in J. Black, 'British Foreign Policy and the War of the Austrian Succession 1740–1748' *Canadian Journal of History* (1986) and J. Black, 'The Problems of the Small State: Bavaria and Britain in the Second Quarter of the Eighteenth Century', *European History Quarterly* (1989). On 1749–54, D. B. Horn, *Sir Charles Hanbury Williams and European Diplomacy* (1930) and 'The Cabinet Controversy on Subsidy Treaties in Time of Peace, 1749–50', *Eng. Hist. Rev.* (1930), and Browning, 'The Duke of Newcastle and the Imperial Election Plan', *Journal of British Studies* (1967–8). On the Seven Years War, Horn, 'The Duke of Newcastle and the Origins of the Diplomatic Revolution' in J. H. Elliott and H. G. Koenigsberger (eds), *The Diversity of History* (1970); P. Doran, *Andrew Mitchell and Anglo-Prussian Diplomatic Relations during the Seven Years War* (New York, 1986); and K. W. Schweizer, *England, Prussia and the Seven Years War* (Lewiston, 1989) are more useful than R. Lodge, *Great Britain and Prussia in the Eighteenth Century* (Oxford, 1923). S. E. Rashed, *The Peace of Paris, 1763* (Liverpool, 1951) does not discuss domestic politics adequately. On 1763–83 the best introduction is H. Scott, 'British Foreign Policy in the Age of the American Revolution' *International History Review* (1984). M. Roberts, *Splendid Isolation, 1763–1780* (Reading, 1970) is misleading. His 'Great Britain and the Swedish Revolution 1772–3', *Historical Journal* (1964) is more useful. D. B. Horn's, *British Public Opinion and the First Partition of Poland* (1945) is excellent. R. van Alstyne, 'Europe, the Rockingham Whigs and the War for American Independence', *Huntington Library Quarterly* (1961–2) 'Great Britain, the War for Independence and the "Gathering Storm" in Europe 1775–1778', *ibid.* (1963–4) and *Empire and Independence. The International History of the American Revolution* (New York, 1965) are useful, as is J. R. Dull, *A Diplomatic History of the American Revolution* (New Haven, 1985). On the negotiations of 1782–3, R. B. Morris, *The Peacemakers* (New York, 1965) and V. T. Harlow, *The Founding of the Second British Empire, 1763–93* (1952, 1964). On 1783–93, J. H. Ehrman, *The Younger Pitt* (1969, 1983); A. Cobban, *Ambassadors and Secret Agents* (1954); T. C. W. Blanning, '. . . George III, Hanover and the *Fürstenbund* of 1785', *Historical Journal* (1977); J. Black, 'The Marquis of Carmarthen and Relations with France 1784–1787', *Francia* (1984), 'Sir Robert Ainslie . . . British Foreign Policy and the International Crisis of 1787' *European History Quarterly* (1984), and 'Anglo-French Relations in the Age of the French Revolution 1787–1793', *Francia* (1987). A general assessment is provided by J. Brewer, *The Sinews of Power, War, Money and the English State, 1688–1783* (1989).

7. THE EIGHTEENTH-CENTURY EMPIRE

Angus Calder's *Revolutionary Empire* (1981) is a brave attempt to encompass the subject matter of this chapter in a single volume. Vincent T. Harlow, *The Founding of the Second British Empire 1763–93*, 2 vols (1952–64) exhaustively examines thirty years from a point of view that has aroused much controversy. Constitutional relations between Britain and her overseas territories are explored through a huge selection of documents in the volumes presented by Frederick Madden (with David Fieldhouse) as *Select Documents on the Constitutional History of the British Empire and Commonwealth*, vol. II, *The Classical Period of the First British Empire, 1689–1783* and vol. III, *Imperial Reconstruction 1763–1840* (New York, 1985, 1987). W. E. Minchinton (ed.), *The Growth of English Overseas Trade in the Seventeenth and Eighteenth Centuries* (1969) is a collection of important articles. They should be supplemented by Ralph Davis, *The Industrial Revolution and British Overseas Trade* (Leicester, 1979). British war and diplomacy outside Europe have attracted much writing; that of Richard Pares remains outstanding, especially his *War and Trade in the West Indies 1739–63* (Oxford, 1936) and his article, 'American versus Continental Warfare, 1739–63', *English Historical Review*, LI (1936) 429–65. For the navy there is a valuable recent collection of essays, *The British Navy and the Use of Naval Power in the Eighteenth Century*, edited by Jeremy Black and Philip Woodfine (Leicester, 1988).

The vast literature on pre-revolutionary and revolutionary America cannot be surveyed in a short space. Current thinking on the colonial period is conveniently summed up in the essays in Jack P. Greene and J. R. Pole (eds), *Colonial British America: Essays in the New History of the Early Modern Era* (Baltimore, 1984). John J. McCusker and Russell R. Menard survey work on *The Economy of British America 1607–1789* (Chapel Hill, 1985). Ian R. Christie and Benjamin W. Labaree have provided the most authoritative single-volume treatment of the Revolution in *Empire or Independence 1760–76* (1976). Stimulating recent interpretations are offered by Robert W. Tucker and David C. Hendrickson, *The Fall of the First British Empire: Origins of the War of American Independence* (Baltimore, 1982) and Edward Countryman, *The American Revolution* (1985). The work of Peter D. G. Thomas, *The Stamp Act Crisis in British Politics: the First Phase of the American Revolution 1763–7* and *The Townshend Duties Crisis: the Second Phase of the American Revolution, 1767–73* (Oxford, 1975, 1987) has displaced earlier studies of the British political response to the colonial problem.

H. B. Neatby, *Quebec: the Revolutionary Age 1760–91* (Toronto, 1966) is a valuable account of Canada after the British conquest. Current interpretations of the eighteenth-century West Indies are dominated by the work of Richard B. Sheridan, many of whose findings are brought together in *Sugar and Slavery: An Economic History of the British West Indies 1623–1775* (Baltimore, 1974). The late eighteenth century has been reinterpreted by Seymour Drescher in *Econocide: British Slavery in the Era of Abolition* (Pittsburgh, 1977). There is important material in J. R. Ward, 'The Profitability of Sugar Planting in the British West Indies', *Economic Historical Review*, 2nd ser., XXXI (1978) 197–213. Roger T. Anstey, *The Atlantic Slave Trade and British Abolition 1760–1810* (1975) and P. E. Lovejoy, *Transformations in Slavery: a History of Slavery in Africa* (Cambridge, 1983) are authoritative works of synthesis on subjects on which the literature is very extensive.

India dominated British eastern expansion. In recent years understanding of the history of the Indian setting in the eighteenth century has taken radically new directions. Attempts have been made to apply this new understanding to the story of the rise of British territorial power in volumes of *The New Cambridge History of India* by C. A. Bayly, *Indian Society and the Making of the British Empire* and P. J.

Marshall, *Bengal the British Bridgehead: Eastern India 1740–1828* (Cambridge, 1988). K. N. Chaudhuri, *The Trading World of Asia and the English East India Company 1660–1760* (Cambridge, 1978) and L. S. Sutherland, *The East India Company in Eighteenth-century Politics* (Oxford, 1952) are fundamental works on the East India Company. For British interests in the Pacific, J. C. Beaglehole, *The Life of Captain James Cook* (1974) should be added to the works on the establishment of New South Wales listed in note 21.

8.   RELIGION IN BRITISH SOCIETY 1740–1790

Several distinguished older surveys of eighteenth-century religion have not lost their value. These include Norman Sykes, *Church and State in England in the Eighteenth Century* (Cambridge, 1934); E. R. Bebb, *Nonconformity and Social and Economic Life, 1600–1800* (1935) and G. F. A. Best, *Temporal Pillars* (Cambridge, 1964). These may be supplemented by Gordon Rupp, *Religion in England 1688–1791* (Oxford, 1986) which, despite the date of its publication, is representative of an older tradition of ecclesiastical scholarship of the eighteenth century; and Anthony Armstrong, *The Church of England, the Methodists and Society, 1700–1850* (1973). Though rather deterministic in method and showing signs of wear A. D. Gilbert's *Religion and Society in Industrial England* (London and New York, 1976) is probably still the best general introduction to the subject and may be used alongside the more comprehensive statistics to be found in R. Currie, A. Gilbert and L. Horsley, *Churches and Churchgoers: Patterns of Church Growth in the British Isles since 1700* (Oxford, 1977). C. G. Brown's *The Social History of Religion in Scotland* (1987) covers the same period in Scotland only with a more flexible methodology. See also E. T. Davies, *Religion in the Industrial Revolution in South Wales* (Cardiff, 1965). There are a number of excellent studies of particular religious traditions including John Bossy, *The English Catholic Community 1570–1850* (1975); M. R. Watts, *The Dissenters from the Reformation to the French Revolution* (Oxford, 1978); R. Davies and G. Rupp, *A History of the Methodist Church in Great Britain*, vol. 1 (1965); D. W. Bebbington, *Evangelicalism in Modern Britain* (1989); and E. R. Norman, *Church and Society in England 1770–1970: A Historical Study* (Oxford, 1976).

Peter Virgin's *The Church in an Age of Negligence: Ecclesiastical Structure and Problems of Church Reform 1700–1840* (Cambridge, 1989) is an important new study of the ecclesiastical structure of the Georgian Church. Other stimulating treatments of the Church of England include J. C. D. Clark, *English Society 1688–1832* (Cambridge, 1985) and F. C. Mather, 'Georgian Churchmanship Reconsidered: Some Variations in Anglican Public Worship 1714–1830', *Journal of Ecclesiastical History*, 36, no. 2 (1985) 255–83. No satisfactory treatment of popular religion exists for this period but Bob Bushaway's *By Rite: Custom, Ceremony and Community in England 1700–1880* (1982) contains some suggestive material on the rural communities of southern England. See also Alan Smith, *The Established Church and Popular Religion* (1971). Further reading on the themes explored in my essay is best followed in the accompanying references, including the academic theses, some of which are to be published within the next few years. All students of this period would profit from reading the many pioneering articles of E. P. Thompson, John Walsh and W. R. Ward, the references to which may be found in the bibliography of David Hempton, *Methodism and Politics in British Society 1750–1850* (1984).

Notes and References

INTRODUCTION   *Jeremy Black*

1. In 1987 *Past and Present* published a critique of his work by Joanna Innes, 'Jonathan Clark, Social History and England's "Ancien régime", and a reply by Clark. There is an important extension of his argument to America in an unpublished paper of Dr Clark's for which I am very grateful to him for letting me have a copy, 'Revolution in the English Atlantic Empire, *c.* 1660–1800: 1688 as a model for 1776'.

2. On the European situation see most recently J. M. Black, *Eighteenth Century Europe 1700–1789* (1990). The most recent studies of Wales are G. H. Jenkins, *The Foundations of Modern Wales: Wales 1642–1789* (Oxford, 1987); T. Herbert and G. E. Jones (eds), *The Remaking of Wales in the Eighteenth Century* (Cardiff, 1988).

3. Besides Clark another valuable study is J. Gunn, *Beyond Liberty and Property: The Process of Self-Recognition in Eighteenth-century Political Thought* (Toronto, 1983). I am grateful to J. Gregory for letting me read a copy of his unpublished paper, 'Anglicanism and the Arts: Religion, Culture and Politics in the Eighteenth Century'.

4. Matlock, Derbyshire CRO 239 M F 8240, Richard Goodwin to William Fitzherbert, 20 Jan. 1750.

5. P. Woodland, 'Extra-Parliamentary Political Organization in the Making: Benjamin Heath and the Opposition to the 1763 Cider Excise', *Parliamentary History* (1985); Woodland, 'Political Atomization and Regional Interests in the 1761 Parliament: The Impact of the Cider Debates, 1763–66', *Parliamentary History* (1989).

6. Paris, Archives Nationales, Archives de la Marine, B7 455, undated anonymous 'Mémoire sur l'Angleterre'.

7. D. R. Schweitzer, 'The Failure of William Pitt's Irish Trade Propositions', *Parliamentary History* (1984).

8. PRO 30/29/1/11 f. 295, Chesterfield to Earl Gower, 11 Nov. 1745.

9. Bedford CRO L30/9/17/3, Glenorchy to Marchioness Grey, 15 Apr. 1746.

10. Worcester CRO 705: 66 BA 42221, Bath to Sir John Rushout, 13 Aug. 1745; Farmington, Weston, vol. 16, Stone to Edward Weston, 13 Aug. 1745; HL STG Box 192 (8), George to Richard Grenville, undated.

11. Farmington, Weston, 3, Sherlock to Weston, 25 May 1746.

12. HL STG Box 212 (28), Chalmers to Grenville, 1 Nov. 1769.

13. Lowther to John Spedding, 8 Dec. 1739, 19 Aug. 1743, Carlisle, Cumbria RO D/Lons/W2/1; Grenville to Duke of Bedford, 27 Dec. 1763, HL ST 7 vol. 1;

Newcastle to Andrew Mitchell, 8 Dec. 1757, BL Add. 6832 f. 31; P. L. C. Webb, 'The Rebuilding and Repair of the fleet 1783–1793', *Bulletin of the Institute of Historical Research* (1977); R. Middleton, 'Naval administration in the age of Pitt and Anson, 1755–1763' in J. Black and P. Woodfine (eds), *The British Navy and the Use of Naval Power in the Eighteenth Century* (Leicester, 1988) pp. 109–27; J. Ehrman, *The Younger Pitt. The Years of Acclaim* (1969) pp. 239–326; J. Brewer, *The Sinews of Power. War, Money and the English State, 1688–1783* (1989).

14. Mount Stuart, Cardiff papers, 9/146, James Dyson to –, – Mar. 1763; Farmington, Horatio Walpole's parliamentary memoranda; Bod. MS North adds c4 f. 144, North to Earl of Guildford, 4 Nov. 1769; Manchester, John Rylands Library, Eng. MSS 940 Jephson to Viscount Townshend, 21 Jan. 1774.

15. Warwick CRO CR 136 B 25/7, Middlesex election 1747 printed papers, flysheet of meeting at Crown Tavern, 18 June.

16. *An Heroic Epistle to the Right Honourable The Lord Craven* (1775); *The Heroic Epistle Answered* (1776); Horace Walpole, *Memoirs of the Reign of King George the Third* 4 vols (1894) I, 190–1.

17. BL Add MSS 35587 f. 56, Sherlock to Hardwicke, 31 Aug. 1742; NeC 596, Stone to Henry Pelham, 26 June 1748; HL MO 1420, Montagu to George Lyttleton, 23 Sept. 1762.

18. Matlock, Derbyshire RO D3155, WH 3461 Thomas Waite to Sir Robert Wilmot, 22 May 1762; HL MO 4592, Montagu to Bath, 23 Oct. 1762; Bod. MS North adds c4 f. 154, North to Guildford, 10 May 1771; Exeter, Devon RO 64/12/29/1/1; New Haven, Beinecke Library, Townshend Boxes, Dixon Hoste to Townshend, 4 Mar. 1790.

19. P. Borsay, *The English Urban Renaissance. Culture and Society in the Provincial Town 1660–1770* (Oxford, 1989); N. McKendrick, J. Brewer and J. H. Plumb, *The Birth of a Consumer Society. The Commercialization of Eighteenth-Century England* (1982); R. Porter, *Health for Sale. Quackery in England 1660–1859* (Manchester, 1989); C. Garrett, *Respectable Folly. Millenarians and the French Revolution in France and England* (Baltimore, 1975); M. Harris, 'Astrology, Almanacs and Booksellers', *Publishing History* (1980); Exeter, Devon RO 64/12/29/1/26.

20. J. Lough, 'Reflections on Enlightenment and Lumières', *British Journal for Eighteenth-Century Studies* (1985) 9; BL Add MSS 24159 f. 112, Rochford to Grantham, 2 July 1773.

21. Anon., *Some Reflections on the Trade Between Great Britain and Sweden* (1756) p. 25; R. A. Houston, 'Geographical mobility in Scotland', 1652–1811', *Journal of Historical Geography*, 11 (1985) 379–94; I. D. Whyte, 'Population Mobility in Early Modern Scotland', in Houston and Whyte (eds) *Scottish Society 1500–1800* (Cambridge, 1989) pp. 37–58.

22. AE CP 415 ff. 78–9.

23. BL Add MSS 23821 f. 107, Trevor to Robinson, 30 Sept. 1745; J. Black, *Culloden and the '45* (Gloucester, 1990). For recent work on Jacobitism, E. Cruickshanks and Black (eds) *The Jacobite Challenge* (Edinburgh, 1988); P. Monod, *Jacobitism and the English People* (Cambridge, 1989).

24. Gloucester, CRO D 1086 F 196.

25. *Jacobite's Journal*, 20 Feb. 1748.

26. Anon., *Some Reflections on the Trade Between Great Britain and Sweden* (1756) pp. 17–18.

27. M. Peters, 'Pitt as a foil to Bute: the public debate over ministerial responsibility and the powers of the Crown' in K. W. Schweizer (ed.), *Lord Bute. Essays in Reinterpretation* (Leicester, 1988) p. 111.

28. Mount Stuart, Cardiff papers, 6/82, Chesterfield to Bute, 9 Apr. 1761.

29. HL MO 1213, 2403, Lyttleton to Elizabeth Montagu, 5 Nov., Elizabeth to Edward Montagu, 18 Nov. 1760.

30. HL MO 4260, Bath to Elizabeth Montagu, 15 June 1762. J. D. Nicholas, 'The Ministry of Lord Bute, 1762–3 (unpublished PhD, University of Wales, Aberystwyth, 1988) is very useful, F. O'Gorman, *Voters, Patrons and Parties. The Unreformed Electorate of Hanoverian England 1734–1832* (Oxford, 1989) qualifies the extent of electoral corruption.

31. WW. RI–1352, Richmond to Rockingham, 22 Jan. 1771.

32. WW. RI–1705, Savile to Rockingham, 15 Jan. 1777.

33. J. W. Derry, *The Regency Crisis and the Whigs, 1788–9* (Cambridge, 1963); Ehrman, *Pitt. Years of Acclaim*, pp. 644–66.

34. HL ST 7 vol. 1, Grenville to Waller, 29 Sept. 1763; HL MO 4447, Bath to Elizabeth Montagu, 6 Nov. 1763. The best guide to politics in this period is I. R. Christie, 'Party in Politics in the Age of Lord North's Administration', *Parliamentary History* (1987) 47–68. J. Brewer, *Party Ideology and Popular Politics at the Accession of George III* (Cambridge, 1976) is valuable but exaggerates the novelty and importance of radical extra-parliamentary political agitation. N. Rogers, *Whigs and Cities. Popular Politics in the Age of Walpole and Pitt* (Oxford, 1989) is important as is P. Langford, 'William Pitt and Public Opinion, 1757', *English Historical Review* (1973). Recent work on support for the American cause includes Langford, 'Old Whigs, Old Tories and the American Revolution', *J. of Imperial and Commonwealth History* (1980); J. E. Bradley, *Popular Politics and the American Revolution in England* (Macon, Georgia, 1986); J. Sainsbury, *Disaffected Patriots. London Supporters of Revolutionary America, 1769–1782* (Kingston, Ontario, 1987). Important regional examples are provided by T. Knox, 'Popular Politics and Provincial Radicalism: Newcastle-Upon-Tyne, 1769–1785', *Albion* (1979) and P. Marshall, 'Manchester and the American Revolution', *Bulletin of the John Rylands Library* (1979).

On Grenville there is a recent study by P. Lawson, *George Grenville, A Political Life* (Oxford, 1984).

35. HL ST 7 vol. 1, Grenville to Earl of Lichfield, 1 Oct. 1763, to Thomas Whatley, 2 July 1764, to Charles Jenkinson, 4 July 1764.

36. HL MO 3088, Montagu to Elizabeth Carter, 26 Nov. 1762; WW RI–1219, Richmond to Edmund Burke, 2 Sept. 1769.

37. Anon., *The Opposition* (1755) p. 5; HL MO 1311, Lyttleton to Elizabeth Montagu, 21 Aug. 1763.

38. HL MO 4583, Montagu to Bath, spring 1763.

1.   BRITISH SOCIETY IN THE EIGHTEENTH CENTURY REVISITED   *Roy Porter*

1. J. C. D. Clark, *English Society, 1688–1832: Ideology, Social Structure and Political Practice During the Ancien Régime* (Cambridge, 1985). Similar strictures equally apply to Clark's subsequent work. *Revolution and Rebellion. State and Society in England in the Seventeenth and Eighteenth Centuries* (Cambridge, 1986). My point has already been made by many earlier commentators on this book: see the excellent discussion by G. S. Rousseau: 'Revisionist Polemics: J. C. D. Clark and the Collapse of Modernity in the Age of Johnson', in P. J. Korshin (ed.), *The Age of Johnson*, vol. 3 (New York, 1989) pp. 423–52: Rousseau approaches the controversy in terms of its rhetoric and polemics, and demonstrates that Clark's own rhetoric and style go far to explain the ensuing controversy. Rousseau also helpfully lists the most important reviews of Clark's work. See also Frank O'Gorman, 'Recent Historiography of the Hanoverian Regime', *Historical Jour-*

nal, 29 (1986) 1005–20; Jeremy Black, '"England's Ancien Régime"?' *History Today*, 38 (1988) 43–51.
I wish to express my gratitude to Jeremy Black, J. C. D. Clark and John Styles, for their extremely helpful comments upon an earlier version of this paper.

2. By contrast, K. Wrightson, *English Society, 1580–1680* (New Brunswick, NJ, 1982) has produced a social history in which few *within* the elite are discussed.

3. J. A. Sharpe, *Early Modern England. A Social History 1550–1760* (1987); Trevor May, *An Economic and Social History of Britain, 1760–1970* (1987).

4. In my view, many of the reviewers of Clark's books have trapped themselves – like Clark himself, but from an opposite viewpoint – in the simplistic assumption that the old political order was incompatible with social change. This issue is evaluated in J. Innes, 'Jonathan Clark, Social History, and England's Ancien Régime', *Past and Present*, 115 (1987) 165–200.

5. Roy Porter, *English Society in the Eighteenth Century* (1982) argues for the enduring strength of the traditional ruling orders; see esp. chs 2 and 3.

6. M. L. Bush, *The English Aristocracy: A Comparative Synthesis* (Manchester, 1984); John Cannon, *Aristocratic Century: The Peerage of Eighteenth Century England* (Cambridge, 1984); J. V. Beckett, *The Aristocracy in England, 1660–1914* (Oxford, 1986); I. R. Christie, *Wars and Revolutions: England 1760–1815* (1982); and especially Christie, *Stress and Stability in Late Eighteenth Century Britain: Reflections on the British Avoidance of Revolution* (Oxford, 1984).

7. Geoffrey Holmes, *Augustan England: Professions, State and Society 1680–1730* (1982); Peter Earle, *The Making of the English Middle Class: Business, Society and Family Life in London, 1660–1730* (1989).

8. John Brewer, *The Sinews of Power* (1989).

9. Peter Mathias, 'Taxation and Industrialization in Britain, 1700–1870', in *The Transformation of England* (New York, 1979); Mathias and Patrick O'Brien, 'Taxation in England and France, 1715–1810. A Comparison of the Social and Economic Incidence of Taxes Collected for the Central Governments', *Journal of European Economic History*, v (1976) 601–50; Patrick O'Brien and Caglar Keyder, *Economic Growth in Britain and France, 1780–1914. Two Paths to the Twentieth Century* (1978).

10. Simon Schama has shown that *ancien régime* France was no less fertile in modernising schemes. The Bourbons were, however, totally unable to make them work: *Citizens. A Chronicle of the French Revolution* (New York, 1989).

11. Clark rightly stresses that party political programmes continued to be organised around principle, as with the Tories under Walpole and beyond. Cf. Linda Colley, *in Defiance of Oligarchy: The Tory Party, 1714–1760* (Cambridge, 1982).

12. John Brewer, *Party Ideology and Popular Politics at the Accession of George III* (Cambridge, 1976); P. Slack (ed.), *Rebellion, Popular Protest and Social Change in Early Modern England* (Cambridge, 1984); Keith Snell, *Annals of the Labouring Poor: Social Change in Agrarian England, 1660–1900* (Cambridge, 1985); J. Stevenson, *Popular Disturbances in England, 1700–1870* (1979). Classic are E. P. Thompson, 'The Moral Economy of the English Crowd', *Past and Present*, no. 50 (1971) 76–136; Thompson, 'Rough Music', *Annales ESC*, xxvii (1972) 285–310; Thompson, 'Patrician Society, Plebeian Culture', *Journal of Social History*, vii (1973–4) 382–405.

13. Earle, *Making of the English Middle Class*. Earle's study affords no support to any view of the radicalism of the London bourgeoisie. For rural religion see J. Obelkevitch, *Religion and Society in South Lincolnshire* (Oxford, 1976).

14. See, for instance, Robert Darnton, *The Great Cat Massacre and Other Episodes in French Cultural History* (New York, 1984); Darnton, *The Business of*

Enlightenment. A Publishing History of the Encyclopédie, 1775–1800 (Cambridge, Mass., 1979); Darnton, *The Literary Underground of the Old Regime* (Cambridge, Mass., 1982).

15. J. Innes and J. Styles, 'The Crime Wave: Recent Writing on Crime and Criminal Justice in Eighteenth Century England', *Journal of British Studies*, xxv (1986) 380–435; J. A. Sharpe, *Crime in Early Modern England 1550–1750* (1984).

16. Linda Colley, 'The Apotheosis of George III: Loyalty, Royalty and the English Nation', *Past and Present*, no. 102 (1984) 94–129; Colley, 'Whose Nation? Class and National Consciousness in England, 1750–1830', *Past and Present*, no. 113 (1986) 96–117; H. Cunningham, 'The Language of Patriotism, 1750–1914', *History Workshop Journal*, xii (1981) 8–33; Gerald Newman, *The Rise of English Nationalism: A Cultural History, 1740–1830* (New York, 1987); Marilyn Butler, *Romantics, Rebels and Reactionaries. English Literature and its Background 1760–1830* (Oxford, 1981); Butler, 'Romanticism in England', in Roy Porter and Mikuláš Teich (eds), *Romanticism in National Context* (Cambridge, 1988) pp. 37–67. Butler's essay valuably emphasises the patriotic political programme prominent in early Romanticism.

17. Jeremy Black, *The English Press in the Eighteenth Century* (1986), offers a corrective to those who instinctively identify the press with its potential for radicalism. See also Michael Duffy (ed.), *The English Satirical Print, 1600–1832*, 7 vols (Cambridge, 1986); Ronald Paulson, *Representations of Revolution 1789–1820* (New Haven, 1983).

18. Earle, *Making of the English Middle Class* says much about how the middle classes defined themselves more by occupation than by political consciousness.

19. See Perry Anderson, *Arguments within English Marxism* (1980); compare P. Corrigan and D. Sayer, *The Great Arch: English State Formation as Cultural Revolution* (Oxford, 1985); Tom Nairn, *The Enchanted Glass. Britain and its Monarchy* (1988).

20. On which see Roy Porter, 'The Scientific Revolution: A Spoke in the Wheel?', in Roy Porter and Mikuláš Teich (eds), *Revolution in History* (Cambridge, 1986) pp. 290–316.

21. N. F. C. Crafts, 'Industrial Revolution in England and France: Some Thoughts on the Question, "Why was England first?"', *Economic History Review*, xxx (1977); Crafts, 'English Economic Growth in the Eighteenth Century: A Re-examination of Deane and Cole's Estimates', *Economic History Review*, xxix (1976) 226–35; Crafts, *British Economic Growth during the Industrial Revolution* (Oxford, 1985); C. Harley, 'British Industrializaton before 1841: Evidence of Slower Growth During the Industrial Revolution', *Journal of Economic History*, xlii (1982) 267–90; Roderick Floud and Donald McCloskey (eds), *The Economic History of Britain since 1700*, 2 vols (Cambridge, 1981). See also David Cannadine, 'The Present and the Past in the English Industrial Revolution, 1880–1980', *Past and Present*, no. 103 (1984) 131–72; M. Fores, 'The Myth of a British Industrial Revolution', *History*, lxvi (1981) 181–9.

22. Maxine Berg, *The Age of Manufactures, 1700–1820* (1985).

23. *Ibid*.

24. David Levine, *Family Formation in an Age of Nascent Capitalism* (New York, 1977); Levine, *Reproducing Families: The Political Economy of English Population History* (Cambridge, 1984).

25. M. Anderson, *Approaches to the History of the Western Family 1500–1914* (1980) is highly suggestive as to the interplay of demographic change, economic development, and the social history of family adjustments.

26. W. A. Cole, 'Factors in Demand', in Floud and McCloskey (eds), *The Economic History of Britain since 1700*, vol. 1; Elizabeth W. Gilboy, 'Demand as a

Factor in the Industrial Revolution', in R. M. Hartwell (ed.), *The Causes of the Industrial Revolution in England* (1967) pp. 121–38.

27. Lorna Weatherill, *Consumer Behaviour and Material Culture, 1660–1760* (1988); Weatherill, 'Consumer Behavior and Social Status in England', *Continuity and Change*, II (1986) 191–216; Weatherill, 'A Possession of One's Own: Women and Consumer Behaviour in England, 1660–1740', *Journal of British Studies*, XXIV (1986) 131–56. Highly illuminating are Tim Breen, 'An Empire of Goods: The Anglicization of Colonial America, 1690–1776', *Journal of British Studies*, XXV (1986) 467–99; and Breen, 'Baubles of Britain: The American and Consumer Revolutions of the Eighteenth Century', *Past and Present* (May, 1988) 73–109; C. Mukerji, *From Graven Images: Patterns of Modern Materialism* (New York, 1983).

28. See Earle, *Making of the English Middle Class*.

29. Grant McCracken, *Culture and Consumption. New Approaches to the Symbolic Character of Consumer Goods and Activities* (Bloomington, 1988).

30. N. McKendrick, John Brewer and J. H. Plumb, *The Birth of a Consumer Society: The Commercialization of Eighteenth-Century England* (1982); N. McKendrick, 'Home Demand and Economic Growth: A New View of the Role of Women and Children in the Industrial Revolution', in N. McKendrick (ed.), *Historical Perspectives: Studies in English Thought and Society* (1974) pp. 152–210; Eric Robinson, 'Eighteenth Century Commerce and Fashion. Matthew Boulton's Marketing Techniques', *Economic History Review*, XVI (1963–4); D. E. C. Eversley, 'The Home Market and Economic Growth in England 1750–1800', in E. L. Jones and C. E. Mingay (eds), *Land, Labour and Population in the Industrial Revolution* (1967) pp. 206–59; E. L. Jones, 'The Fashion Manipulators: Consumer Tastes and British Industries, 1660–1800', in L. P. Cain and P. J. Uselding (eds), *Business Enterprise and Economic Change* (Kent State, Ohio, 1973) pp. 198–226. There are interesting insights in Alan Macfarlane, *The Culture of Capitalism* (Oxford, 1987). A study of Thomas Bewick's business methods is forthcoming from John Brewer and Stella Tillyard.

31. See Roy Porter, *Health for Sale: Quack Medicine in Eighteenth Century England* (Manchester, 1989); Dorothy Porter and Roy Porter, *Patient's Progress* (Cambridge, 1989).

32. Asa Briggs, *Victorian Things* (1988).

33. Peter Lindert, 'English Occupations, 1670–1811', *Journal of Economic History*, XL (1980), 701–7; Lindert, 'Remodelling British Economic History: A Review Article', *Journal of Economic History*, XLIII (1983) 988–90; Lindert and Jeffrey G. Williamson, 'Revising England's Social Tables, 1688–1812', *Explorations in Economic History*, XIX (1982) 385–408; XX (1983) 94–109; P. J. Corfield, 'Class by Name and Number in Eighteenth Century Britain', *History*, LXXII (1987).

34. For shops, see Brewer, *The Sinews of Power*; for newspaper advertising, see J. J. Looney, 'Advertising and Society in England, 1720–1820: A Statistical Analysis of Yorkshire Newspaper Advertisements' (Princeton University PhD thesis, 1983). Obviously urbanisation was an important factor: see Peter Borsay, 'The English Urban Renaissance: The Development of Provincial Urban Culture, c. 1680–1760', *Social History*, V (1977); P. J. Corfield, *The Impact of English Towns 1700–1800* (Oxford, 1982); J. Walvin, *English Urban Life, 1776–1851* (1984). Indispensable background is F. Braudel, *Civilization and Capitalism. 15th–18th Century*. Vol. i: *The Structures of Everyday Life*; vol. ii: *The Wheels of Commerce*; vol. iii: *The Perspective of the World* (New York, 1985).

Rival explanations of the rise of consumerism are sensibly discussed in D. Miller, *Material Culture and Mass Consumption* (1987); Colin Campbell, *The Romantic Ethic and the Spirit of Modern Consumerism* (1987); Mary Douglas and Baron Isherwood, *The World of Goods: Towards an Anthropology of Consumption* (1980).

35. John Brewer, 'Commercialization and Politics', in McKendrick, Brewer and Plumb, *The Birth of a Consumer Society* pp. 197–264. On meanings, compare A. Appadurai (ed.), *The Social Life of Things* (Cambridge, 1986); R. Barthes, *Mythologies* (1972); Pierre Bourdieu, *Distinction. A Social Critique of the Judgement of Taste* (Cambridge, Mass., 1984), and Jean Baudrillard, *Le Système des Objets* (Paris, 1968). Peter Burke, *The Historical Anthropology of Early Modern Italy* (Cambridge, 1987) has much to say upon surface meanings in a face-to-face society.

36. Simon Schama, *The Embarrassment of Riches: An Interpretation of Dutch Culture in the Golden Age* (New York, 1987); see also his 'The Unruly Realm: Appetite and Restraint in Seventeenth-Century Holland', *Daedalus*, CVIII (1979) 103–23. For England, see Earle, *Making of the English Middle Class*.

37. John Sekora, *Luxury: The Concept in Western Thought, Eden to Smollett* (Baltimore, 1977); J. G. A. Pocock, *Virtue, Commerce and History* (Cambridge, 1985); Joyce Appleby, 'Ideology and Theory: The Tension between Political and Economic Liberalism in Seventeenth Century England', *American Historical Review*, LXXXI (1976) 499–515.

38. Ann Kussmaul, *Servants in Husbandry in Early Modern England* (Cambridge, 1981).

39. J. Rule, *The Experience of Labour in Eighteenth Century Industry* (1981); R. Glen, *Urban Workers in the Early Industrial Revolution* (1984); H. Cunningham, *Leisure in the Industrial Revolution* (1980); R. Malcolmson, *Popular Recreations in English Society 1700–1850* (Cambridge, 1973); E. P. Thompson, 'Time, Work-Discipline and Industrial Capitalism', *Past and Present*, no. 38 (1967) 56–97; David Vincent, *Bread, Knowledge and Freedom. A Study of Nineteenth Century Working Class Autobiography* (1981); John Burnett, *The Annals of Labour. Autobiographies of British Working Class People, 1820–1920* (Bloomington, 1974).

40. R. Trumbach, *The Rise of the Egalitarian Family: Aristocratic Kinship and Domestic Relations in Eighteenth Century England* (New York, 1978); Lawrence Stone, *The Family, Sex and Marriage in England, 1500–1800* (1977); Stone and Jeanne C. Fawtier Stone, *An Open Elite? England 1540–1880* (Oxford, 1984); P. Laslett, *The World We have Lost, Further Explored*, 3rd edn (1983).

41. On this range of topics see above all L. Jordanova, *Sexual Visions. Images of Gender in Science and Medicine Between the 18th and the 20th Centuries* (Madison, 1989). See also Trumbach, *Rise of the Egalitarian Family*; Judith S. Lewis, *In the Family Way: Childbearing in the British Aristocracy 1760–1860* (New Brunswick, NJ, 1986).

42. Michael Anderson, *Family Structure in Nineteenth Century Lancashire* (Cambridge, 1971).

43. Ford K. Brown, *Fathers of the Victorians. The Age of Wilberforce* (Cambridge, 1961).

44. C. Lasch, *Haven in a Heartless World* (New York, 1977).

45. See above all Levine, *Family Formation in an Age of Nascent Capitalism*: and Levine, *Reproducing Families: The Political Economy of English Population History*, and Carole Shammas, 'The Domestic Environment in Early Modern England and America', *Journal of Social History*, XIV (1980) 1–24; E. Shorter, *Making of the Modern Family* (New York, 1975).

46. E.g. I. Pinchbeck, *Women Workers and the Industrial Revolution, 1750–1850* (1981; 1st edn, 1930).

47. Arthur Calder Marshall, *The Grand Century of the Lady* (1979); R. Brimley Johnson, *Blue Stocking Letters* (1926).

48. Alice Clark, *Working Life of Women in the Seventeenth Century* (1968; 1st edn, 1919).

49. And, one should add, prostitution, the classic consumerisation of gender

242   BRITISH POLITICS AND SOCIETY 1742–1789

relations. See R. Trumbach, 'Modern Prostitution and Gender in *Fanny Hill*: Libertine and Domesticated Fantasy', in G. S. Rousseau and Roy Porter (eds), *Sexual Underworlds of the Enlightenment* (1987) pp. 69–85; Stanley Nash, 'Prostitution and Charity: The Magdalen Hospital, A Case Study', *Journal of Social History*, XVII (1984) 617–28; Nash, 'Social Attitudes towards Prostitution in London, from 1752 to 1829' (PhD thesis, New York University, 1980); V. Bullough, 'Prostitution and Reform in Eighteenth Century England', in R. P. Maccubbin (ed.), *'Tis Nature's Fault. Unauthorized Sexuality during the Enlightenment* (Cambridge, 1987) pp. 61–74.

50. Snell, *Annals of the Labouring Poor: Social Change in Agrarian England, 1660–1900*.

51. Though see Peter Earle, 'The Female Labour Market in London in the late Seventeenth and early Eighteenth Centuries', *Economic History Review*, 2nd series, XLII, no. 3 (1989) 328–53; Mary Prior (ed.), *Women in English Society, 1500–1800* (1985); Lindsey Charles and Lorna Duffin (eds), *Women and Work in Pre-Industrial England* (1985); E. Richards, 'Women in the British Economy since about 1700: An Interpretation', *History*, LIX (1974) 337–57; and, more generally, Olwen Hufton, 'Women in History: Early Modern Europe', *Past and Present*, no. 101 (1983).

52. K. M. Rogers, *Feminism in Eighteenth Century England* (Chicago, 1982); Bridget Hill, *Eighteenth Century Women: An Anthology* (1984); Dale Spender, *Mothers of the Novel: 100 Good Women Novelists Before Jane Austen* (1986).

53. See, in particular, Leonore Davidoff and Catherine Hall, *Family Fortunes: Men and Women of the English Middle Class, 1780–1850* (1987), a work based on extensive archival research on Midlands society; their 'The Architecture of Public and Private Life. English Middle Class Society in a Provincial Town, 1780–1850', in D. Fraser and A. Sutcliffe (eds), *The Pursuit of Urban History* (1983), is also relevant. See also S. Amussen, *An Ordered Society: Class and Gender in Early Modern England* (Oxford, 1988). More generally see Joan Scott, 'Gender: A Useful Category of Historical Analysis', *American Historical Review*, XCI (1986).

54. K. V. Thomas, 'The Double Standard', *Journal of the History of Ideas*, XX (1959) 195–216.

55. T. Laqueur, 'Orgasm, Generation, and the Politics of Reproductive Biology', *Representations*, XIV (1986) 1–14; C. Gallagher and T. Laqueur (eds), *The Making of the Modern Body. Sexuality and Society in the Nineteenth Century* (Berkeley, 1987); P.-G. Boucé (ed.), *Sexuality in Eighteenth Century Britain* (Manchester, 1982); Roy Porter, '"The Secrets of Generation Display'd": *Aristotle's Master-Piece* in Eighteenth Century England', in Maccubbin (ed.), *'Tis Nature's Fault. Unauthorised Sexuality During the Enlightenment* (1987) pp. 7–21.

56. See N. F. Cott, 'Passionlessness; an Interpretation of Victorian Sexual Ideology, 1890–1850', in J. W. Leavitt (ed.), *Women and Health in America* (Madison, 1984) pp. 57–69; E. Showalter, *The Female Malady* (New York, 1986); F. J. Barker-Benfield, *The Horrors of the Half-Known Life* (New York, 1976); M. Foucault, *A History of Sexuality*, vol. 1. *Introduction* (1978). For a broader discussion see also Jordanova, *Sexual Visions*; Jordanova, 'Naturalising the Family: Literature and the Bio-Medical Sciences in the Late 18th Century', in Jordanova (ed.), *Languages of Nature* (1986); Jordanova, 'Conceptualising Power over Women', *Radical Science Journal*, XII (1982), 124–8; Jordanova, 'Natural Facts: a Historical Perspective on Science and Sexuality', in C. MacCormack and M. Strathern (eds), *Nature, Culture and Gender* (Cambridge, 1980) pp. 42–69; C. Duncan, 'Happy Mothers and Other Ideas in 18th Century Art', *Art Bulletin*, LX (1973) 570–83. And see the general discussion in the 'Introduction' to Rousseau and Porter (eds), *Sexual Underworlds of the Enlightenment*.

57. C. N. Degler, 'What Ought to be and What was: Women's Sexuality in the Nineteenth Century', in Leavitt (ed.), *Women and Health in America*, pp. 40–56. Anna Clark, *Women's Silence, Men's Violence: Sexual Assault in England, 1770–1845* (1987); the issues raised by Clark are discussed in Antony E. Simpson, 'Vulnerability and the Age of Female Consent: Legal Innovation and its Effect on Prosecutions for Rape in Eighteenth Century London', in Rousseau and Porter (eds), *Sexual Underworlds of the Enlightenment*, pp. 181–205; Roy Porter, 'Rape – Does it have a Historical Meaning?', in Sylvana Tomaselli and Roy Porter (eds), *Rape* (Oxford, 1986) pp. 216–36.

58. P. Gay, *The Bourgeois Experience, Victoria to Freud*, vol. 1, *A Sentimental Education*, vol. 2, *The Tender Passion* (New York, 1984 and 1986).

59. Roy Palmer, *The Sound of History, Songs and Social Comment* (Oxford, 1988). For independent women see Liz Stanley (ed.), *The Diaries of Hannah Cullwick, Victorian Maidservant* (New Brunswick, 1984); Helena Whitbread (ed.), *I Know my Own Heart. The Diaries of Anne Lister 1791–1840* (1988).

60. For the following dicussion of childbirth and rearing see especially A. Wilson, 'Participant or Patient?', in R. Porter (ed.), *Patients and Practitioners* (Cambridge, 1985) pp. 129–44; Wilson, 'William Hunter and the Varieties of Man-midwifery', in W. F. Bynum and Roy Porter (eds), *William Hunter and the Eighteenth Century World* (Cambridge, 1985) pp. 343–69; E. Shorter, *A History of Women's Bodies* (1983).

61. On this point see the discussion in Roy Porter, 'A Touch of Danger: The Man Midwife as Sexual Predator', in Rousseau and Porter (eds), *Sexual Underworlds of the Enlightenment*, pp. 206–32.

62. V. Fildes, *Breasts, Bottles and Babies. A History of Infant Feeding* (Edinburgh, 1986); Fildes (ed.), *Women as Mothers in Pre-Industrial England* (1989); Fildes *Wetnursing* (Oxford, 1988).

63. From their profoundly divergent viewpoints, the following all agree that much attention was lavished on Georgian children: Linda Pollock, *Forgotten Children: Parent-Child Relations from 1500 to 1900* (Cambridge, 1983); Pollock, *A Lasting Relationship: Parents and Children over Three Centuries* (1987); J. H. Plumb, 'The New World of Children in Eighteenth Century England', in McKendrick, Brewer and Plumb, *Birth of a Consumer Society: The Commercialization of Eighteenth-Century England*, pp. 286–315; Stone, *Family, Sex and Marriage in England, 1500–1800*; Trumbach, *Rise of the Egalitarian Family*.

64. Jean Donnison, *Midwives and Medical Men. A History of Interprofessional Rivalries and Women's Rights* (1977).

65. Roy Porter, 'The Enlightenment in England', in Roy Porter and Mikuláš Teich (eds), *The Enlightenment in National Context* (Cambridge, 1981) pp. 1–18.

66. Peter Gay, *The Enlightenment: An Interpretation*, vol. 2 (New York, 1969). See also Roy Porter, 'Was There a Medical Enlightenment in Eighteenth Century England?', *British Journal for Eighteenth Century Studies*, 5 (1982) 46–63.

67. Ruth Richardson, *Death, Dissection and the Destitute: A Political History of the Human Corpse* (1987); C. Gittings, *Death, Burial and the Individual in Early Modern England* (1984); Roy Porter and Dorothy Porter, *In Sickness and in Health. The British Experience, 1650–1850* (1988) ch. 13; Porter and Porter, *Patient's Progress. The Dialectics of Doctoring in 18th Century England*, ch. 9; P. Ariès, *The Hour of our Death* (1981). See also R. Houlbrooke (ed), *Death, Ritual and Bereavement* (1989). An illuminating angle on the secularization of death is what happened to suicide: see Michael MacDonald, 'The Secularization of Suicide in England, 1660–1800', *Past and Present*, no. 111 (1986) 50–100; and also O. Anderson, *Suicide in Victorian and Edwardian England* (Oxford, 1987).

68. Peter Burke, *Popular Culture in Early Modern Europe* (1978); J. M. Golby

and A. W. Purdue, *The Civilization of the Crowd: Popular Culture in England, 1750–1900* (1984).

69. R. Muchembled, *Popular Culture and Elite Culture in France, 1400–1750* (Baton Rouge, 1985).

70. M. Foucault, *Discipline and Punish*, trans. A. Sheridan (1977): M. Ignatieff, *A Just Measure of Pain: The Penitentiary in the Industrial Revolution, 1750–1850* (New York, 1978).

71. Peter Burke, 'Popular Culture between History and Ethnology', *Ethnologi Europaea*, XIV (1984) 5–13; Burke, 'Revolution in Popular Culture', in Porter and Teich (eds), *Revolution in History*, pp. 206–25.

72. The abandonment of elite interest in astrology is instructive. See Patrick Curry (ed.), *Astrology, Science and Society: Historical Essays* (Woodbridge, 1987).

73. M. Fissell, 'The Physic of Charity: Health and Welfare in the West Country, 1690–1834' (PhD thesis, University of Pennsylvania, 1988). This should be compared with J. Barry, 'The Cultural Life of Bristol, 1640–1775' (DPhil thesis, Oxford University, 1986).

74. A. J. Vickery, 'Women's Consumption and Material Culture: Elizabeth Shackleton of Alkincoats, 1726–81' (seminar paper delivered at the Victoria and Albert Museum, 1987) is highly informative on what belongings meant to a Lancashire lady. See also her forthcoming PhD thesis, 'Women of the Local Elite in Lancashire, c. 1760–1828'.

75. F. Barker, *The Tremulous Private Body* (1984) is an example of this genre. It attempts to make bold statements about the changing perception of the body in bourgeoisie perception from the seventeenth to the nineteenth centuries on the basis of deconstructionist readings of texts, without recourse to external historical information. Its conclusions seem to me wholly fallacious.

76. Roger Lonsdale (ed.), *The New Oxford Book of Eighteenth Century English Verse* (Oxford, 1984). On this point see John Barrell, *English Literature in History, 1730–80: An Equal, Wide Survey* (1983).

77. W. A. Speck, *Society and Literature, 1700–1760* (Dublin, 1983).

78. John Barrell, *The Dark Side of the Landscape. The Rural Poor in English Painting, 1730–1840* (Cambridge, 1983); Barrell, *The Idea of Landscape and the Sense of Place, 1730–1840* (Cambridge, 1972); Barrell, *The Political Theory of Painting from Reynolds to Hazlitt* (New Haven, 1986); Ronald Paulson, *Book and Painting: Shakespeare, Milton and the Bible. Literary Texts and the Emergence of English Painting* (Knoxville, 1982); Paulson, *Emblem and Expression. Meaning in English Art of the Eighteenth Century* (1975); Paulson, *Literary Landscape. Turner and Constable* (New Haven, 1982); Paulson, *Popular and Polite Art in the Age of Hogarth and Fielding* (Notre Dame, 1979). See also Peter Stallybrass and Allon White, *The Politics and Poetics of Transgression* (Ithaca, 1986), and Roy Porter, 'Seeing the Past', *Past and Present*, no. 118 (1988) 186–205.

79. G. S. Rousseau, 'Science and Literature, the State of the Art', *Isis*, LXIX (1978) 583–91; Rousseau, Literature and Medicine: The State of the Field', *Isis*, LXVII (1981) 406–24.

80. Bob Bushaway, *By Rite: Custom, Ceremony and Community in England, 1700–1880* (1982) is exemplary in the interpretation of folklore as the site of values contested between popular and polite culture, J. Obelkevitch, 'Proverbs and Social History', in Peter Burke and Roy Porter (eds), *The Social History of Language* (Cambridge, 1987) pp. 43–72, massively advances our understanding of the place of proverbs, and guides historians as to how to make use of them.

81. Roy Palmer, *The Sound of History. Songs and Social Comment* (1988) does not entirely avoid the pitfalls of reading off 'people's history' from 'people's song'.

82. As is illuminatingly demonstrated in John Brewer, *The Common People and*

Politics, 1750–1790s (Cambridge, 1986). It goes without saying that we need good studies of the meaning and use of the language itself. Still useful in this respect is Raymond Williams, *Keywords. A Vocabulary of Culture and Society* (1983); Olivia Smith, *The Politics of Language* (Oxford, 1984). See also Peter Burke 'Introduction', to Burke and Porter (eds), *The Social History of Language*, pp. 1–20.

2. THE BRITISH ECONOMY IN TRANSITION, 1742–1789   *William Hausman*

1. R. M. Hartwell, 'The Causes of the Industrial Revolution: An Essay in Methodology', in R. M. Hartwell (ed.), *The Causes of the Industrial Revolution in England* (1967) p. 53.

2. E. J. Hobsbawm, *Industry and Empire* (1968) p. 13. An equally bold statement can be found in E. A. Wrigley, *Continuity, Chance, and Change: The Character of the Industrial Revolution in England* (Cambridge, 1988) p. 7.

3. A few historians object to use of the term 'industrial' revolution. This has been expressed most forcefully by Michael Fores, 'The Myth of a British Industrial Revolution', *History*, 66 (June 1981) 181–98.

4. M. W. Flinn, *Origins of the Industrial Revolution* (1966) p. 2.

5. Rondo Cameron, 'A New View of European Industrialization', *Economic History Review*, 2nd series, XXXVIII (Feb. 1985) 3.

6. Arnold Toynbee, *Toynbee's Industrial Revolution* (reprinted New York, 1969) p. 27.

7. Cameron, 'New View', p. 3; T. S. Ashton, *The Industrial Revolution, 1760–1830* (1972, first published 1948).

8. Charles Wilson, *England's Apprenticeship, 1603–1763* (1965) p. 376; J. H. Plumb, *England in the Eighteenth Century (1714–1815)* (1950) p. 77.

9. W. W. Rostow, *The Stages of Economic Growth* (Cambridge, 1960) ch. 4.

10. Phyllis Deane and W. A. Cole, *British Economic Growth, 1688–1958*, 2nd edition (Cambridge, 1969) ch. II.

11. C. K. Harley, 'British Industrialization Before 1841: Evidence of Slower Growth During the Industrial Revolution', *Journal of Economic History*, XLII (June 1982) 267–89.

12. Toynbee, *Toynbee's Industrial Revolution*, p. 85.

13. Phyllis Deane, *The First Industrial Revolution* (Cambridge, 1965) p. 1.

14. Douglass C. North, *Structure and Change in Economic History* (New York, 1981) ch. 12.

15. Paul Mantoux, *The Industrial Revolution in the Eighteenth Century*, revised edition (New York, 1961) p. 189.

16. David S. Landes, *The Unbound Prometheus* (Cambridge, 1969) ch. 1.

17. François Crouzet, 'Editor's Introduction', in Crouzet (ed.), *Capital Formation in the Industrial Revolution* (1972) p. 69.

18. Hobsbawm, *Industry and Empire*, p. 56.

19. Rostow, *Stages*, pp. 53–5.

20. E. A. Wrigley, 'The Supply of Raw Materials in the Industrial Revolution', in Hartwell (ed.), *Causes of the Industrial Revolution*, p. 113.

21. Cameron, 'New View', p. 4; also see Wrigley, 'Supply of Raw Materials', pp. 113–17, and D. C. Coleman, 'Industrial Growth and Industrial Revolutions', in E. M. Carus-Wilson (ed.), *Essays in Economic History*, vol. 3 (New York, 1966) p. 348.

22. Deane and Cole, *British Economic Growth*. An important precursor of this type of analysis was T. S. Ashton, *Economic Fluctuations in England, 1700–1800* (Oxford, 1959).

23. R. M. Hartwell, 'Introduction', in Hartwell (ed.), *Causes of the Industrial Revolution*, p. 8.

24. Hartwell, 'Causes', in *ibid.*, p. 79.

25. N. F. R. Crafts, *British Economic Growth during the Industrial Revolution* (Oxford, 1985).

26. *Ibid.*, p. 69.

27. Joel Mokyr, 'The Industrial Revolution and the New Economic History', in Joel Mokyr (ed.), *The Economics of the Industrial Revolution* (Totowa, NJ, 1985), p. 5.

28. Flinn, *Origins*, p. 13; Ashton, *Industrial Revolution*, p. 4.

29. Peter Mathias, 'British Industrialization: Unique or Not?', in Peter Mathias, *The Transformation of England: Essays in the Economic and Social History of England in the Eighteenth Century* (New York, 1979) p. 11.

30. Mokyr, 'Industrial Revolution', p. 2.

31. *Ibid.*, p. 28; also see Maxine Berg, *The Age of Manufactures, 1700–1820* (New York and Oxford, 1986) Introduction.

32. Deane, *First Industrial Revolution*, pp. 3–4.

33. Population figures are from R. D. Lee and R. S. Schofield, 'British Population in the Eighteenth Century', in Roderick Floud and Donald McCloskey (eds), *The Economic History of Britain Since 1700*, vol. 1, *1700–1860* (Cambridge, 1981) pp. 17, 21; rates of growth were calculated by R. V. Jackson, 'Growth and Deceleration in English Agriculture, 1660–1790', *Economic History Review*, 2nd series, XXXVIII (Aug. 1985) 340.

34. E. S. Wrigley and R. S. Schofield, *The Population History of England, 1541–1871: A Reconstruction* (Cambridge, Mass., 1981) pp. 418–19.

35. *Ibid.*, p. 333.

36. *Ibid.*, p. 473.

37. M. W. Flinn, 'The Population History of England, 1541–1871', *Economic History Review*, 2nd series, XXXV (Aug. 1982) 457. For additional criticism see Peter H. Lindert, 'English Living Standards, Population Growth, and Wrigley-Schofield', *Explorations in Economic History*, 20 (April 1983) 131–55.

38. Adapted from N. F. R. Crafts, 'British Economic Growth, 1700–1831: A Review of the Evidence', *Economic History Review*, 2nd series, XXXVI (May 1983) 187.

39. N. F. R. Crafts, 'The Eighteenth Century: A Survey', in Floud and McCloskey, *Economic History of Britain*, p. 3.

40. Crafts, *British Economic Growth* (1985) p. 62.

41. N. F. R. Crafts, 'British Economic Growth, 1700–1850; Some Difficulties of Interpretation', *Explorations in Economic History*, 24 (July 1987) 256.

42. His results are summarised in C. H. Feinstein, 'Capital Accumulation and the Industrial Revolution', in Floud and McCloskey (eds), *Economic History of Britain*, pp. 128–42.

43. Crafts, *British Economic Growth* (1985) p. 73.

44. Jeffrey G. Williamson, 'Debating the British Industrial Revolution', *Explorations in Economic History*, 24 (July 1987) 285.

45. Feinstein, 'Capital Accumulation', p. 133.

46. Deane and Cole, *British Economic Growth*, p. 49.

47. François Crouzet, 'Toward an Export Economy: British Exports during the Industrial Revolution', *Explorations in Economic History*, 17 (Jan. 1980) 51.

48. Deane and Cole, *British Economic Growth*, p. 83. This view is not universally accepted. See, for example, R. P. Thomas and D. N. McCloskey, 'Overseas Trade and Empire 1700–1860' in Floud and McCloskey (eds), *Economic History of Britain*, pp. 87–102.

49. Deane and Cole, *British Economic Growth*, p. 83.

50. W. A. Cole, 'Factors in Demand 1700–80', in Floud and McCloskey (eds), *Economic History of Britain*, p. 45. For an econometric test of Deane and Cole's original propositions see T. J. Hatton, John S. Lyons and S. E. Satchell, 'Eighteenth-Century British Trade: Homespun or Empire Made?,' *Explorations in Economic History*, 20 (Apr. 1983) 163–82.

51. All overseas trade figures are from the tables accompanying Ralph Davis, 'English Foreign Trade, 1700–1774', in W. E. Minchinton (ed.), *The Growth of English Overseas Trade in the 17th and 18th Centuries* (1969) pp. 99–120.

52. Crouzet, 'Export Economy', p. 92.

53. E. H. Phelps Brown and Sheila V. Hopkins, 'Seven Centuries of the Prices of Consumables, Compared with Builders' Wage-Rates', in E. M. Carus-Wilson (ed.), *Essays in Economic History*, vol. 2 (New York, 1966) pp. 179–96.

54. L. D. Schwarz, 'The Standard of Living in the Long Run: London, 1700–1860', *Economic History Review*, 2nd series, xxxviii (Feb. 1985) 24–41.

55. E. W. Gilboy, *Wages in Eighteenth-Century England* (Cambridge, Mass., 1934).

56. E. H. Hunt and F. W. Botham, 'Wages in Britain during the Industrial Revolution', *Economic History Review*, 2nd series, xl (Aug. 1987) 380–99.

57. Feinstein, 'Capital Accumulation', p. 136.

58. W. A. Cole, 'Factors in Demand 1700–1800', in Floud and McCloskey (eds), *Economic History of Britain*, p. 62.

59. E. L. Jones, 'Agriculture 1700–1800', in Floud and McCloskey (eds), *Economic History of Britain*, p. 68.

60. *Ibid.*, pp. 66–86.

61. Jackson, 'Growth and Deceleration', p. 333.

62. Michael Turner, 'English Open Fields and Enclosures: Retardation or Productivity Improvements', *Journal of Economic History*, xlvi (Sept. 1986) 669–92.

63. Jones, 'Agriculture', p. 85.

64. Michael Turner, *Enclosures in Britain, 1750–1830* (1984) p. 16.

65. Jones, 'Agriculture', pp. 83–4.

66. J. R. Wordie, 'The Chronology of English Enclosure, 1500–1914', *Economic History Review*, 2nd series, xxxvi (Nov. 1983) 502.

67. Turner, *Enclosures*, ch. 2.

68. Turner, 'English Open Fields', pp. 687–88. Robert C. Allen and Cormac Ó Grada, 'On the Road Again with Arthur Young: English, Irish, and French Agriculture during the Industrial Revolution', *Journal of Economic History*, xlviii (Mar. 1988) 116, argue that the only clear benefactors of enclosure were the landlords.

69. Jackson, 'Growth and Deceleration', p. 351.

70. Adapted from Crafts, *British Economic Growth* (1985) p. 22.

71. Berg, *Age of Manufactures*, pp. 199–202.

72. Crafts, *British Economic Growth* (1985) p. 23.

73. S. D. Chapman, *The Cotton Industry in the Industrial Revolution* (1972), ch. 1.

74. Landes, *Unbound Prometheus*, p. 84.

75. Deane, *First Industrial Revolution*, ch. 6.

76. *Ibid.*, pp. 98–9.

77. Berg, *Age of Manufactures*, pp. 226–8, 236.

78. Immanuel Wallerstein, *The Modern World-System III: The Second Era of Great Expansion of the Capitalist World-Economy, 1730–1840s* (London and San Diego, 1989) p. 27.

79. Philip Riden, 'The Output of the British Iron Industry before 1870', *Economic History Review*, 2nd series, xxx (Aug. 1977) 448.

80. Charles K. Hyde, *Technological Change and the British Iron Industry, 1700–1870* (Princeton, 1977) p. 56.

81. Riden, 'British Iron Industry', p. 448.

82. Hyde, *Technological Change*, ch. 5.

83. Michael W. Flinn, *The History of the British Coal Industry, Vol. 2, 1700–1830: The Industrial Revolution* (Oxford, 1984) p. 26.

84. *Ibid.*, p. 252.

85. *Ibid.*, p. 445.

86. Eric Pawson, *Transport and Economy: The Turnpike Roads of Eighteenth Century Britain* (London and New York, 1977) p. 60.

87. *Ibid.*, p. 289.

88. Flinn, *British Coal Industry*, pp. 181–2.

89. *Ibid.*, pp. 182–3.

90. Gerard Turnbull, 'Canals, Coal and Regional Growth during the Industrial Revolution', *Economic History Review*, 2nd series, xl (Nov. 1987) 552.

91. Richard Sullivan, 'England's "Age of Invention": The Acceleration of Patents and Patentable Invention during the Industrial Revolution', *Explorations in Economic History*, 26 (Oct. 1989) 424–52.

92. Wilson, *England's Apprenticeship*, p. 313.

93. All expenditure and debt figures are from B. R. Mitchell and Phyllis Deane, *Abstract of British Historical Statistics* (Cambridge, 1971).

94. Peter Mathias, 'Taxation and Industrialization in Britain, 1700–1870', in Mathias, *Transformation of England*, p. 117.

95. Jeffrey G. Williamson, 'Why Was British Growth So Slow During the Industrial Revolution?', *Journal of Economic History*, xliv (Sept. 1984) 687–712. For a criticism of this view see Joel Mokyr, 'Has the Industrial Revolution been Crowded Out? Some Reflections on Crafts and Williamson', *Explorations in Economic History*, 24 (July 1987) 293–325.

96. Peter Mathias and Patrick O'Brien, 'Taxation in Britain and France, 1715–1810. A Comparison of the Social and Economic Incidence of Taxes Collected for the Central Government', *Journal of European Economic History*, 5 (Winter 1976) 605, 613.

97. Mathias, 'Taxation and Industrialization', p. 129.

98. Toynbee, *Toynbee's Industrial Revolution*, p. 255.

3.   SCOTLAND AND IRELAND 1742–1789   *Bruce Lenman*

1. *The Jacobite Attempt of 1719*, ed. William K. Dickson, Scottish History Society, vol. 19 (Edinburgh, 1895).

2. *Private Correspondence of Chesterfield and Newcastle 1744–46*, ed. Sir Richard Lodge, Royal Historical Society, Camden Third Series, vol. 44 (1930) pp. 25, 33, 36, 40, 43, 48–9, 53, 57, 58. The quotation is from Chesterfield to Newcastle, 30 Mar. NS, 1745, p. 36.

3. Edith Mary Johnston, *Ireland in the Eighteenth Century*, Gill History of Ireland, vol. 8 (Dublin, 1974) pp. 103–4.

4. S. J. Connolly, 'Albion's Fatal Twigs: Justice and Law in the Eighteenth Century', in *Economy and Society in Scotland and Ireland: 1500–1939*, ed. Rosalind Mitchison and Peter Roebuck (Edinburgh, 1988) p. 120.

5. Chesterfield to the Rev. Dr Madden, 15 Apr. 1749, *The Letters of Philip Dormer Stanhope 4th Earl of Chesterfield*, ed. Bonamy Dobrée, vol. 4, 1748–51 (1932) pp. 1328–30.

6. Chesterfield to Newcastle, 11 Mar. 1746, *ibid.*, vol. 3, p. 742.

7. Chesterfield to Newcastle, 5 Oct. 1745, *Correspondence of Chesterfield and Newcastle*, pp. 72–3.

8. Samuel Shellabarger, *Lord Chesterfield and His World* (Boston, 1951) p. 223.

9. Chesterfield to Newcastle, 11 Mar. 1746, *Letters of Lord Chesterfield*, vol. 3, pp. 745–8.

10. John S. Gibson, *Playing the Scottish Card: The Franco-Jacobite Invasion of 1708* (Edinburgh, 1988) pp. 143–4.

11. Bruce P. Lenman, *The Jacobite Risings in Britain 1689–1746* (1980).

12. Bruce P. Lenman, *The Jacobite Clans of the Great Glen 1650–1784* (1984), chs 6–8.

13. *The True Patriot and the History of Our Own Times*, no. 1, Tuesday 5 Nov., 1745, reprinted in *The True Patriot and Related Writings*, ed. W. B. Coley, in The Wesleyan Edition of the Works of Henry Fielding (Middletown, Connecticut, 1987) pp. 113–15.

14. Geoffrey Stell, 'Highland Garrisons 1717–23: Berera Barracks', *Post-Medieval Archaeology*, vol. 7 (1973) pp. 20–30, and Ian MacIvor, *Fort George* HMSO Official Guide (1970).

15. A. J. Youngson, *After the '45: the Economic Impact on the Scottish Highlands* (Edinburgh, 1973).

16. Lawrence A. Stone and J. C. Fawtier Stone, *An Open Elite* (Oxford, 1984); John Cannon, *Aristocratic Century* (Cambridge, 1984); and Eileen Spring and David Spring, 'The English Landed Elite, 1540–1879', *Albion*, 17 (1985) 149–66, and 'Social Mobility and the English Landed Elite', *Canadian Journal of History*, 21 (1986) pp. 333–51.

17. Cannon, *Aristocratic Century*, pp. 20–1.

18. I owe this point to a seminar paper delivered by Dr Keith Brown.

19. James Hayes, 'Scottish Officers in the British Army, 1714–63', *Scottish Historical Review*, 37 (1958) 23–33.

20. Geoffrey S. Holmes, *Augustan England: Professions, State and Society, 1680–1730* (1982) pp. 178–81.

21. Lewis Mansfield Knapp, *Tobias Smollet: Doctor of Men and Manners* (Princeton, 1949); *The Poetical Works of T. Smollet M.D. with the Life of the Author* (n.d.).

22. *The Cambridge Guide to English Literature*, ed. Michael Stapleton (Cambridge, 1988) p. 803.

23. Francis Godwin James, *Ireland in the Empire 1688–1777* (Cambridge, Mass., 1973) pp. 132–3, 160–1, 286.

24. Edith Mary Johnston, *Ireland in the Eighteenth Century* (Dublin, 1974) chs 5–6.

25. James, *Ireland in the Empire*, p. 1; T. Christopher Smout, 'Where had the Scottish Economy got to by the Third Quarter of the Eighteenth Century?', in Istvan Hont and Michael Ignatieff (eds), *Wealth and Virtue* (Cambridge, pbk edn, 1985) pp. 45–72; L. M. Cullen, T. C. Smout and A. Gibson, 'Wages and Comparative Development in Ireland and Scotland, 1565–1780', in Rosalind Mitchison and Peter Roebuck (eds), *Economy and Society in Scotland and Ireland 1500–1939* (Edinburgh, 1988) pp. 105–14.

26. Thomas F. Moriarty, *The Harcourt Viceroyalty in Ireland, 1772–1777* (University Microfilms, Ann Arbor, 1971, from 1964 Notre Dame PhD).

27. Robin F. A. Fabel, *Bombast and Broadsides: the Lives of George Johnstone* (Tuscaloosa and London, 1987) pp. 94–9.

28. James C. Beckett, *Confrontations: Studies in Irish History* (New Jersey, 1972) p. 131.

29. Ronald M. Sunter, *Patronage and Politics in Scotland 1707–1832* (Edinburgh, 1986).

4. THE CHANGING NATURE OF PARLIAMENTARY POLITICS, 1742–1789   *Ian R. Christie*

1. J. C. D. Clark, 'A General Theory of Party, Opposition and Government, 1688–1832', *Historical Journal*, 23 (1980) 295–325, esp. 302–6.
2. The suggestion by Dr B. W. Hill, that a Whig–Tory polarisation continued after 1760 (*British Parliamentary Parties, 1742–1832*, 1985, pp. ix, 37–44) does not appear viable in the face of a close analysis of the personnel of the Commons – Ian R. Christie, 'Party in Politics in the Age of Lord North's Administration', *Parliamentary History*, vol. 6, p. I (1987) pp. 47–68.
3. Ian R. Christie, 'The Anatomy of the Opposition in the Parliament of 1784', accepted for publication in *Parliamentary History*.
4. For full detail on the parliamentary manoeuvres of the years 1742–6 see J. B. Owen, *The Rise of the Pelhams* (1957), and Linda Colley, *In Defiance of Oligarchy. The Tory Party 1714–1760* (Cambridge, 1982) pp. 236–51.
5. Eveline Cruickshanks, *Political Untouchables. The Tories and the '45* (1979) p. 29. Not only were very few offices offered to the Tories but the Place Act of 1742 excluding revenue officers from the House of Commons was far from satisfying their demands for constitutional reforms designed to aid their recovery of an ascendancy in Parliament; on their programme see p. pp. 104–5 below.
6. Chesterfield to Newcastle, 13 Apr. 1745, quoted Cruickshanks, *Political Untouchables*, p. 74.
7. As the Lord Chancellor, Lord Hardwicke, observed, there was 'no man of business or even of weight left in the House of Commons capable of leading or conducting an opposition'. Quoted in A. S. Foord, *His Majesty's Opposition 1714–1830* (Oxford, 1964) p. 257.
8. For a summary of the arguments about the mid-eighteenth-century parties see W. Speck, 'Whigs and Tories dim their glories: English political parties under the first two Georges', in *The Whig Ascendancy. Colloquies on Hanoverian England*, ed. John Cannon (1981) pp. 51–70. The shift in interpretation of the Tory role and sense of identity can be seen by comparing J. B. Owen, *The Rise of the Pelhams* (1957) pp. 66–9, with Linda Colley, *The Tory Party*, esp. ch. 4.
9. Colley, *Tory Party*, pp. 247–8.
10. *Ibid.*, p. 101; cf. Eveline Cruickshanks, *Political Untouchables*, pp. 34–5.
11. *The History of Parliament. The House of Commons, 1715–1754*, ed. Romney Sedgwick (2 vols, 1970), I, pp. 62–78; Cruickshanks, *Political Untouchables*, passim; F. J. McLynn, 'Issues and Motives in the Jacobite Rising of 1745', *The Eighteenth Century*, 23, no. 2 (1982) 97–133.
12. Colley, *Tory Party*, p. 41; Cruickshanks, *Political Untouchables*, p. 38; P. D. G. Thomas, 'Jacobitism in Wales', *Welsh History Review*, I (1962) 296–9.
13. Ian R. Christie, 'The Tory Party, Jacobitism and the 'Forty-five: A Note', *The Historical Journal*, 30, no. 4 (1987) 921–31. In brief, it does not appear to me that the conclusion that the Tories were 'a predominantly Jacobite party' up to 1745 can be sustained, but a large and significant minority fell into that category, larger – and therefore more dangerous in the event of a French pro-Jacobite expedition – than has sometimes been allowed.
14. On Prince Frederick as 'leader of the Opposition' from 1746 to 1751 see A. N. Newman, 'The Political Patronage of Frederick Louis, Prince of Wales', *Historical Journal*, 1 (1958) 68–75; Newman, 'Leicester House Politics, 1749–51', *English Historical Review*, LXXVI (1961) 577–89; Newman (ed.), 'Leicester House

Politics, 1750–60, from the papers of John, Second Earl of Egmont', Royal Historical Society, Camden 4th series, 7 (1969) *Camden Miscellany XXIII*, pp. 85 *seq.*; Foord, *His Majesty's Opposition*, pp. 262–5.

15. Foord, *Opposition*, p. 264 and n. 2; Colley, *Tory Party*, pp. 253–5; *House of Commons, 1715–54*, ed. Sedgwick, I, p. 75.

16. Foord, *Opposition*, pp. 269–70; *Camden Miscellany XXIII*, pp. 86–9.

17. Colley, *Tory Party*, pp. 260–2. Heat was created by debates on the 'Jew Bill' but this did not shake the administration's majority in the Commons (Thomas W. Perry, *Public Opinion, Propaganda, and Politics in Eighteenth-Century England: A Study of the Jew Bill of 1753*, Cambridge, Mass., 1962).

18. Not only have Newcastle's abilities been underestimated, but the dismissal of his claims on the ground that only a premier in the Commons could maintain a workable administration overlooks other conspicuous examples of peers acting in this role. Except for about five years, peers were prime ministers throughout the years 1806–41 and one of them, Lord Liverpool, had an unbroken tenure for fifteen years: the exceptions acting as prime ministers in the Commons were Perceval, 1809–12, Canning for four months in 1827, Peel for four months, 1834–5.

19. For detail see J. C. D. Clark, *The Dynamics of Change. The crisis of the 1750s and English party systems* (Cambridge, 1982) chs 1–5; Marie Peters, *Pitt and Popularity. The Patriot Minister and London opinion during the Seven Years War* (Oxford, 1980) chs I–II; Colley, *Tory Party*, ch. 10.

20. Clark, *Dynamics of Change*, ch. 6.

21. For detailed analysis see Clark, *Dynamics of Change*, pp. 354–477.

22. *Ibid.*, p. 454. See also Dr Colley's analysis of the apparent attraction of Pitt for the Tories in 1756 as the man of the future connected with the king to come, *Tory Party*, pp. 271–2; and on the inability of the party to make conditions, *ibid.*, p. 278.

23. Marie Peters, '"Names and Cant": Party Labels in English Political Propaganda, *c.* 1755–1765', *Parliamentary History*, 3 (1984) 103–27, esp. 104–7, 109–13, 120–1.

24. Clark, *Dynamics of Change*, pp. 125, 147–8, 298; 'The decline of party, 1740–1760', *English Historical Review*, xciii (1978) 517–18.

25. Colley, *Tory Party*, p. 267.

26. *Ibid.*, pp. 273–5, 278; Peters, *Pitt and Popularity*, p. 43.

27. Philip Jenkins, *The Making of a Ruling Class. The Glamorgan Gentry, 1640–1790* (Cambridge, 1983) pp. 66–7; Marie Peters, '"Names and Cant"', p. 116, and *Pitt and Popularity*, pp. 136–9, 140–1, 151, 154–7; Colley, *Tory Party*, pp. 281–5.

28. Jenkins, *Glamorgan Gentry*, p. 181; Colley, *Tory Party*, pp. 278–9, 281–5; Peters, *Pitt and Popularity*, pp. 136–9, and '"Names and Cant"', pp. 111–14.

29. Clark, 'The Decline of Party', p. 526. Cf. Colley, *Tory Party*, p. 282 – 'A coalition including Pitt would be more advantageous to them than its only alternative, unadulterated Pelhamite or Foxite supremacy'.

30. Linda J. Colley, 'The Loyal Brotherhood and the Cocoa Tree: The London Organization of the Tory Party, 1727–1760', *Historical Journal*, 20 (1977) 87–8; Sir Lewis Namier and John Brooke, *The History of Parliament. The House of Commons, 1754–1790* (3 vols, 1964), III, pp. 197, 638.

31. See text and n. 40 below.

32. *Camden Miscellany XXIII*, p. 226.

33. Sir Lewis Namier, *England in the Age of the American Revolution* (2nd edn, 1961) pp. 193–7.

34. In the mid 1750s the Glamorganshire MP supported by both Whigs and Tories was the freethinker, T. W. Mathews, 'who thought the Bible was only a

barbarous record of ancient tribes'. Jenkins, *Glamorgan Gentry*, p. 177.

35. J. C. D. Clark, *English Society, 1688–1832* (Cambridge, 1985) pp. 179–82.

36. One leading Tory who absented himself on this occasion declared that while he considered Wilkes 'an impudent, worthless fellow', he would not support 'dismantling the fences of their liberties' in order to punish him, a sentiment he held in common with many *soi-disant* Whigs of the 1760s and 1770s. Colley, *Tory Party*, p. 288.

37. Namier, *England in the Age of the American Revolution*, pp. 136, 137, 140.

38. 'Heads of my conversation with Mr. Pitt, June 1765', *The Correspondence of King George III*, ed. Sir John Fortescue (6 vols, 1927–8) I, p. 124.

39. Peters, '"Names and Cant"', pp. 116–17.

40. P. D. G. Thomas, 'Sir Roger Newdigate's Essays on Party, *c*. 1760', *English Historical Review*, CII (1987) 394–400. However, rather than conclude that these essays confirm *tout court* the existence of a Court–Country polarisation of politics under George II, I suggest that they reflect a response to the ineluctable necessity of a redefinition of their role imposed on erstwhile Tories by the political transformation of the later 1750s; see also J. Black, 'Party Politics in Eighteenth-Century Britain', *Lamar Journal of the Humanities*, 15 (1989). Dr Colley I think unnecessarily post-dates the impact of this change (*Tory Party*, pp. 283, 284, and note 54 at p. 359).

41. *Horace Walpole's Memoirs of the Reign of King George III*, ed. G. F. Russell Barker (4 vols, 1894) I, p. 4; Burke, 'Thoughts on the Cause of the Present Discontents', in *The Works of Edmund Burke* (Bohn edn, 8 vols, 1894–1900) I, p. 308.

42. Namier, *England in the Age of the American Revolution*, pp. 409–21.

43. Sir W. Codrington (Tewkesbury), W. Dowdeswell (Worcs.), R. Glover (Weymouth), Sir R. Glyn (London), C. Lloyd (Cardigan boroughs),T. Staunton (Ipswich), C. Tudway (Wells). This conclusion is indicated by their biographies in the *History of Parliament*.

44. Christie, 'Party in Politics in the Age of Lord North's Administration', pp. 50–8.

45. The phrase appears in Frank O'Gorman, *The Rise of Party in England. The Rockingham Whigs, 1760–1782* (1975) p. 33.

46. On this see Romney Sedgwick (ed.), *The Letters of George III to Lord Bute, 1756–1766* (1939) the introduction, esp. pp. li–lix; Namier, *England in the Age of the American Revolution*, pp. 83–93.

47. R. Pares, *King George III and the Politicians* (Oxford, 1953) pp. 70–1, 115–16; Sedgwick (ed.), *Letters to Bute*, no. 215 at p. 155, no. 217, no. 232 at p. 167, no. 337 at p. 242, no. 339 at p. 253; *Correspondence of King George III*, ed. Fortescue, I, nos. 425, 430, 519, 521, 537.

48. Paul Langford, 'Old Whigs, Old Tories, and the American Revolution', *Journal of Imperial and Commonwealth History*, VIII (1980) 107–8.

49. The Rockingham party's strength before the dissolution of 1768 is estimated at only 54, of which 34 were former friends of Newcastle – hardly even a shadow of the Old Corps of the 1750s. O'Gorman, *The Rise of Party*, p. 191; Paul Langford, *The First Rockingham Administration, 1765–1766* (1973), pp. 274–6; Christie, 'Party in Politics in the Age of Lord North's Administration', the appendix – my findings about the scattering of erstwhile 'Tories' and the extent of support for North from erstwhile 'Whigs' seem to raise problems of reconciliation with the implications of some of Dr Langford's arguments in 'Old Whigs, Old Tories, and the American Revolution', particularly at pp. 123–5.

50. O'Gorman, *The Rise of Party*, provides a judicious and exhaustive exploration of this theme, and for some brief general reflections see his *The Emergence of the British Two-Party System, 1760–1832* (1982) pp. x–xi.

51. See p. 126.

52. J. R. G. Tomlinson, 'The Grenville Papers, 1763–1765', M.A. thesis, University of Manchester, 1956, pp. 77–101; *Additional Grenville Papers, 1763–1765*, ed. Tomlinson (Manchester, 1962) pp. 90–1; W. C. Costin and J. Steven Watson, *The Law and Working of the Constitution: Documents, 1660–1914* (2 vols, 1952) I, p. 307; G. F. S. Elliot, *The Border Elliots and the Family of Minto* (Edinburgh, 1897) p. 391; Philip Lawson, *George Grenville. A Political Life* (Oxford, 1984) pp. 167–8, 174–80.

53. Langford, *First Rockingham Administration*, pp. 109–98; P. D. G. Thomas, *British Politics and the Stamp Act Crisis. The first phase of the American Revolution, 1763–1767* (Oxford, 1975) pp. 154–252; Ian R. Christie, 'William Pitt and American Taxation. A Problem of Parliamentary Reporting', *Studies in Burke and his Times*, 17 (1976) 167–79.

54. Reed Browning, *The Duke of Newcastle* (New Haven, 1975) pp. 293, 304, 319–20; *The Jenkinson Papers, 1760–1766*, ed. Ninetta S. Jucker (1949) pp. 405–6; Ross J. S. Hoffman, *The Marquis. A Study of Lord Rockingham, 1730–1782* (New York, 1973) pp. 141–2, 160–76; O'Gorman, *The Rise of Party*, pp. 204–5, 220; Thomas, *Stamp Act Crisis*, pp. 310–15, 325–8, 368–9; John Brooke, *The Chatham Administration, 1765–1766* (1956) pp. 203–10.

55. Dr Lawson's doubts about there being a royal veto on Grenville's return to high office (*George Grenville*, pp. 241–2) do not tally with George III's own avowal, which was going the rounds in 1767, that he would rather see the Devil in his closet than Grenville (John Brooke, *King George III* (1972) p. 119).

56. The Opposition's commitment to this myth is outlined in Ian R. Christie, *Myth and Reality in Late Eighteenth-century British Politics and other Papers* (1970) pp. 27–54, and receives fuller treatment in O'Gorman, *The Rise of Party, passim*. Cf. Hoffman, *The Marquis*, pp. 135, 141–2, 143, 167–8, 177, 232–6.

57. See p. 126.

58. O'Gorman, *The Rise of Party*, pp. 403–5, and *The Emergence of the Two-Party System*, pp. 7–9.

59. O'Gorman, *The Rise of Party*, p. 320.

60. See pp. 188–9.

61. O'Gorman, *The Rise of Party*, p. 299.

62. For the parliamentary conflicts over the Company see L. S. Sutherland, *The East India Company in Eighteenth-Century Politics* (Oxford, 1952) and O'Gorman, *The Rise of Party*, pp. 191–2, 197–9, 298–302, 555, 589–90.

63. See pp. 139–40

64. For a brief outline of the development of government policy, see Ian R. Christie and Benjamin Woods Labaree, *Empire or Independence, 1760–1776. A British–American Dialogue on the coming of the American Revolution* (1976) pp. 183–96, 214–34, and for more detail Bernard Donoughue, *British Politics and the American Revolution. The Path to War, 1773–1775* (1964). For the Opposition see O'Gorman, *The Rise of Party*, pp. 309–52.

65. For detail on 1779–82 and for the Opposition's attempt to profit from wider public agitation for 'economical reform' in its promotion of place bills, see H. Butterfield, *George III, Lord North and the People, 1779–1780* (1949); Ian R. Christie, *The End of North's Ministry, 1780–1782* (1958) esp. pp. 26–9, 304–69, and *Wilkes, Wyvill and Reform. The Parliamentary Reform Movement in British Politics, 1760–1785* (1962) pp. 70–7, 79–80, 85–9, 95–9, 101–4; O'Gorman, *The Rise of Party*, ch. 19. On the popular agitation for reform see pp. 137–8.

66. O'Gorman, *The Rise of Party*, ch. 21; John Norris, *Shelburne and Reform* (1963) ch. ix; L. G. Mitchell, *Charles James Fox and the Disintegration of the Whig Party, 1782–1794* (1971) pp. 9–37.

67. J. A. Cannon, *The Fox–North Coalition: Crisis of the Constitution, 1782–*

1784 (Cambridge, 1969) ch. 1. More critical of the Foxite role during these two years is the summary in Ian R. Christie, *Wars and Revolutions. Britain 1760–1815* (1982) pp. 143–53.

68. On the politics of Shelburne's fall, Cannon, *The Fox–North Coalition*, chs 2–3; Norris, *Shelburne and Reform*, ch. xiii; Mitchell, *Fox and the Whig Party*, pp. 37–46.

69. Mitchell, *Fox and the Whig Party*, pp. 47–64; Cannon, *The Fox–North Coalition*, chs 3–5.

70. Christie, *War and Revolutions*, pp. 147–53.

71. John Ehrman, *The Younger Pitt. The Years of Acclaim* (1969) pp. 102–4.

72. The most detailed treatment is in Cannon, *The Fox–North Coalition*, chs 6–7. See also L. S. Sutherland, *East India Company*, pp. 392–406; Ehrman, *The Younger Pitt*, pp. 118–27.

73. Cannon, *The Fox–North Coalition*, chs 8–11; Ehrman, *The Younger Pitt*, pp. 127–53; Mitchell, *Fox and the Whig Party*, pp. 75–96.

74. Paul Kelly, 'British Parliamentary Politics 1784–1786', *Historical Journal*, xvii (1974) 733–53.

75. For the Regency Crisis of 1788–9 which might have but in the event did not break this pattern see John W. Derry, *The Regency Crisis and the Whigs, 1788–9* (Cambridge, 1963); Ehrman, *The Younger Pitt*, pp. 644–66; Mitchell, *Fox and the Whig Party*, pp. 118–52.

5.   RADICALS AND REFORMERS IN THE AGE OF WILKES AND WYVILL
H. T. Dickinson

I am grateful to my colleague, Dr F. D. Dow, for helpful comments on an earlier draft of this essay.

1. The importance of the aristocratic elite has been stressed most recently in John Cannon, *Aristocratic Century* (Cambridge, 1984) and J. C. D. Clark, *English Society 1688–1832* (Cambridge, 1985). For the vitality of popular and radical politics before 1760, see H. T. Dickinson, 'Popular Politics in the Age of Walpole', in Jeremy Black (ed.), *Britain in the Age of Walpole* (1984) pp. 45–68; H. T. Dickinson, 'The Precursors of Political Radicalism in Augustan Britain', in Clyve Jones (ed.), *Britain in the First Age of Party 1680–1750* (1987) pp. 63–84; J. G. A. Pocock, 'Radical Criticism of the Whig Order in the Age between Revolutions', in Margaret Jacob and James Jacob (eds), *The Origins of Anglo-American Radicalism* (1984) pp. 35–57; Nicholas Rogers, 'The Urban Opposition to Whig Oligarchy, 1720–60', in *ibid.*, pp. 132–48; and Linda Colley, 'Eighteenth-Century English Radicalism before Wilkes', *Trans. Royal Hist. Soc.*, 5th ser., xxxi (1981) 1–19.

2. For this section, see H. T. Dickinson, *Liberty and Property* (1977) ch. 6.

3. For the hostility to Bute, see John Brewer, 'The Misfortunes of Lord Bute: A Case-study in Eighteenth-century Political Argument and Public Opinion', *Historical Journal*, xvi (1973) 3–43; and John Brewer, 'The Faces of Lord Bute: a visual contribution to Anglo-American political ideology', *Perspectives in American History*, vi (1972) 95–116.

4. Edmund Burke, 'Thoughts on the Cause of the Present Discontents' (1770), in *The Works of Edmund Burke* (6 vols, Bohn edn, 1854–6), I, 313.

5. Ian R. Christie, *Wilkes, Wyvill and Reform* (1962) pp. 97–8.

6. *Public Advertiser*, 8 Feb. 1769.

7. On the impact of the American issue on British extra-parliamentary politics, see Colin C. Bonwick, *English Radicals and the American Revolution* (Chapel Hill, 1977); James E. Bradley, *Popular Politics and the American Revolution in England*

(Macon, 1986); John Sainsbury, *Disaffected Patriots: London Supporters of Revolutionary America 1769–1782* (Gloucester, 1987); Paul Langford, 'London and the American Revolution', in John Stevenson (ed.), *London in the Age of Reform* (Oxford, 1977) pp. 55–78; Paul Langford, 'Old Whigs, Old Tories, and the American Revolution', *Journal of Imperial and Commonwealth History*, VIII (1980) 106–30; and John Brewer, *Party Ideology and Popular Politics at the Accession of George III* (Cambridge, 1976) pp. 201–16.

8. On the ideological debate at this time, see Dickinson, *Liberty and Property*, ch. 6; Bonwick, *English Radicals and the American Revolution*, chs 1–5; Clark, *English Society 1688–1832*, pp. 307–23; J. G. A .Pocock, 'Radical Criticism of the Whig Order in the Age between Revolutions', in Margaret Jacob and James Jacob (eds), *Origins of Anglo-American Radicalism*, pp. 35–57; and Isaac Kramnick, 'Republican Revisionism Revisited', *Amer. Hist. Rev.*, 87 (1982) 629–64.

9. Christopher Wyvill, *Political Papers*, 6 vols (York, 1794–1804) II, 20–1; III, 66, 69.

10. William Cobbett, *The Parliamentary History of England*, XVIII (1775–6) 1287–97.

11. John Brewer, 'English Radicalism in the Age of George III', in J. G. A. Pocock, *Three British Revolutions: 1641, 1688, 1776* (Princeton, 1980) pp. 344–8; John Brewer, 'The Wilkites and the law, 1763–1774', in John Brewer and John Styles (eds), *An Ungovernable People* (1980) pp. 128–71; and Peter D. G. Thomas, 'John Wilkes and the Freedom of the Press (1771)', *Bull. Inst. Hist. Res.*, XXXIII (1960) 86–98.

12. John W. Osborne, *John Cartwright* (Cambridge, 1972) chs 1–2.

13. On Price and Priestley, see Caroline Robbins, *The Eighteenth-Century Commonwealthman* (Cambridge, Mass., 1959) ch. IX; D. O. Thomas, *The Honest Mind: The Thought and Work of Richard Price* (Oxford, 1977), chs VIII–X; Margaret Canovan, 'Paternalistic Liberalism: Joseph Priestley on Rank and Inequality', *Enlightenment and Dissent*, 2 (1983) 23–37; and Anthony Lincoln, *Some Political and Social Ideas of English Dissent 1763–1800* (Cambridge, 1938), chs 4–5.

14. James Burgh, *Political Disquisitions* (3 vols, 1774), I, 26–8, 36–8, 51–4, 87–94, 106–27. See also Carla H. Hay, 'The Making of a Radical: The Case of James Burgh', *Journal of British Studies*, XVIII (1979) 90–117.

15. John Cartwright, *Take Your Choice!* (1776) p. 19.

16. Wyvill, *Political Papers*, I, 228–43; and *The Report of the Sub-Committee of Westminster* (1780) pp. 3–8.

17. Dickinson, *Liberty and Property*, pp. 228–9.

18. *Ibid.*, pp. 229–31. See also the introduction to H. T. Dickinson (ed.), *The Political Works of Thomas Spence* (Newcastle upon Tyne, 1982).

19. Brewer, *Party Ideology and Popular Politics*, pp. 163–77.

20. *Ibid.*, p. 197; Brewer, 'English Radicalism in the Age of George III', in *Three British Revolutions*, pp. 331–4; and Thomas R. Knox, 'Popular Politics and Provincial Radicalism: Newcastle upon Tyne, 1769–1785', *Albion*, II (1979) 227.

21. Christie, *Wilkes, Wyvill and Reform*, pp. 71–2.

22. John Brewer, 'Commercialization and Politics', in Neil McKendrick, John Brewer and J. H. Plumb, *The Birth of a Consumer Society* (1982) pp. 254–8; Brewer, *Party Ideology and Popular Politics*, ch. 8; Robbins, *The Eighteenth-Century Commonwealthman*, ch. IX; and C. C. Bonwick, 'An English Audience for American Revolutionary Pamphlets', *Historical Journal*, XIX (1976) 355–74.

23. George Rudé, *Wilkes and Liberty* (Oxford, 1962), ch. VI; George Rudé, 'Wilkes and Liberty, 1768–9', *Guildhall Miscellany*, I (1952) 3–24; and Walter J. Shelton, *English Hunger and Industrial Disorders* (1973).

24. Rudé, *Wilkes And Liberty*, chs v, viii, x.

25. Brewer, 'Commercialization and Politics', in *The Birth of a Consumer Society*, pp. 203–16.

26. *Ibid.*, pp. 241–60.

27. There is a considerable debate about how far the Dissenters in general, as distinct from the leading Rational Dissenters who were responsible for much radical propaganda, were involved in extra-parliamentary politics. See Clark, *English Society 1688–1832*, pp. 307–24; C. C. Bonwick, 'English Dissenters and the American Revolution', in H. C. Allen and Roger Thompson (eds), *Contrast and Connection* (1976) pp. 88–112; Russell E. Richey, 'The Origins of British Radicalism: The Changing Rationale for Dissent', *Eighteenth-Century Studies*, 7 (1973–4) 179–92; James E. Bradley, 'Whigs and Nonconformists: "Slumbering Radicalism" in English Politics, 1739–1789', *ibid.*, 9 (1975–6) 1–27; James E. Bradley, 'Religion and Reform at the Polls: Nonconformity in Cambridge Politics, 1774–1784', *Journal of British Studies*, 23 (1984) 55–78; and John Seed, 'Gentlemen Dissenters: The Social and Political Meanings of Rational Dissent in the 1770s and 1780s', *Historical Journal*, 28 (1985) 299–325.

28. Clark, *English Society 1688–1832*, pp. 216–29, 235–9; Henry P. Ippel, 'British Sermons and the American Revolution', *Journal of Religious History*, 12 (1982) 191–205; and Paul Langford, 'The English Clergy and the American Revolution', in Eckhart Hellmuth (ed.), *The Transformation of Political Culture; England and Germany in the Late Eighteenth Century* (Oxford, 1989) pp. 275–307.

29. Brewer, 'English Radicalism in the Age of George III', in *Three British Revolutions*, pp. 331–3; Sainsbury, *Disaffected Patriots*, *passim*; Bradley, *Popular Politics and the American Revolution in England*, ch. vi; William Purdie Treloar, *Wilkes and the City* (1917) *passim*; Thomas R. Knox, 'Popular Politics and Provincial Radicalism: Newcastle upon Tyne, 1769–1785', *Albion*, ii (1979) 224–41; Thomas R. Knox, 'Wilkism and the Newcastle Election of 1774', *Durham University Journal*, 72 (1979) 23–37; John A. Phillips, 'Popular Politics in Unreformed England', *Journal of Modern History*, 52 (1980) 599–625; P. T. Underdown, 'Bristol and Burke', in Patrick McGrath (ed.), *Bristol in the Eighteenth Century* (Newton Abbot, 1972) pp. 41–62; Peter Marshall, 'Manchester and the American Revolution', *Bulletin of the John Rylands University Library of Manchester*, 62 (1979) 168–86; and John Money, *Experience and Identity: Birmingham and the West Midlands 1760–1800* (Manchester, 1977), chs 7–8.

30. Verner W. Crane, 'The Club of Honest Whigs: Friends of Science and Liberty', *William and Mary Quarterly*, 3rd ser., xxiii (1966) 210–33.

31. Brewer, 'Commercialization and Politics', in *The Birth of a Consumer Society*, pp. 217–36.

32. Brewer, 'English Radicalism in the Age of George III', in *Three British Revolutions*, pp. 331–2, 342, 357–8; and Brewer, *Party Ideology and Popular Politics*, pp. 180, 194–9, 206.

33. Brewer, 'Commercialization and Politics', in *The Birth of a Consumer Society*, pp. 234–8.

34. For Wyvill's achievements, see Christie, *Wilkes, Wyvill and Reform*, chs iii–vi; John Cannon, *Parliamentary Reform 1640–1832* (Cambridge, 1973) ch. 4; and George S. Veitch, *The Genesis of Parliamentary Reform* (1913) chs 3–4.

35. For the SCI, see Black, *The Association*, ch. v; Veitch, *The Genesis of Parliamentary Reform*, pp. 71–5, 86–9; Carl B. Cone, *The English Jacobins* (New York, 1968) pp. 61–2, 65–70; Edward Royle and James Walvin, *English Radicals and Reformers 1760–1848* (1982) pp. 29–32; and Günther Lottes, *Politische Aufklärung und plebejisches Publikum* (Munich, 1979) pp. 29–52.

36. For these elections, see the references to the various constituencies in Sir

Lewis Namier and John Brooke (eds), *The House of Commons 1754–1790*, 3 vols, (1964); Christie, *Wilkes, Wyvill and Reform*, pp. 60–2; Sainsbury, *Disaffected Patriots*, pp. 66–8; Bradley, *Popular Politics and the American Revolution in England*, pp. 86–7; John A. Phillips, 'Popular Politics in Unreformed England', *Journal of Modern History*, 52 (1980) 599–625; Thomas R. Knox, 'Wilkism and the Newcastle Election of 1774', *Durham University Journal*, 72 (1979) 23–37; and Money, *Experience and Identity*, ch. 7.

37. Treloar, *Wilkes and the City*, *passim*; Rudé, *Wilkes and Liberty*, ch. IX; Sainsbury, *Disaffected Patriots*, pp. 22–54; and Langford, 'London and the American Revolution', in Stevenson (ed.), *London in the Age of Reform*, pp. 55–78.

38. See the accounts of these constituencies in Namier and Brooke (eds), *The House of Commons 1754–1790*.

39. Brewer, 'The Wilkites and the law, 1763–74', in Brewer and Styles (eds), *An Ungovernable People*, pp. 128–71.

40. Peter D. G. Thomas, 'John Wilkes and the Freedom of the Press (1771)', *Bull. Inst. Hist. Res.*, XXXIII (1966) 86–98.

41. H. T. Dickinson, *Radical Politics in the North-East of England in the Later Eighteenth Century* (Durham, 1979) p. 8.

42. On the press, see Brewer, *Party Ideology and Popular Politics*, pp. 139–60; Brewer, 'Commercialization and Politics', in *The Birth of a Consumer Society*, pp. 254–8; Solomon Lutnick, *The American Revolution and the British Press 1775–1783* (Columbia, Mo., 1967) *passim*; Bradley, *Popular Politics and the American Revolution in England*, pp. 110–11; and Money, *Experience and Identity*, ch. 6.

43. C. C. Bonwick, 'An English Audience for American Revolutionary Pamphlets', *Historical Journal*, 19 (1976) 355.

44. Brewer, *Party Ideology and Popular Politics*, pp. 146, 154–5.

45. Sainsbury, *Disaffected Patriots*, p. 29.

46. Brewer, *Party Ideology and Popular Politics*, pp. 171–4; and Breackley, *The Life of John Wilkes*, pp. 189–90.

47. Royle and Walvin, *English Radicals and Reformers*, p. 30.

48. Brewer, 'Commercialization and Politics', in *The Birth of a Consumer Society*, pp. 238–41; and John Brewer, 'The Number 45: A Wilkite Political Symbol', in Stephen Baxter (ed.), *England's Rise to Greatness* (Los Angeles, 1983) pp. 349–80.

49. Sainsbury, *Disaffected Patriots*, p. 91.

50. Rudé, *Wilkes and Liberty*, chs VII–VIII; Cannon, *Parliamentary Reform*, pp. 62–3; and John A. Phillips, 'Popular Politics in Unreformed England', *Journal of Modern History*, 52 (1980) 601–5.

51. Bradley, *Popular Politics and the American Revolution in England*, pp. 121–49.

52. Christie, *Wilkes, Wyvill and Reform*, chs III–VI; Cannon, *Parliamentary Reform*, ch. 4; Black, *The Association*, chs II–III; and Veitch, *The Genesis of Parliamentary Reform*, chs III–IV.

53. Brewer, *Party Ideology and Popular Politics*, pp. 178–90.

54. Dickinson, *Radical Politics in the North-East of England in the Later Eighteenth Century*, p. 6.

55. Brewer, *Party Ideology and Popular Politics*, pp. 189–90; Rudé, *Wilkes and Liberty*, ch. VI; and George Rudé, 'Wilkes and Liberty, 1768–9', *Guildhall Miscellany*, I (1957), 3–24.

56. D. L. Keir, 'Economical Reform, 1779–1787', *Law Quarterly Review*, L (1934) 368–85; A. S. Foord, 'The Waning of "The Influence of the Crown"', *English Historical Review*, LXII (1947) 484–507; and John A. Phillips, 'Popular

Politics in Unreformed England', *Journal of Modern History*, 52 (1980) 599–625.

57. Christopher Hibbert, *King Mob, passim*; George Rudé, 'The Gordon Riots: A Study of the Rioters and their Victims', *Trans. Royal Hist. Soc.*, 5th ser., VI (1956) 93–114; and Nicholas Rogers, 'Crowd and People in the Gordon Riots', in Hellmuth (ed.), *The Transformation of Political Culture: England and Germany in the Late Eighteenth Century*, pp. 39–55.

58. Witt Bowden, *Industrial Society in England Towards the End of the Eighteenth Century* (New York, 1925) pp. 169–81; G. M. Ditchfield, 'The campaign in Lancashire and Cheshire for the Repeal of the Test and Corporation Acts, 1787–1790', *Trans. Historic Soc. of Lancs. and Cheshire*, 126 (1977) 109–38; and James Walvin, 'The Propaganda of Anti-Slavery', in James Walvin (ed.), *Slavery and British Society 1776–1846* (1982) pp. 49–68.

59. Langford, 'The English Clergy and the American Revolution', in Hellmuth (ed.), *The Transformation of Political Culture: England and Germany in the Late Eighteenth Century*, pp. 275–307; Lutnick, *The American Revolution and the British Press 1775–1783*, pp. 12–34; Bradley, *Popular Politics and the American Revolution in England*, ch. IV; Henry P. Ippel, 'Blow the Trumpet, Sanctify the Fast', *Huntington Library Quarterly*, XLIV (1980) 43–60; and Henry P. Ippel, 'British Sermons and the American Revolution', *Journal of Religious History*, 12 (1982) 191–205.

60. Paul Kelly, 'Radicalism and Public Opinion in the General Election of 1784', *Bull. Inst. Hist. Res.*, 45 (1972) 73–88; and M. Dorothy George, 'Fox's Martyrs: the general election of 1784', *Trans. Royal Hist. Soc.*, 4th ser., XXI (1939) 133–68.

6.   FOREIGN POLICY AND THE BRITISH STATE 1742–1793   *Jeremy Black*

I would like to thank Philip Woodfine for his comments on an earlier draft and the British Academy, Wolfson Foundation and the Staff Travel and Research Fund of Durham University for their support of archival research.

1. NeC 642: Newcastle to Pelham, 21 July 1748; RA CP 40/130: Cumberland to Newcastle, 20 Oct. 1748; BL Add. MSS 35464 f. 133, Sandwich and Robinson to Keith, envoy in Vienna, 20 Oct. 1748; AST LM Ing. 55: Ossorio to Charles Emmanuel III, 31 Mar. 1749. H. M. Scott, 'The True Principles of the Revolution': The Duke of Newcastle and the Idea of the Old System' in Black (ed.), *Knights Errant and True Englishmen. British Foreign Policy* (Edinburgh, 1989) pp. 55–91.

2. RA CP 40/166: Newcastle to Cumberland, 22 Oct. 1748.

3. RA CP 41/238: Newcastle to Cumberland, 25 Nov. 1748.

4. C. Nordmann, 'Choiseul and the last Jacobite attempt of 1759', in E. Cruickshanks (ed.), *Ideology and Conspiracy. Aspects of Jacobitism, 1689–1759* (Edinburgh, 1982) pp. 201–17.

5. Mount Stuart, Cardiff Papers 6/143: Bute to Mitchell, 9 Apr. 1762.

6. K. W. Schweizer, *England, Prussia and the Seven Years War* (Lewiston, New York, 1989) pp. 104–260.

7. Black, 'The Crown, Hanover and the Shift in British Foreign Policy in the 1760's', in Black (ed.), *Knights Errant*, pp. 113–34.

8. PRO SP 91/72 f. 109, Earl of Sandwich to Earl of Buckinghamshire, 23 Sept. 1763.

9. M. Roberts, *Splendid Isolation 1763–1780* (Reading, 1970).

10. AE CP Ang. 450 f. 498, D'Eon to Praslin, 20 July 1763.

11. AST LM Ing. 78, Scarnafis to Charles Emmanuel III, 13 Nov. 1772.

12. A. Cobban, *Ambassadors and Secret Agents, The Diplomacy of the First Earl of Malmesbury at The Hague* (1954); Black, 'The Marquis of Carmarthen and relations with France 1784–1787, *Francia*, 12 (1984) 283–303; Black, 'Sir Robert

Ainslie: His Majesty's Agent-provocateur? British Foreign Policy and the International Crisis of 1787', *European History Quarterly*, 14 (1984) 253–83.

13. T. C. W. Blanning and C. Haase, 'George III, Hanover and the Regency Crisis' in Black (ed.), *Knights Errant*, pp. 135–50; A. Cunningham, 'The Oczakow Debate' *Middle Eastern Studies*, 1 (1964–5) 209–37.

14. Black, 'Anglo-French Relations in the Age of the French Revolution 1787–1793', *Francia*, 15 (1987) 407–33; *ibid.*, 'The British Press and the French Revolution', in M. Vovelle (ed.), *La Révolution Française*, 3 vols (Paris, 1989) I, 371–7.

15. J. B. Owen, 'George II Reconsidered', in A. Whiteman, J. S. Bromley and P. G. M. Dickson (eds), *Statesmen, Scholars and Merchants* (Oxford, 1973) pp. 113–34; J. Clark, *The Dynamics of Change: The Crisis of the 1750s and English Party Systems* (Cambridge, 1982); S. Baxter, 'The Conduct of the Seven Years' War' in Baxter (ed.), *England's Rise to Greatness 1660–1763* (Berkeley, Cal., 1983) pp. 323–48; M. Roberts, 'Great Britain and the Swedish Revolution, 1772–73', *Historical Journal*, 7 (1964) 1–46; T. C. W. Blanning, '"That Horrid Electorate" or "Ma Patrie Germanique"? George III, Hanover and the *Fürstenbund* of 1785', *Historical Journal*, 20 (1979) 311–44; P. Mackesy, *War Without Victory: The Downfall of Pitt, 1799–1802* (Oxford, 1984).

16. BL Add. MSS 35363 f. 341, Joseph to Philip Yorke, 14 Dec. 1753; J. G. Droysen *et al.* (eds), *Politische Correspondenz Friedrichs des Grossen*, 46 vols (Berlin, 1879–1939) X, 149–50.

17. Cobbett, XIII, 356; R. Hatton, *The Anglo-Hanoverian Connection 1714–1760* (1982).

18. BL Add. MSS 32812–3, Newcastle to Sandwich, 5 Apr., 13 July 1748.

19. *Politische Correspondenz*, IV, 324; PRO SP 84/454, Newcastle to Holdernesse, 5 Jan. 1750.

20. BL Add. MSS 35514, Hugh Elliot, envoy at the Imperial Diet, to Sir Robert Murray Keith, envoy in Vienna, 11 Aug. 1778.

21. Cambridge, University Library, Add. MSS 6958, Carmarthen to Pitt, 4 Jan. 1786, Richmond to Pitt, 30 July 1787.

22. PRO SP 84/449 f. 68, Holdernesse to Newcastle, 8 July 1749; RA CP 32/303, Newcastle to Cumberland, 15 Mar. 1748.

23. Cobbett, XIII, 379.

24. BL Add. MSS 35363 f. 283, Joseph to Philip Yorke, 12 June 1751.

25. RA CP 20/415, Newcastle to Cumberland, 17 Mar. 1747.

26. AST LM Ing. 56, Perron to Charles Emmanuel III, 1 Jan. 1750.

27. NeC 487: Walpole to Pelham, 12 Aug. 1747.

28. J. R. Jones, *Britain and the World, 1648–1815* (1980) pp. 13, 185; G. C. Gibbs, 'English attitudes towards Hanover and the Hanoverian Succession in the First Half of the Eighteenth Century', in A. N. Birke and K. Kluxen (eds), *England and Hanover* (Munich, 1986) p. 44. But see Black, 'The House of Lords and British Foreign Policy, 1720–48', in C. Jones (ed.), *A Pillar of the Constitution. The House of Lords in British Politics, 1640–1784* (1989) pp. 113–36.

29. Bod. MS D. D. Dashwood B11/12/6, Vernon to Sir Francis Dashwood, 29 July 1749.

30. PRO SP 98/55 f. 96, Bedford to Consul Goldsworthy, 28 Nov. 1748; BL Add. MSS 32813 f. 41–2, Mann to Bedford, 16 July 1748; PRO SP 94/135 f. 8, Bedford to Keene, 19 Jan. 1749; *Sbornik imperatorskago Russkago istoricheskago obshchestvo* (148 vols, St Petersburg, 1867–1916) 148 p. 399; PRO SP 80/191, Newcastle to Keith, 20 Apr. 1753.

31. London, Bedford Estate Office, Papers of the 4th Duke, vol. 23, meeting in Cornhill, 23 Jan., Hardwicke to Bedford, 2 Feb. 1749; PRO SP 84/452 f. 136, Newcastle to Dayrolle, 13 Sept. 1751.

32. Bedford, CRO Lucas papers, 30/14/308/ 3–6, Pitt to Grantham, 8 Oct., Grantham to Pitt, 11 Oct. 1782.

33. T. R. Clayton, 'The Duke of Newcastle, the Earl of Halifax, and the American Origins of the Seven Years War', *Historical Journal*, 24 (1981); Mount Stuart, 1761 papers No. 458, Bedford to Bute, 13 June 1761.

34. Black, 'Naval Power and British Foreign Policy in the Age of Pitt the Elder', in Black and Woodfine (eds), *The British Navy and the Use of Naval Power in the Eighteenth Century* (Leicester, 1988) pp. 91–107.

35. Mount Stuart, Cardiff Papers 5/4, John Paterson to Bute, 9 Oct. 1762.

36. Bod. Firth G 18, 'A Full and Particular Account of the Scandalous and treasonable libel which is to be publicly burnt tomorrow'.

37. Aylesbury, Buckinghamshire CRO Trevor papers vol. 36, Stair to Trevor, 2 Dec. 1743.

38. NeC 489, Walpole to Pelham, 3 Sept. 1747; AE CP Ang. 427 f. 411, Abbé de La Ville, Angleterre-sur l'état politique de ce Royaume, 1749; AE CP Prusse 171 f. 260–1, Saint-Contest to La Touche, envoy in Berlin, 22 May 1753; AE CP Ang. 432 f. 35, Mirepoix to Puysieulx, 18 June 1751.

39. Warwick, CRO CR 136 B 2539/17, 11 Apr. 1746; Paris, Archives Nationales KK. 1372, Puysieulx to Marshal Richelieu, 29 June 1748.

40. PRO 30/29/1/11, f. 313, 318, 311, Pelham to Earl Gower, 18 Aug. 1748, 22 Aug. 1749, 9 Aug. 1748, NeC 573, Legge to Pelham, 24 May 1748.

41. M. Peters, *Pitt and Popularity. The Patriot Minister and London Opinion during the Seven Years War* (Oxford, 1980); R. Middleton, *The Bells of Victory. The Pitt–Newcastle Ministry and the Conduct of the Seven Years War 1757–1762* (Cambridge, 1985).

42. Mount Stuart, Cardiff papers, 6/82, Chesterfield to Bute, 9 Apr., 1761 papers, No. 457, Newcastle to Bute, 13 June 1761.

43. Aberdeen, University Library, 2727/1/2/4, Sir James Kinloch to Lord Braco, 5 Jan. 1749.

44. BL Add. MSS 32949 f. 252, Hardwicke to Newcastle, 1 July 1763; J. Brewer, *Sinews of Power. War, Money and the English State, 1688–1763* (1989) pp. 39–41.

45. D. A. Baugh, 'Why did Britain lose command of the sea during the war for America?', in Black and Woodfine (eds), *British Navy*, pp. 149–69.

46. Black, *Natural and Necessary Enemies. Anglo-French Relations in the Eighteenth Century* (1986) p. 68.

7. THE EIGHTEENTH-CENTURY EMPIRE   *P. J. Marshall*

1. Jack P. Greene, 'A Posture of Hostility: A Reconsideration of some Aspects of the Origins of the American Revolution', *Proceedings of the American Antiquarian Society*, LXXXVII (1977) 33.

2. For a recent statement of this view, see John M. Murrin, 'Political Development' in Jack P. Greene and J. R. Pole (eds), *Colonial British America: Essays in the New History of the Early Modern Era* (Baltimore, 1984) pp. 432–41.

3. Richard L. Bushman, 'American High Styles and Vernacular Cultures' in Greene and Pole, *Colonial British America*, pp. 346–83. See also studies of the British Caribbean by Jack P. Greene and of British America by Michael Zuckerman in Nicholas Canny and Anthony Pagden (eds), *Colonial Identity in the Atlantic World 1500–1800* (Princeton, 1987) pp. 115–58, 213–66.

4. Bernard Bailyn, *The Ideological Origins of the American Revolution* (Cambridge, Mass., 1967) is the classic statement. For further discussion, see R. Shallhope, 'Republicanism and Early American Historiography', *William and Mary Quarterly*, 3rd ser., XXXIX (1982) 334–56.

5. For recent assessments of the largest colonial communities, see Rhys Isaac, *The Transformation of Virginia* (Chapel Hill, 1982) and Richard L. Bushman, *King and People in Provincial Massachusetts* (Chapel Hill, 1985).

6. L. S. Sutherland, *The East India Company in Eighteenth-century Politics* (Oxford, 1952) pp. 261–31.

7. R. Davis, 'English Foreign Trade 1700–74', *Economic History Review*, 2nd ser., xv (1962) 285–303.

8. K. N. Chaudhuri, *The Trading World of Asia and the English East India Company 1660–1760* (Cambridge, 1978) pp. 277–312.

9. John J. McCusker and Russell R. Menard, *The Economy of British America 1607–1789* (Chapel Hill, 1985) p. 279.

10. F. Crouzet, 'Towards an Export Economy: British Exports during the Industrial Revolution', *Explorations in Economic History*, xvii (1980) 69.

11. A. Anderson, *An Historical and Chronological Deduction of the Origins of Commerce . . . Containing an History of the Commercial Interests of the Great British Empire*, 2 vols (1764) I, xv.

12. Kathleen Wilson, 'Empire, Trade and Popular Politics in Mid-Hanoverian Britain: the Case of Admiral Vernon', *Past and Present*, no. 121 (1988) 74–109.

13. Cited in T. R. Clayton, 'The Duke of Newcastle, The Earl of Halifax and the American Origins of the Seven Years War', *Historical Journal*, xxiv (1981) 576.

14. R. Koebner, *Empire* (Cambridge, 1961) pp. 70–85.

15. White migration has recently been studied in Bernard Bailyn with Barbara DeWolfe, *Voyagers to the West: A Passage in the Peopling of America on the Eve of the Revolution* (New York, 1986).

16. R. B. Sheridan, 'The British Credit Crisis of 1772 and the American Colonies', *Journal of Economic History*, xx (1960) 161–86.

17. The case for continuing growth is cogently argued in Seymour Drescher, *Econocide: British Slavery in the Era of Abolition* (Pittsburgh, 1977).

18. See contributions by Roger Anstey, Philip D. Curtin and J. E. Inikori in *Journal of African History*, xvii (1976) 197–223, 595–627; David Richardson, 'Slave Exports from West and West-Central Africa, 1700–1810. New Estimates of Volume and Distribution', *ibid.*, xxx (1989) 1–22.

19. Events in Bengal are analysed in P. J. Marshall, *Bengal: the British Bridgehead: Eastern India 1740–1828* (Cambridge, 1988). For a wider perspective, see C. A. Bayly, *Indian Society and the Making of the British Empire* (Cambridge, 1988).

20. Ralph Davis, *The Industrial Revolution and British Overseas Trade* (Leicester, 1979) pp. 89, 113.

21. Important articles on these controversies are collected in Ged Martin, *The Founding of Australia: The Argument about Australian Origins* (Sydney, 1978). Alan Frost, *Convicts and Empire: a Naval Question 1776–1811* (Melbourne, 1980); David Mackay, *A Place of Exile: The European Settlement of New South Wales* (Melbourne, 1985); and Margaret Steven, *Trade, Tactics and Territory: Britain and the Pacific, 1783–1823* (Melbourne, 1983) are later contributions to the debate.

22. Lord Halifax on 10 Dec. 1755, in R. C. Simmons and P. D. G. Thomas (eds), *Proceedings of the British Parliaments Respecting North America 1754–83* (New York 1983–) I, 115. Clayton, 'American Origins', *Historical Journal*, xxiv, 571–603, analyses the decision to commit troops to America.

23. Cited in Michael Duffy, *Soldiers, Sugar and Seapower: The British Expeditions to the West Indies and the War against Revolutionary France* (Oxford, 1987) p. 371.

24. Davis, *Industrial Revolution and Overseas Trade*, p. 19.

25. Thomas Pownall, *The Administration of the Colonies*, 2nd edn (1765) p. 9.

26. Koebner, *Empire*, pp. 193, 196.

27. *The Present State of the British Empire in Europe, America, Africa and Asia* (1768) p. v.

28. *The Works of the Right Honourable Edmund Burke*, Bohn's British Classics, 8 vols (1854–89) VII, 10.

29. See articles by Linda Colley, 'The Apotheosis of George III: Loyalty, Royalty and the British Nation 1760–1820', *Past and Present*, no. 102 (1984) 94–129, and 'Whose Nation? Class and National Consciousness in Britain 1750–830', *ibid.*, 113 (1986) 97–117.

30. Koebner, *Empire*, p. 240.

31. C. Ross (ed.), *The Correspondence of Charles, First Marquis Cornwallis*, 3 vols (1859) III, 562.

32. *The Colonial Background to the American Revolution* (New Haven, 1924) pp. 123–6.

33. (1952–64).

34. Robert W. Tucker and David C. Hendrickson, *The Fall of the First British Empire: Origins of the War of American Independence* (Baltimore, 1982) p. 194. See also Ian R. Christie and Benjamin W. Labaree, *Empire or Independence 1760–1776* (1976) p. 20.

35. D. L. Mackay, 'Direction and Purpose in British Imperial Policy, 1783–1801', *Historical Journal*, xvii (1974) 497, 500.

36. M. E. Yapp, '"The Brightest Jewel": The Origins of a Phrase', in Kenneth Ballhatchet and John Harrison (eds), *East India Company Studies* (Hong Kong, 1986) pp. 31–68.

37. Jack P. Greene, *Peripheries and Center: Constitutional Development in the Extended Polities of the British Empire and the United States* (1987).

38. J. R. Pole, *The Gift of Government: Political Responsibility from the English Restoration to the American Revolution* (Athens, Ga., 1983) p. 145.

39. Peter D. G. Thomas, *The Townshend Duties Crisis: the Second Phase of the American Revolution 1767–73* (Oxford, 1987) p. 264.

40. *Journals of the House of Commons*, xxxix, 5.

41. *Burke Works*, VII, 16.

42. xxxiii, 91.

43. *Journals of the House of Commons*, xliii (1788) 212.

44. See the material in P. J. Marshall, 'British Assessments of the Dutch in Asia in the Age of Raffles', *Itinerario*, xii (1988) 1–15.

45. Andrews, *Colonial Background*, p. 124.

8.   RELIGION IN BRITISH SOCIETY 1740–1790   David Hempton

I am grateful to Dr Ian Green and Dr John Walsh for pointing me to materials I would otherwise have missed.

1. See A. D. Gilbert, *Religion and Society in Industrial England* (London and New York, 1976), and C. G. Brown, *The Social History of Religion in Scotland since 1730* (London and New York, 1987).

2. R. Currie, A. Gilbert and L. Horsley, *Churches and Churchgoers: Patterns of Church Growth in the British Isles since 1700* (Oxford, 1977).

3. E. T. Davies, *Religion in the Industrial Revolution in South Wales* (Cardiff, 1965) p. 13.

4. The most commonly cited are Diana McClatchey, *Oxfordshire Clergy 1777–1869* (Oxford, 1960), and Arthur Warne, *Church and Society in Eighteenth-Century Devon* (Newton Abbot, 1969).

5. E. R. Norman, *Church and Society in England 1770–1970* (Oxford, 1976) p. 15.

6. For Burke's views and for a wider analysis of the intellectual underpinnings of the Church of England see J. C. D. Clark, *English Society 1688–1832* (Cambridge, 1985).

7. S. J. C. Taylor, 'Church and State in England in the Mid-Eighteenth Century: The Newcastle Years 1742–1762' (Cambridge PhD thesis, 1988).

8. Peter Virgin, *The Church in an Age of Negligence: Ecclesiastical Structure and Problems of Church Reform 1700–1840* (Cambridge, 1989) pp. 191–6.

9. Christopher Clay, '"The Greed of Whig Bishops"?: Church Landlords and their Lessees 1660–1760', *Past and Present*, no. 87 (May 1980) 128–57; D. R. Hirschberg, 'Episcopal incomes and expenses, 1660–c. 1760', in R. O'Day and F. Heal (eds), *Princes and Paupers in the English Church 1500–1800* (Leicester, 1981) pp. 211–30.

10. Ian Green, 'The First Years of Queen Anne's Bounty', in O'Day and Heal (eds), *Princes and Paupers*.

11. Virgin, *The Church in an Age of Negligence*, pp. 138–42.

12. W. R. Ward, 'The Tithe Question in England in the Early Nineteenth Century', *Journal of Ecclesiastical History*, 16 (1965) 67–81.

13. I am grateful to Professor Thompson for allowing me to refer to these unpublished tables.

14. Virgin, *The Church in an Age of Negligence*, pp. 109–30.

15. R. B. Walker, 'Religious Changes in Cheshire, 1750–1850', *Journal of Ecclesiastical History*, 17 (1966) 77–94.

16. M. A. Smith, 'Religion and Industrial Society: the Case of Oldham and Saddleworth, 1780–1865' (Oxford DPhil thesis, 1987).

17. E. J. Evans, 'Some Reasons for the Growth of English Rural Anticlericalism c. 1750–1830', *Past and Present*, no. 66 (1975) 84–109.

18. Ward, 'The Tithe Question in England', p. 67.

19. P. J. Rycroft, 'Church, Chapel and Community in Craven, 1764–1851', (Oxford DPhil thesis, 1988).

20. F. C. Mather, 'Georgian Churchmanship Reconsidered: Some Variations in Anglican Public Worship 1714–1830', *Journal of Ecclesiastical History*, 36 (1985) 255–83.

21. D. A. Spaeth, 'Common Prayer? Popular Observance of the Anglican Liturgy in Restoration Wiltshire', in Susan Wright (ed.), *Parish, Church and People* (1988) pp. 125–51.

22. E. P. Thompson, 'Patrician Society, Plebeian Culture', *Journal of Social History*, 7 (1974) 382–405; and 'Anthropology and the Discipline of Historical Context', *Midland History*, 1 (1972) 41–55.

23. Clark, *English Society 1688–1832*, pp. 161–73.

24. Bob Bushaway, *By Rite: Custom, Ceremony and Community in England 1700–1800* (1982) p. 87.

25. D. M. Valenze, 'Prophecy and Popular Literature in Eighteenth-Century England', *Journal of Ecclesiastical History*, 29 (1987) 75–92; and Susan Pedersen, 'Hannah More Meets Simple Simon: Tracts, Chapbooks, and Popular Culture in Late Eighteenth-Century England', *Journal of British Studies*, 25 (1986) 84–113.

26. W. R. Ward, 'The Relations of Enlightenment and Religious Revival in Central Europe and in the English-speaking World', *Studies in Church History*, Susidia 2 (1979) 281–305; and 'Power and Piety: the Origins of Religious Revival in the early Eighteenth Century' *Bulletin of the John Rylands University Library of Manchester*, 63 (1980) 231–52.

27. John Walsh, 'Religious Societies: Methodist and Evangelical 1738–1800', *Studies in Church History*, 23 (1986) 279–302.

28. David Hempton, 'Methodism and the Law, 1740–1820', *Bulletin of the John Rylands University Library of Manchester*, 70, no. 3 (1988) 93–107.

29. D. W. Bebbington, *Evangelicalism in Modern Britain* (1989) pp. 42–50.

30. Lambeth Palace Library MSS, Secker Papers, 8 (Methodists).

31. D. M. Valenze, *Prophetic Sons and Daughters* (Princeton, 1985).

32. D. W. Lovegrove, *Established Church, Sectarian People: Itinerancy and the Transformation of English Dissent, 1780–1830* (Cambridge, 1988).

33. Brown, *Social History of Religion in Scotland*, p. 16.

34. C. D. Field, 'The Social Structure of English Methodism: eighteenth-twentieth centuries', *British Journal of Sociology*, 28, no. 2 (1977) 199–225; and J. Q. Smith, 'Occupational Groups among the Early Methodists of the Keighley Circuit', *Church History*, 57, no. 2 (1988) 187–96.

35. John Bossy, *The English Catholic Community 1570–1850* (1975).

36. C. M. Haydon, 'Anti-Catholicism in Eighteenth-Century England *c.* 1714–*c.* 1780', (Oxford DPhil thesis, 1985); J. M. Black, 'The Catholic Threat and the British Press in the 1720s and 1730s', *Journal of Religious History*, 12 (1983) 364–81.

37. Clark, *English Society 1688–1832*, ch. 5.

38. J. E. Bradley, 'Whigs and Nonconformists: "Slumbering Radicalism" in English Politics, 1739–1789', *Eighteenth Century Studies*, 9, no. 1 (1975) 1–27.

39. John Seed, 'Gentlemen Dissenters: The Social and Political Meanings of Rational Dissent in the 1770s and 1780s', *Historical Journal*, 28, no. 2 (1985) 299–325.

40. N. U. Murray, 'The Influence of the French Revolution on the Church of England and its Rivals, 1789–1802' (Oxford DPhil thesis, 1975).

41. Wright, *Parish, Church and People*, pp. 152–202.

Notes on Contributors

JEREMY BLACK is a lecturer in the History Department of Durham University. Graduating from Queens' College, Cambridge, with a starred first, he did research at St John's College, Oxford, and held a Harmsworth Senior Scholarship at Merton College, Oxford. He is the author of *British Foreign Policy in the Age of Walpole* (1985), *The British and the Grand Tour* (1985), *Natural and Necessary Enemies. Anglo-French Relations in the Eighteenth Century* (1986), *The English Press in the Eighteenth Century* (1987), *The Collapse of the Anglo-French Alliance 1727–31* (1987), *Eighteenth Century Europe, 1700–89* (1990), *Sir Robert Walpole and the Nature of Politics in Early Eighteenth-Century Britain* (1990), *The Rise of the European Powers, 1679–1793* (1990); *A Military Revolution? Military Change and Governmental Development, 1550–1800* (1991); *Culloden and the '45* (1990), and *British Foreign Policy 1660–1793* (1991). Editor of *Britain in the Age of Walpole* (1984), *The Origins of War in Early Modern Europe* (1987) and *Knights Errant and True Englishmen. British Foreign Policy 1660–1800* (1989), and co-editor of *Essays in European History in Honour of Ragnhild Hatton* (1985), *The Jacobite Challenge* (1988), *The British Navy and the Use of Naval Power in the Eighteenth Century* (1988) and *Politics and the Press in Hanoverian Britain* (1989).

IAN R. CHRISTIE recently retired as Astor Professor of British History at University College, London. A Fellow of the British Academy, he is the author of numerous works including *The End of North's Ministry 1780–1782* (1958), *Wilkes, Wyvill and Reform* (1962), *Crisis of Empire. Great Britain and the American Colonies 1754–1783* (1966), *Myth and Reality in Late Eighteenth-Century British Politics* (1970), *Wars and Revolutions. Britain 1760–1815* (1982), *Stress and Stability in Late Eighteenth-Century Britain* (1984) and with B. W. Labaree, *Empire or Independence, 1760–1776. A British-American dialogue on the coming of the American Revolution* (1976).

H. T. DICKINSON is Richard Lodge Professor of British History at the University of Edinburgh and Concurrent Professor of History at the University of Nanjing, China. He is the author of *Bolingbroke* (1970), *Walpole and the Whig Supremacy* (1973), *Liberty and Property: Political Ideology in Eighteenth-Century Britain* (1977), *British Radicalism and the French Revolution 1789–1815* (1985) and *Caricatures and the Constitution 1760–1832* (1986); the editor of *The Correspondence of Sir James Clavering* (1967), *Politics and Literature in the Eighteenth Century* (1974), *The Political Works of Thomas Spence* (1982) and *Britain and the French Revolution 1789–1815* (1989); and a contributor of essays to many books and learned journals.

265

266   BRITISH POLITICS AND SOCIETY 1742–1789

WILLIAM J. HAUSMAN is Professor of Economics at the College of William and Mary in Williamsburg, Virginia. He is the author of *Public Policy and the Supply of Coal to London, 1700–1770* (1981) and journal articles on the coal industry and tax policy in the eighteenth century.

DAVID HEMPTON is Lecturer in Modern History, Queen's University, Belfast, formerly a research student at St Andrews University. He is the author of *Methodism and Politics in British Society 1750–1850*, which was awarded the Whitfield Prize of the Royal Historical Society. He has in preparation a social history of religion in Britain during the industrial revolution and a study of evangelicalism in Irish society 1750–1900.

BRUCE P. LENMAN is Reader in Modern History in the University of St Andrews. His publications include From *Esk to Tweed* (1975), *An Economic History of Modern Scotland* (1975), *The Jacobite Risings in Britain 1689–1746* (1980), *Integration, Enlightenment and Industrialization; Scotland 1746–1832* (1981), *Jacobite Clans of the Great Glen* (1984) and *The Jacobite Cause* (1986).

P. J. MARSHALL is Rhodes Professor of Imperial History, King's College, London. He is the author of *The Impeachment of Warren Hastings* (1965), *Problems of Empire: Britain and India 1757–1813* (1968), *The British Discovery of Hinduism in the Eighteenth Century* (1970), *East Indian Fortunes: The British in Bengal in the Eighteenth Century* (1976), with Glyndwr Williams, *The Great Map of Mankind: British Perceptions of the World in the Age of Enlightenment* (1982), *Bengal: the British Bridgehead: Eastern India 1740–1828* (1988), and editor of *The Correspondence of Edmund Burke*, vols V, VII and X, and *The Writings and Speeches of Edmund Burke*, vol. V, *Madras and Bengal 1774–85* (1981).

ROY PORTER is Senior Lecturer in the Social History of Medicine at the Wellcome Institute for the History of Medicine. His publications include *English Society in the Eighteenth Century* (1982), *Mind Forg'd Manacles* (1987) and *A Social History of Madness* (1987). Among the books he has co-edited are *The Enlightenment in National Context* (1981), *Revolution in History* (1986) and *Romanticism in National Context* (1988).

Index

267